*Read what these people in the know
have to say about the man
and his book PAUL*

"I found *PAUL* to be both honest and introspective; an incisive, self-confronting challenge for the reader!"

Richard H. Jury,
Entrepreneur/Stock Broker

"C'mon in, the water's fine! Paul Stearns' lucid account of growing up, success, despair and rejuvenation is an example for all who wish to explore the innermost aspects of their beings. Stearns, a successful businessman and politician, turned his talents inward in *PAUL*, to chronicle a voyage of self-discovery that took him to his roots—and beyond, to his very soul. The autobiographical model he uses beckons anyone who seriously wants to answer that most ancient of questions: *Who am I?*"

Robert M. Steed
Managing Director, Performance Plus
Consultants to Management
Rye, New York

"This is not simply just one man's recovery story. The story of *PAUL* is the re-telling and re-discovery of the wonder of living in a world fueled by competition. This entrepreneur shares a lively tale of success in business which is laced with not-so-successful ventures in personal growth. The story of *PAUL* is more than a real life story of the old pop tune "Growing Up is Hard to Do!" It's an exciting glimpse into the life of each one of us who will stop just long enough to reflect on that elusive happiness to which we aspire. In his glance backward, you will follow Paul, the entrepreneur, from a community and political leader as a "Citizitician" (the author's blending of citizen and politician) to a childhood "clogdancer" (his inner-child) and back again. At each turn, you'll be surprised by a delightful piece of self-penned poetry or a memory that touches your inner-child or a flash of vision in which you find yourself recovering your balance in this competitive world."

Richard E. Murdoch,
Clinical Member American
Association for Family and
Marriage Therapy; Clergyman

"I find *PAUL* fascinating. This book is the clear testamony of a successful businessman being driven by his childhood abuses and his failure to accept his own success. Readers will come away with a clearer sense of the struggle to integrate oneself into one's life, accepting both the reality of the past and the responsibility to transcend it in a mindful fashion."

Mike Munsell,
Editor, FatherTime
a newsletter for men

"*PAUL* is a compelling, truthful accounting of a man journeying through the mountains and valley's of life. *PAUL* is proof that people can successfully overcome the valley's and attain the mountains."

Bobbie L. Clift, RN, BSN
Medical/Oncology Manager
Lansing General Hospital
Lansing, Michigan

"As a long term business attorney, I realize that the self-made person, the entrepreneur, is a special breed. A breed that all too often feel after they have achieved their long sought success, 'is this all there is?' They either then drive themselves harder to achieve greater success or they quit the game and turn to alcoholism, gambling, infidelity or some other form of self-defeating conduct. Here is a story of one of those men who refused to lower himself to such actions. He sought his own personal form of salvation and enlightenment. His story can help many who face the same pressures."

J. Michael Warren
Warren, Price, Cameron & Faust, P.C.

"Paul gives us a sensitive portrayal of growing up in the 40's in rural Oklahoma where . . . *folks already knew all the answers in life* especially his harsh abusive father. Programmed for failure through enormous self-doubt, Paul's quest in business, politics, family and the spiritual instead produced an effective, contributing, successful man whose story can touch everyone who reads the book."

Dee Kinzel
Long Term Care
Insurance Agent

"The story of *PAUL* took me back to my own childhood. It gave me many clues as to why achievement has not brought the contentment I hoped it would. *PAUL* has caused me to begin my own quest for personal discovery."

Wayne Wagoner,
Business Executive

"Paul Stearns reveals with clarity, honesty and unpretentiousness his tortuous quest to find his true self. The reader rides a roller coaster of emotion as he takes us from the joy, confidence and enthusiasm of the Clog dancer through the turmoil of his adult life, showing the way to recapture the wonder of the inner child. He takes us along the path of his quest, opens new doors and never once lets us down."

Thomas McCormack,
Writer
Royal Oak, Michigan

"Paul Stearns looks the way he writes: rugged and honest. From the 6-year old clog dancer and high school basketball star to the successful entrepreneur to the wounded and crippled fighter, his story sparkles with insight. The "inward journey" to healing grips the reader. *PAUL* displays a recovery you won't forget."

W. Fred Graham, Ph.D.
Department of Religious Studies
Michigan State University

PAUL

PAUL

A STORY OF DISCOVERY, RECOVERY AND HEALING

Paul W. Stearns

AMMOND PUBLISHING CORPORATION

Additional copies of this book may be ordered through bookstores or by sending $19.95 plus $2.50 for postage and handling to Ammond Publishing Corporation, P.O. Box 32433, Columbus, Ohio 43232

Copyright © 1992 by Paul W. Stearns

Publisher's Cataloging-in-Publication Data

Stearns, Paul W., 1937-
Paul: a story of discovery, recovery and healing/
by Paul W. Stearns—Lansing, MI : Ammond
Publishing Corporation
  p. cm.
ISBN 0-9630245-0-7
1. Stearns, Paul W. 2. Self-realization—
Case studies. I. Title
BF637.S4S74   1991
158 [B]—dc20   91-73270
Manufactured in the United States of America

Dedicated

to my Wife
Libby, who held the light

to Scott and Jeff
make your own footprints

ACKNOWLEDGEMENTS

This work is a product of a painful journey, first toward discovery, then to recovery and healing. There is no way I can list all the wonderful people who have helped me find healing in community. Still some stand out and deserve, not only acknowledgement, but my profound gratitude for helping *PAUL* become a reality. They include Professor Gordon Rohman and Mike Smith whose advice and counsel were invaluable and Annabelle McIlnay and Pam Irwin who guided me through the process and a very special last word of appreciation to my wife, Libby, whose optimism and encouragement kept me going, even when my own faltered. I also want to express my profound gratitude to Valerie Scandling, my long time accountant whose faith in me will always be appreciated.

CONTENTS

THE CLOG DANCER

Paul W. Stearns

He's only 6 years old in 1943
He's wearing overalls
He's wearing clod hoppers
He's got a corn cob pipe in his mouth
He's got the spirit
My can he dance
Look at him dance
He loves that fiddle
He loves that guitar
He loves those drums
He loves the audience
He loves the feeling
His sister doesn't have the spirit
His brother doesn't have the spirit
The bus ride home is long
The words are cutting
Why do they say these sharp cutting words
They are inadequate
They are fearful
They are wounded
They are children too
What will my mom say
What will my dad say
Will the clog dancer ever dance again?

INTRODUCTION

> Clogging is the country cousin to tap danc-
> ing, a rhythmic dance of folk origins. It
> spread from Appalachia to the Southeastern
> and Southwestern parts of the United States.

PAUL is a story of discovery, recovery and healing.
This is my story about my quest for relief from betrayal,
pain, depression and despair.

Although my quest was for recovery I could not have
stated it that way at the beginning. *PAUL, The Clog Dancer*
was who I recovered.

PAUL was the free spirit who followed his bliss without
the constraints of someone else's problems. At age six he
was active, curious, outgoing, and energetic, but the signals
he received from his family were that something was wrong
with him. He liked to perform at school, but when he went
home he suffered verbal and physical abuse.

I began my quest for recovery on November 12, 1987. A
path of despair is what I had followed. A spiritual path, one
of hope and recovery, is what I found.

Webster defines "quest" as a search, a pursuit, an investigation. I did all these and did them with a desperation
filled with anxiety every step of the way. The urgency I felt
pushed me on, though there were days I didn't think I could.

I read over one hundred books, reviewed over one hundred hours of audio and video tapes. I attended over one hundred and fifty hours of seminars and work shops. The subjects included psychology (including dream interpretation, imagery and meditation), religion, mythology, spirituality (including the twelve step programs), and self-help.

I was deeply wounded and betrayed by forces which I tried and failed to control. My life was out of control! I was powerless.

In business and politics I had transformed myself into the desirable person of my dreams; an outgoing, confident and successful person who exerted self-control and control over the way people looked at me. But when I looked in a mirror, I saw a person I didn't like—a guarded individual who couldn't relax, who righteously judged every situation and person. I couldn't do enough to be okay. God knows I tried!

Long ago I isolated myself from others, fearing if they knew me they wouldn't like me. My anxiety was focused on being an individual I thought others might like, as well as on sexual fantasies, worry, and work. These I thought I might be able to control. The problem? I lost *PAUL*.

I was like an engine, frozen because it had not been lubricated nor getting the fuel required to run! I felt nothing.

Early in my quest I enrolled in a continuing education course at Michigan State University described as "A course on self discovery." Its title was "How To Write An Autobiography." The instructor, Professor Gordon Rohman, stressed two points I will always remember. One was "We live life forward, but we understand it backwards, if at all." He also said "If each of you will research and write your autobiography the result will be to place your life in perspective. You will also find the exercise to be therapeutic." Now that my writing is complete it is clear that what Gordon told the class was true. It happened to me!

I am indebted to Gordon and many others for sharing with me the paths they trod and were disappointed by. Rabbi Harold Kushner, in his book *When All You've Ever Wanted Isn't Enough* repeated a Hasidic story which tells of a man who went for a walk in the forest and got lost. He wandered around for hours trying to find his way back to town, trying one path after another, but none led him out. Then abruptly he came across another hiker walking through the forest.

He cried out, "Thank God for another human being. Can you show me the way back to town?"

The other man replied, "No, I'm lost too. But we can help each other in this way. We can tell each other which paths we have already tried and been disappointed in. That will help us find the one that leads out."

My hope when I began was to probe the mysteries of my life and find out who I am. Writing became a guide to discovery! My purpose was to identify and place on paper the events of my life, thereby providing a sense of order and perspective.

I'm pleased to share with you my self-discovery and how I recovered *PAUL*. How I negotiated the path of the recovery and healing!

I hope you too will find your path!

PART I

THE OUTWARD JOURNEY

CHAPTER ONE

THE FAILURE

THE VIGIL

Paul W. Stearns

He drove a truck from midnight till dawn
He drove a truck from midnight till dawn
Said he drove a truck from midnight till dawn
He drove across the hills of Montana
His payload was vigilance
Said his payload was vigilance
Can't sleep when you're vigilant
Viet Nam scarred him don't you see
He witnessed his buddy being slaughtered
He felt responsible—said he felt responsible
He's on duty, he's on guard—can't let it happen again
He'll drive a truck from midnight till dawn

"Mike, why do I feel like such a failure? I'm tired and can't get enough rest. I can't find the way to peace or serenity. I'm fifty years old and know nothing but anxiety, pain and despair. I'm in a state of fear all the time. I haven't considered suicide, but I know clearly why people do. If the rest of my life is to be like this, life isn't worth living!"

Mike Smith, my friend of over twenty years, and I had just finished lunch. We were ready to say good-by to each other when I blurted out my message of pain and despair. I didn't feel out of place doing it because Mike had shared personal things with me.

9

Mike was shocked. "Paul! You a failure? A man who has it all! A fine wife and two boys; one graduating from Boston University <u>Summa Cum Laude</u>. The other a freshman at the University of Michigan. A man with the financial success and political success you have in this community. You, with all your accomplishments, feel like a failure?"

"Yes, Mike" I replied. The pain and despair I'm in does not go away. I don't feel anything!"

I came to a point on November 12, 1987 which I never anticipated. I had worked too hard to avoid being a failure, much less feel like one. Yet that's how I felt, a failure!

I always thought if I worked hard and did the right thing success would come. Someday, I would arrive and when that day came I would not only be a success, I would feel like one as well. The success would be measured in position, cars, housing, family, community respect and church respect. Now I had all of them, but I still felt like a failure.

I was almost crippled by physical ailments which I learned stemmed from stress; I could barely go on. I went to my office, but I felt like throwing up. My back and neck chronically caused me difficulty, to do anything without great pain was a problem. I had been to psychiatrists, osteopaths, chiropractors, medical doctors, massage therapists, and nothing seemed to help permanently. For me, the closer I got the further success moved away, but I couldn't give up.

Mike said, "Paul, clearly you are having a bad day, but you need to know that by anyone's standards, you are a success, and have been for all the years I've known you and that dates back to when you first came to the community over twenty-three years ago, with no money and in debt up to your eyeballs. I've been envious of your success! You are my friend and you have made many other friends with all your endeavors. That alone makes you a success beyond most people's fondest dreams." He thought a moment. "I have to go now. But I have a booklet I want to share with you, I'll get it to you later this afternoon."

True to his word, Mike dropped off the booklet; *Conscious Contact, A Partnership With A Higher Power*, written anonymously by Gail N. and published by Hazelden in Center City, Minnesota.

What Mike didn't know is that I read the fifteen page booklet in the next 20 minutes. What I didn't know is that I would weep uncontrollably like a child. The content of the booklet pricked an emotional charge the way a pin pricks an inflated balloon. It was filled with feeling and emotions which had been crying to be released. When the crying stopped I called Mike and thanked him for the booklet.

Reading about Gail N. took me back to a time when I had a child-like trust, when I had been spontaneous, joyful and happy. I had lost that ability to trust and be spontaneous. I was despairing. I could no longer fake being joyful and happy. I was fifty years old and somewhere along the way I "lost control."

I behaved inappropriately. Sometimes I showed rage and hostility; more importantly, I could not control it when it came. Afterwards, I felt bad, embarrassed and mentally beat myself.

Since graduating from college I relentlessly pursued the American Dream; self-employment, 2.8 kids, two cars, a house and cottage, etc. etc. I was determined to measure up, be somebody, prove to my father I was somebody. In the final analysis everything I did was done in an attempt to fill the deep emptiness I felt. I was always looking for something more, something different.

I recalled a Viet Nam veteran I had read about. To cope with the residuals of his war experience he left his house each night and drove aimlessly across the hills of Montana until he was so exhausted he couldn't drive. This went on day after day, month after month for twenty years. I knew the way he felt.

My family of origin said there was something wrong with me. I tried to find what it was and fix it! My drive accelerated when I was twenty-five and went through a divorce. From that time on I tried to fix all the faults and frailties I was told I had!

Our youngest son Jeff, a freshman at the University of Michigan, was struggling to find himself and a direction for his life. He thought he should know what he wanted to study and what he wanted to do with his life. He was miserable. His mother and I became miserable with him.

I felt I failed him. I became convinced I had passed on to him the things I hated from my childhood, my insecurity, my lack of confidence and ignorance. I had not healed myself from the wounds of my past childhood and now he was suffering from them. Jeff was my child and I loved him with all my heart. I felt I had not adequately prepared him.

Our oldest son, Scott, was going to graduate from Boston University. He had loaded his schedule. He was frustrated. He used us as a sounding board to relieve his frustration. When he spoke I heard insecurity, fear, and inferiority.

My deepest desire for Scott and Jeff was to help them feel confident, and be secure and fearless. I had suffered these frailties enough for all three of us and wanted to shield them from that suffering.

Early in Scott's life I worried that he was my guinea pig. There are no manuals or do-it-yourself kits on how to raise kids or be a father. I saw myself passing on to Scott some things I learned which I knew had harmed me. I wanted to stop but I didn't know how.

Libby, my wife, was going through the empty nest syndrome. She was unsettled about her life and worried about both boys. But with them being gone all she could do was worry. When they were home there were things she could do. I felt I should be able to create an environment to give her security. I believed that security would give her serenity. At that point she was neither secure or serene.

I spent the first ten years of my career, after college, working for national corporations. I thought that was the answer. It wasn't! I then became an entrepreneur running my own business. I went from Spartan Oil Corporation to Hammond Mfg. Corporation to Valley Building Centers Corporation, and finally into the real estate development business. Each was supposed to be the answer. They weren't!

I tried religion and politics and was betrayed by both!

Each path I chose took me full circle! Each was taken to save me, but only dug a deeper hole for me.

The real estate development business was very profitable, but not something I liked to do, however I kept doing it. Growing up I was taught not to be a quitter and always finish what you start! I disciplined myself to do what I didn't like to do. That's what I had always done. It was all I knew. The real estate business was supposed to be the be all and end all to defeat the feelings I swore I would defeat when I started. It didn't.

The Hammond Mfg. Corporation experience was fraught with union conflicts which traumatized me and I looked over my shoulder daily for something bad to happen. Hammond negated the confidence I built up through Spartan Oil and my political success.

Neither Spartan Oil Corporation, Hammond Mfg. Corporation, nor Valley Building Centers Corporation was the big company I said I was going to build and I had not gone public. I could accept that but what I couldn't accept were the feelings of fear that ultimately motivated me to sell each company and move on. Here I was again—in the real estate development business, paranoid with fear that I was going broke. Though there was no legitimate reason for the fear, I had it.

I withdrew from the community, I didn't feel liked. I was sure when people called, it was to use me in some way. It was sort of like the women you hear talking about men. They say all men want is their bodies. I felt all people wanted was what I could give them.

My attitude toward my church changed. I lost faith because I believed our Senior Minister deceived me. I admired him, helped him, then he left his wife for a female Associate Pastor twenty-five years his junior. This was against all my beliefs and his teachings and I was unable to accept what I felt was a betrayal.

Politics and my contribution had backfired. The Governor had betrayed a promise to me and I looked bad to over three hundred small business people who served with me on the Small Business Council. Finally all of my efforts in my political activities made me feel like an egomaniac.

My father had betrayed me! He had been dead seven

years, but I still hated the "son of a bitch." All my life I tried to gain his acceptance! He was no longer around, so how could I prove or show him I could be somebody, that I was not as bad as he said I was? My sister and brother treated me as if I were invisible, except when they were attacking me.

I had deep wounds. My sense of betrayal was devastating. I felt betrayed by my father, politics and church.

I was addicted to smoking again. After smoking cigarettes—two packs a day—for many years and quitting for ten years, I was smoking cigars and inhaling them. I burned holes in my tailor made suits. I was so addicted that if I ran out of cigars and the stores were closed, I'd rummage through trash dumpsters looking for cigar butts.

Michigan passed a law limiting places where we could smoke. People were aggressive and even asked me not to smoke my cigars in smoking areas. I was an outcast and it was degrading. I continued smoking cigars, growing more defensive and angry! I finally was able to stop smoking the same day I read the *Conscious Contact, A Partnership With A Higher Power* booklet Mike Smith gave me.

In addition to smoking, twenty-four hours a day my thoughts had to do with sex, and the relief it might bring. I did not let myself have an affair because of Lib and the boys. I felt like a sexual deviate. I could not share my feelings with anyone. The pressure continued to build!

I displaced sexual thoughts by concentrating on work. Once in a while a little validation came in community acceptance which eased the pain and yearning for fleeting moments.

The more money I made the more I wanted and needed. I hoarded it! Now that I had become a multi-millionaire, I worried about losing it. What I originally thought would bring me control and security was controlling me. Instead of security, it brought more responsibility to manage it properly and there was never a day I didn't worry about going broke.

Responsibility and more of it was certainly not what I needed. I had the responsibility for my boys, wife, employees and when someone asked me to do something, I took that responsibility too, whether it be community or church.

No matter how much money I made, which country club I joined, what big car I drove, which jewelry or art I purchased, my sense of failure stayed with me.

I always felt that my greatest attributes were enthusiasm, vitality and energy. My greatest strength was my endurance. Now they were all but gone.

I couldn't go to church because "Our Father which art in Heaven" was worse than my Father had been. The Old Testament, fire and brimstone I was told about made me fearful and I couldn't worship a God that would punish me, not with all my sins!

What could I do? I couldn't surrender; that would show weakness. If I did, to whom or what would I surrender?

I reached a point where I was battling phantoms. I was worn out, totally exhausted all the time. I found there was no fatigue as tiring as that which self-doubt engenders. I felt an unknown adversary looming above me. Yet I couldn't stop. I was sure I could fight my way back. I always had!

I connected with the title song of a successful Broadway musical called *Starlight Express*. Its lyrics haunted me. "How many times have you found though you were firm on the ground, still the world around you sways, you notice all that you've got does not add up to a lot and way aheads a maze, you've used everything inside you, so maybe it's time you tried to find a brand new power to shine a light. . .a light to brighten up your darkest hour. . .Starlight Express, hears your distress, He's there all around, Starlight Express will answer you yes, he's waiting to be found."

I realized I had to find a power to live by. I couldn't go on using work and sex to salve the pain. They were, at best, momentary anesthetics which led to a dead end. Shame and guilt resulted in more pain or lower self-esteem. It was a vicious cycle and I had been in it for fifty years. Worse, I had no idea if there was a way to get off.

My quest had not begun so I did not know that surrender was the only acceptable payment for a ticket to a path to recovery. I did not know that vulnerability has its own strength. I didn't know I could change. I didn't know I would need to change.

My childhood culture never taught me that to birth the new I had to let the old die. It is now clear to me that all through life our willingness to learn is challenged. Our willingness to change is a key. I've learned change is necessary. We who fight change suffer painful consequences.

CHAPTER TWO

THE EARLY YEARS

ON CONTROL
Paul W. Stearns

There were no door knobs on the inside of my room
There were door knobs on the outside of my room
My dad controlled the door knobs to my room
My dad crossed the boundaries to my room
He told me I must be perfect
He told me I wasn't perfect
Since then I've been striving for perfection for my own
    protection
I'm in control now—I must be in control now
I control the animate and the inanimate
Won't let my boundaries be crossed again
I'm out of control trying to control
Too much control leads to pain, despair and mistrustful
    isolation
The need for control is as old as creation
I gotta let go of control now
I gotta surrender control now
God I gotta trust you to control now.

The stock market crash in '29 started the "Great Depression", which was still in full force in Oklahoma in 1937. A drought induced "Dust Bowl" added misery to the times. These terrible conditions caused a great out migration of people from Oklahoma. The emigration continued

17

into the forties. "Times were hard" --a sad time for a state and its people.

I came into the world kicking and screaming late Tuesday evening, March 9, 1937, with extensive damage to my neck and base of my head. I carry scars to this day. The resistance I showed seemed to forewarn that I knew I would be facing what the natives had come to call "hard times."

Ruby and Kenneth Stearns lived in a one room house on a farm located outside the town of Osage, Oklahoma, a rural part of the state thirty miles to the west and slightly north of Tulsa.

The town of Osage, in Osage County, Oklahoma, might as well have been one hundred miles from Tulsa, instead of thirty. In 1937 the automobile and road systems in Oklahoma were still in their infancy.

Ruby was pregnant with her third child and had just gone into labor. Kenneth had started the model "A" pick-up truck to take her 1/4 mile away to the main farm house where his mother, Minnie and his father William, lived. Kenneth continued on to Cleveland, Oklahoma, to fetch Dr. Melvin Saddarus to help with the delivery. The nearest hospital, in Tulsa, was rarely used by rural folks.

Dr. Saddarus arrived and proceeded with a forced (forceps) delivery. The procedure produced a damaged baby boy weighing just over ten pounds. The name Paul had been selected if the child was a boy.

Uncle Chesley had come to Oklahoma in the mid-twenties to work in the oil fields, and from his pay acquired eighty acres of sand dunes, which he called a farm.

My Grandpa Stearns (William) emigrated from England to Boston and then to the frontiers of Ohio and Indiana, where Grandpa worked his dad's farm in Southern Indiana. Here he married my Grandma (Minnie) and raised eight children. My Grandfather was barely making it in Indiana, when Uncle Chesley convinced him things would be easier in Oklahoma.

Grandpa Stearns wasn't an ambitious man. He left the pushing and shoving to Grandma. Grandma Stearns was a tough, demanding, righteous, God-fearing lady. She passed her religious zest on to her children and packed them all, except for the baby—my Father—off to God's Bible School in Cincinnati, Ohio. As a result he always considered himself the black sheep of the family.

I was born to parents possessing nothing of material value and possessing little understanding of how the world worked. They and their peers were literally characters straight out of the *The Grapes of Wrath*. Steinbeck's book talked about disasters and tragedies to the land and its people.

This past summer I saw the New York Broadway revival of *The Grapes of Wrath*. I saw it with the added perspective that I was a native Oklahoman. I wanted to see if I could understand why the novel and play spoke to so many millions of people throughout the world.

Whatever else, *The Grapes of Wrath* was about people, my people. Their innocence clothed in ignorance, pain and disconcerting uncertainty. The book revealed a spirit which spoke to our collective spirit.

Mother was the oldest of the seven children of Gertrude and John Calvin Stephens. She married my father in 1931, when she turned sixteen. John, my Grandad, was an ornery old cuss who insisted on being called Grandad, not Grandpa. He was part Cherokee Indian. His grandmother, a Cherokee, had been relocated from Tennessee across the Trail of Tears to Oklahoma in the early 1800's by the Federal Government.

Due to the drought and depression, John, a farmer, could not make a living for his big family. So, at the age of 53, he loaded all his belongings and kids onto and into an old model "A" and headed to Holtville, California.

The year I was born marked thirty years since Oklahoma had been granted statehood. Tulsa was being called the oil capital of the world. The state was in terrible financial shape. Nationally, Franklin Roosevelt was trying to end the great depression and still delivering his fireside chats. The CIO and UAW Labor Unions were on strike at the Hudson, Chrysler, and Desoto Motor car companies. Radio was king and television was thirteen years in the future. A bottle of

Coca Cola was five cents and a quart of Texaco Motor Oil was a quarter.

Internationally, King Edward VI of England would be crowned King of England on May 12, 1937. Germany and Japan were on their way to developing massive war machines, although at the time no-one knew World War II would start two years later.

My Father, using an old model "A" truck, hired himself and his truck out for $2.00 per day. In 1938, dad's brother Charlie, who had followed Chesley to Oklahoma, had a foreman's job for the Sunray Oil Company. He tried to hire Dad but Dad failed the physical; Dad was a highly nervous man and during the physical had heart palpitations. The doctor said he had a heart condition and flunked him. Sunray did not hire him.

That year Dad got a job working for the Barnsdall Oil Company and we moved from Osage to Barnsdall (population 1,000) thirty miles away. Barnsdall was a vibrant oil town in the heart of Osage County and the only city in the United States to have an operating oil well on Main Street.

My brother Bob was born in Barnsdall in 1938 and in 1939 we moved to a smaller town called Avant, ten miles to the south.

Avant was our final move. My sister, brothers and I went from the first through twelfth grades in Avant public schools. Although Dad died in 1980, my Mother continued to live there.

In the twenties, State Highway 11 ran out of Tulsa twenty-five miles northwest to Avant. It was constructed of concrete and barely wide enough to allow two model "A"'s to pass each other. It looks pretty much the same today as it did back then.

Avant was named for Ben Avant, an Osage Indian. Ben, a cattleman and trader owned a ranch on the north edge of town and a two-story building in town, in which he operated a hotel and restaurant. During the early boom days Avant had been a hot bed of illegal activities and the citizens hired Marshall Pennequine to clean up the town. Ben was shot and killed by Pennequine in 1922; the act marked the end of the wild and wooly era of Avant.

When my family arrived in Avant, there were only about 250 people left. That number remained fairly constant from then to today. Floods from Bird Creek and fires took buildings and caused damage to the point where most of the commercial buildings no longer exist, but most of the housing is still there.

In Avant the only businesses that still existed in 1939 were a drug store and post office operated by Shorty Higdon and three grocery stores, one operated by Edna Schwartz, and a second store was owned and operated by Fair King. At the north edge of the town stood a gasoline station with two pumps. The third store was across the street. One quarter mile to the east was the Hilltop Bar.

We rented a house in town while a new four room house was being built on an oil lease two and a half miles to the south. It was not completed for six months, but our life in Avant had begun. At the end of six months, we moved to the new house in the country, a company house owned by the Barnsdall Oil Company.

Gas was piped to the house supplying heat and gas mantles were used for lighting. Our toilet facilities consisted of an outdoor john, a "one holer." We drilled a well and had cold running water piped to the house but no water heater, so no hot water.

To approach our new home we took the Hill road from Avant to Skiatook. It was a dirt road. When it wasn't muddy your car left a trail of dust as far as you could see, and when it rained was almost impassable. We lived two miles south of Avant.

The newly built house sat on an oil lease next to an oil pumping power plant where my Father was the pumper and gauger. They were called oil leases because oil companies leased the land from owners, they rarely bought the land. Along with the land lease they acquired the mineral rights to the land. Finally Ruby and Kenneth Stearns had their first new home, where Virginia, eight years old, Dale, six years old, Bob a new born, and I, a two year old, settled in.

Ours was a company house, it was common for oil companies to own and provide houses for their workers. The closest neighbor was Ray Parks, a quarter mile down the road. He was a bachelor. The next closest was a half mile further down the road and a mile in the other direction. Three other families lived at the top of the hill in the oil company power plant compound.

The centerpiece of our social life was the Methodist Church in Avant where liberal doses of hell fire and brimstone of the Old Testament were dispensed twice on Sunday, as well as Wednesday night prayer meeting. Dad took mother and us kids to church faithfully each Sunday. Each time he dropped us off and continued downtown where he visited with other town people, sitting on a bench outside Higdon's drug store, chewing tobacco and whittling. When the time came for church to end Dad was there to pick us up. The only time Dad went to church was on Sunday nights. Summertime brought Church School which ran daily for two weeks. Crafts were taught and Bible stories told.

In that little church we were taught some good values and principles like honesty, work ethics, coming to the aid of people in distress and trouble. Flood and fire victims were helped by the church. The entire community came to their aid with food, clothes, and needed items. Affection was never shown, but love was shown through acts of mercy in times of emergency. Children didn't know it was love, but that is what it was.

Reverend Bowerly was not only a minister but a pretty good artist—he used a 20" x 30" note pad set on an easel and while he was preaching, drew pictures depicting what he was saying. Flames of hell, and the devil, all red and with horns were always in the drawings. He always ended his sermons with a threat, "If you die tonight you must avoid going to hell," and point to the picture he had drawn of the most vivid, terrifying hell you could imagine. "You will go there unless you're saved tonight."

His wife was the pianist and choir leader and always started the first stanza of a tear-jerking rendering of "Just As I Am." Reverend Bowerly had her and the congregation repeat the stanza six or seven times. At the end of each one he'd ask members of the congregation to come forward to receive Jesus. If they did then they wouldn't go to hell. I didn't understand what all this meant but I saw that people were visibly upset and crying. I was scared to death every time that happened!

Early on, my nature said this religion—a religion where when people were inside the building, their behavior was one way and outside the building, their behavior was another way—was seriously flawed. But another side asked, what if they are right.

I wondered why we couldn't learn the value of religion without fear, until I learned that in Avant religion was a way of keeping young people in line. In Avant religion was a system of beliefs, but my feelings convinced me spirituality was not a part of that religion. The way religion was practiced in Avant killed the spirit in me.

Anyone who has studied plants knows the root systems are tough and for protection, if they are damaged, grow tougher, and the systems go deeper. People who practice a sick religion have a root system which goes deep as well.

Little did I know my first branches developed from a troubled root system.

In 1940 the first tragedy struck our family. Grandma Stearns died. She and Grandpa still lived on the farm in Osage and people from miles around came to the little country church to show their respect, then to their home, bringing comfort and food to the family.

Uncle Chesley and his wife Freda lived near Grandpa. Their sons Robert, Ray Allen, and Donald were near our ages and played with us in the sand dunes around and near the house. We had a great time playing cowboys and Indians. Grandpa still had teams of work horses, which we occasionally got to ride. Aunt Freda and mother prepared the Sunday meal.

A Sunday meal was a grand occasion at Grandpa's. The kitchen and dining room buzzed with activity.

The ham or beef, straight from the smoke house, was baked to perfection. Mashed potatoes were topped with white gravy made from flour and milk. Big red radishes and crisp onions were fresh picked. Black eyed peas, fried okra, green beans were brought from the cellar. All were served with piping hot yeast rolls and fresh churned butter. We had milk straight from a cow to drink. For dessert, strawberry shortcake.

In 1941 Jerry was born in the house on the oil lease. It was fun having a baby and we felt important helping mom care for him.

During the summers we swam in creeks (keeping a watch out for the water moccasin snakes) explored the hills, valleys, woods, caves, of the area. But the rock crusher was off limits to us. We could roam for a mile or two any direction from the house and encounter only six neighbors. We discovered mystical stump water for wart removal. We learned to be alert for copper head and rattle snakes, especially since we went barefoot as much of the time as we could. We went barefoot partly because it was fun and partly to cut down on the expense of shoes.

It's a wonder we survived growing up in the country. There were hazards everywhere and what we didn't find, we invented.

I wanted to be a pole vaulter and once, after seeing it done, tried it over a barbed wire fence. As I dove over the fence my leg caught on a barb cutting a five inch gash in my leg. I still have the scar as a reminder.

Dad traded some hay for an old used Schwinn bicycle. All the accessories, including the fenders, had been stripped. All that remained was the frame, two wheels, tires and handle bars. For us it was a grand prize. It was a community toy. We had equal access. One day Dale proposed he trade with Bob and me so I could own the bicycle outright, and Bob could own a bat. In exchange Dale wanted the Christmas gifts from other years, boxing gloves, etc. He still brags about getting the best of the deal. Little did he know how badly I wanted that bike.

I got the bike but almost lost my life. The fun of the bike was to push it to the top of a nearby steep hill and then ride back down. One day the chain slipped and came off. The only brake on the bike was the chain, hence, no brakes. The bike started to gain momentum. I hung on and hung on and when I reached the bottom of the hill, I sped past the house lickety split. Not being able to make the curve in the road, I headed straight for the "holler." I was sure I was going to die. There was no way to stop. About 100 feet before the cliff which had a drop of about 75 feet, I hit a huge rock. I went straight over the rock and landed in another pile of rocks. I lay there bloody and hurt all over. Finally, ignoring my bleeding wounds, I got up and carried the bike to the house a couple of hundred yards away. I arrived crying at the top of my lungs, hurt but alive.

One night a week we went to town to watch the silent movies. An old brick building was converted to an outdoor theater by a white bed sheet being hung on the side of it. The projector started as soon as darkness fell. The evenings cost was five cents per person and one cent per bag for the pop-corn.

I was getting ready to start first grade in September of 1943, when the second great tragedy struck. One day Old Yeller, our dog, came into the yard foaming at the mouth. The dog was dying and according to my dad had been bitten either by a copperhead or rattle snake, both of which are deadly poisonous. Dad had to shoot the dog putting him out of his misery. That ended the years before school.

The impact my Father had on me dominated every fiber of my being. That is not unusual, but in a family system and atmosphere that is negative and dark for whatever reason it causes conscious or sub-conscious pain. This discomfort caused memory suppression to hide the pain.

My Dad was a stern, tough, volatile, unpredictable task-master. But his righteousness was arbitrary! He would not tolerate any questioning or back-talk. Although I never saw Dad hit Mom, he treated her like the kids in all other ways. His word was the final word! It never occurred to me or my sister or brothers to cross him. It may have occurred to Mom to cross him, but she never did.

I can't remember a time when I was not physically or mentally afraid of my Father. From my very first memories he told us how to act, what to think, and how to feel. He enforced his will with his tongue, and whipped us with a belt or freshly cut switch. Other times he ignored us.

Dad never once in my entire life told me he loved me. Spewed words of condemnation, demeaned, and degraded me and filled me as water does a sponge. My memories of him saying repeatedly and at different times, "Paul, you're a coward," "You're selfish," "You really aren't worth anything," "You're lazy," "You're a quitter and always will be," "You're going to be an alcoholic," "You're an embarrassment to your family," "You're no good," "You never will be worth anything," "Your brother can whip you."

These words were so devastating at times I thought I would explode. They hurt far worse than the whippings, yet at times the whippings were so fierce I often dropped to my knees, begging him to stop. Crying uncontrollably, I remember saying, "Dad, don't hit me, please don't, Dad I love you, don't hurt me!" I wanted him to love me and build me up, but the reverse is what I got. He would say, "Learn to take it like a man Paul, or you'll never be worth anything."

At times I could see his hate as he jerked my arm, pulling me to my feet and continuing the whipping. I was powerless.

I learned the hate stemmed from my begging him to stop. I was supposed to take it like a man. "Men don't cry!" I couldn't help it, I cried and admitted I would do anything to get him to stop. After begging, I felt humiliated. I had wimped out! I hadn't taken it like a man. I would swear the next time would be different, but it was always the same.

Dale took it like a man. He didn't wimp out. Although Dale got whipped as hard as I did, he never cried. I only saw his eyes well up once. The pain was great, but he wouldn't cry. "Why can't you take it like Dale?" Dad sneered.

My most vivid feeling after punishment was not that I had done something wrong, but there was something wrong with me. There had to be for my Dad to treat me the way he did. He never told me what, but never-the-less, I knew there had to be something wrong with me. Little did I know I would spend most of my life trying to find and fix that wrong. Always looking for what it might be. I was without grace, but why?

I learned early in my life to try to anticipate what might get me into trouble with Dad. The feelings and moods that developed made me feel like the sky was coming down, compressing me. The feelings were so ominous at times I thought I would explode before they passed. I had no one to turn to for help. No way to escape. I understood how prisoners of war felt and why when tortured they would do anything their persecutors wanted them to do.

Evidence indicates that the family Dad came from was as unforgiving as he was. Their righteousness had been inculcated in him and, though he didn't practice what he preached, he preached what he had received. He forcefully executed the lessons.

Today if Dad did what was done then he would be in jail for child abuse. So would some others in my childhood community, because angry, uncontrolled and unrelenting punishment was not openly condemned.

Dad liked massages and pedicures, although in rural Oklahoma they were not called that! They were called "back-rubs" and "pick my toes." I remember at nine being designated as the primary child to rub his neck and back, as well as cut his toe nails and clean them. It was a sickening job, and I hated it. It was a debasing and humiliating job to pick Dad's toes! When a request was not honored it became a demand and I had to move quickly to avoid punishment. At nine I wasn't big enough to defend against some forms of injustice. It is now clear to me how victims of incest feel!

The pain a child represses seems to make it go away. I handled my father's behavior toward me by repressing the pain. However, it did not make it go away forever. It simmered within me until it could no longer be repressed. When I showed anger, Dad whipped me for getting angry. He said I was not supposed to get angry. Now at age 50 the painful memories are as vivid as if they happened yesterday. I learned grieving them is the necessary way to deal with, and heal them.

I did anything to get Dad to love me, praise me, validate

me. At an early age I found one good way to do that was work. In work I could get a little of what I yearned. If I dug the longest and widest ditch there might be a little back handed praise. "At least Paul's ditch doesn't look as bad as yours," Dad would say.

The lost, empty, lowdown feelings which came from my father's whippings or tongue lashing were the most damaging experiences of my life. (When I left home I vowed never to let anyone else ever do that to me.) To be denied my fathers love and affection was torture. At times I tried to hug him, to show my love and to get his love. He became angry and said, "Quit begging Paul, you have to learn to be a man!" as he shoved me away.

Values in Avant were never re-examined! The totalitarianism practiced as I grew up can be traced all the way back to our country's founding generation.

The mores of the early day Americans helped form the American character represented in Avant. The three central strands of our culture are biblical, republican and modern individualist. The Puritans brought the rigid biblical mores blindly practiced in Oklahoma as I grew up. The founding generation of the American Republic produced American individualism (see *Habits of the Heart: Individualism and Commitment in American Life* by Robert Bellah and others).

In Avant the way individualism was practiced, as in most towns and cities across America, left the individual in terrifying isolation. Self-reliance was deemed a virtue, but in Avant it was practiced in a way that left the individual isolated! Feelings and emotions were never shared except when a major crisis existed, as when a house burned down. Otherwise you were expected, at a very early age, to make it on your own.

ODE TO MY DAD

Paul W. Stearns

How did you learn what you learned?
Where did you learn what you learned?
Can you un-learn what you've learned?
What if what you learned is to control?
What if what you learned is to fear?
Can modification be learned?
Does fear ever go away?
Will surrender protect you?
Control is an illusion—I've come to that conclusion.

CHAPTER THREE

SCHOOL YEARS

THE SLAVE

Paul W. Stearns

Look at that slave working in the field
He works bareback to the sun
He has scars on his back
Weary though he be, works as though he's free
Whip cracks 40 times—40 scars
Can't kill his spirit!
Look at that male child fritter from here to there
He works in a different way—his work is his play
Cheery though he be—he's not free
He's a slave to tongues used like whips
Whip cracks 40 times—40 scars
Can kill his spirit

      Our lives in Avant revolved around work, family, church and school. The schools, both public and church, were important to the small town rural community. What we were taught at church and school re-enforced what was taught at home. There was a feeling that folks already knew all the answers in life. Those answers were passed on by the parents at home. Your views were shaped by the immediate and extended family, not by the school. Once a truth was pronounced it was the law and never to be changed. It was not debatable. The school was expected to reinforce truths, not foster searching for them. Public schools delivering any

31

more than the basic rudiments of the three R's were not to be trusted.

In Avant, our contact with the community revolved around the school. To be educated in urban America residents talk about the broader community and environment. People in our world seldom did!

Age six, in my family, was an important time. For one thing all the Stearns boys started learning to steer a car by sitting on Dad's knee. It was the age we started school too!

September, 1943, my first day of school, I entered a new world and was expected to find my own way. I felt defenseless and scared. Loneliness was something I had already learned so it seemed no worse on this day. I left my parent's world to share with the outside world.

The school year began in mid-September and ended in the middle of May. Most of the students were farmer's kids and needed in the fields to help with spring planting or the fall harvest.

My dress attire for the first day of school was overalls, a handmade sack cloth shirt and clodhoppers. The clodhoppers were ankle high, lace-up, cowhide shoes, worn principally by farmers. Being ankle high and lace-up they kept dirt out while walking in the fields. Sack cloth shirts were made out of livestock feed sacks. The cotton fabric came in various prints.

The first day of school each year, although scary, was pretty special, and exciting.

If you had anything new on the first day of school, like clothes, pencils, or books this was the time to show them off. My shirt was brand spanking new (even though it was homemade) as were my overalls. The clodhoppers had seen better days, but at least they didn't have holes in the soles, nor was one sole completely loose or flopping. When they started to wear out they sometimes did that until you could get them sewn back up.

At school the unofficial dress code required snap button western shirts and Levi pants. Levi's were coveted as Ralph Lauren pants are today. And I was described as a "hillbilly." The social class distinction was clear. Little did the people doing the name calling know that everyone in Tulsa considered people in Avant rednecks. Of course Tulsans were city slickers to us.

Times were improving, but still difficult, in Avant. At home we still had water gravy from time to time, instead of gravy made with milk. Our food was very simple. Now we've learned why the life expectancy of people back then was so short. All the foods were high in cholesterol, fat content, and starch. A typical meal included fried potatoes, bacon, gravy, mush, and okra. All still taste very good to me today despite their poor nutritional value.

On that fateful first day the school bus came to a stop just up the road from Mrs. Baker's house. She would be my first grade teacher, and as a matter of fact, the only teacher the first grade had. She taught everything we were expected to learn!

Mrs. Baker's husband was a field foreman for the McBride Oil Company, an important job, so the Bakers were important people. Their house was within one hundred yards of the dirt road to Skiatook in one direction and Avant in the other. The same road ran to our house which was one and a half miles from the bus stop.

As the school bus came to a stop, Sis would yell, "Dale, Paul, we're going to miss the bus if we don't run." Then she would take off like a flash. Our hearts were pumping as we approached the bus with the metal stop sign flipped straight out from its side, it came to a stop and the doors cantilevered open. Ray Maloy, driving the bus, greeted us. "You kids want a ride, better be on time tomorrow." I was scared to death! It never occurred to this six year old kid that Ray Maloy would have waited forever if he saw us. He was a friend to all kids; we were his flock.

My sister Virginia (I thought her name was Sis, that's all any of us ever called her) was in the sixth grade and Dale was in fourth. They were old hands at catching the bus. While I relied on them that first morning it was still pretty scary.

We climbed into the bus panting and it was full except for one seat which Sis took. The bus had two more stops to make before we arrived at the school house. On most days only six kids had to stand up.

When the bus reached school everyone got off and went their separate ways. Unfortunately I had no idea where to go. My older brother and sister were concerned about themselves. Little Jr. Anthony had just gotten off the bus and his uncle, Big Jr. Anthony, a sixth grader, was with him. Thankfully Little Jr. noticed me and said, "I'm going to the first grade, follow us." Big Jr. had him by the hand and took us to Mrs. Baker's class. Big Jr. and Little Jr. were named after their respective fathers who had the same first and last names, but different middle names.

Our first grade class met in what was called the grade school when built in 1910. It was the only school. It was constructed of dark brown brick and had two stories. In the late twenties another school, called the high school, was built. The two facilities sat twenty feet apart. Grades one through eight met in the grade school, grades nine through twelve met in the high school.

Big Jr. dropped us off at Mrs. Baker's class. She welcomed us and showed us where to place our coats, sweaters, sack lunches. The lockers were wooden and covered with chicken wire. You could see through them. They had two compartments, a top where the sack lunch and books went, and a bottom with hooks to hang coats and place galoshes if you had them. My galoshes were clodhoppers.

The bell rang at 9:00. Since we had arrived at 8:45 we had little time for chatter or getting acquainted. Mrs. Baker's classroom was rectangular with a wooden floor, and windows all along one side. A chalk board ran the full width of the front of the room, with a rail at the bottom to hold erasers and chalk. We each had a desk with a chair affixed to it. The desk top raised as a lid and exposed space for our pencils, books and papers. The top, or lid, had an indentation to hold pencils from rolling off and slanted top when closed. It also had a hole called an ink well, which would hold a bottle of Schaefer ink. As the class began, Mrs. Baker asked us to get out our crayons and take the blue crayon out of the box. It seemed everyone had new boxes and new crayons except me. My crayons were hand-me-downs from Sis and Dale.

I leaned forward and tapped Barbara Okerson on the shoulder and said, "Can you tell me which crayon is blue?"

She laughed and said "That one is." I didn't say thank you because we had been interrupted with laughter. She and the other kids sitting next to us thought it was funny that I asked about a color. No one, including me, knew at the time that I was color blind.

Mrs. Baker was conscientious and a real disciplinarian. If a student did not toe the line, she called him or her forward and bent the offender over her knee. There, with a specially built paddle (it had holes in it so the air wouldn't hold the paddle back) she gave each student four or five swats with the paddle. Her rules were unbreakable and if broken, punishment was swift and sure.

My Father had a cardinal rule; if you got whipped at school, you got another whipping when you got home. It didn't matter to him if you were guilty of an infraction. The fact that you got whipped was all he needed. I remember only two school whippings in my twelve years. Yes, Dad followed up!

Recess came and we all ran out to the playground. The playground had two merry-go-rounds, three banks of swings, three big slides and a small softball diamond at one end. It was a frenzy of activity. The entire school, grades one through twelve were on the same general playground at recess, at the same time. I had never seen that many people together at one time, in one place in my life.

Recess was over as quickly as it began and as we started back to the classes, we had to walk by the lockers containing our sack lunches. The aroma of bananas, apples, cookies, bologna and peanut butter sandwiches was strong. The sacks had become stained with cooking oil. It was almost 11:00 and I hadn't eaten since breakfast at 6:00 that morning. I was so hungry I felt as if my stomach was stapled to my spine. My love affair with noon lunch began at that instant. What the other kids brought always looked better than mine. Some had metal lunch pails and maybe that's what made them look better.

Each afternoon, after recess, we took naps. After school on that first day, Little Jr. Anthony and I went directly to the bus staging area. We met Big Jr., my sister and brother there. The bus ride home was as thrilling as the morning had been, although the walk home was uneventful.

The days passed, each of us taking our turns cleaning chalk boards and erasers. The first grade was a time of innocence, but also one of initiation that continued throughout grade school. The initiation seemed endless. I never really felt I had my feet on the ground.

The next day I began to learn the rituals that probably had been going on as long as there had been school buses. We arrived at the bus stop but the bus was not there. Two other kids joined us so the five of us got in a little horseplay. Then someone yelled out, "Here comes the bus." It stopped and the sign flipped out to the side of the bus. The doors opened and we crawled on. The others found seats at the front of the bus and I went to the rear and found a seat. Behind me were Little Jr. and Big Jr. The bus jolted forward and as it did something hit my ear and the sting was painful. I looked behind me and several kids laughed. I said, "Who did that?" It was apparent someone had flipped my ear with his finger, but no one owned up to it. I faced forward and it happened again. Again I looked back and asked who did it. Everyone laughed and yelled in unison, neh, neh, na, neh, neh. I started to cry, partly because my ear hurt, but mostly because of the humiliation of everyone laughing at me. I couldn't fight back, I was powerless. When we arrived at school I was glad to get off the bus. I didn't know it but I had just encountered the first bully of my life and I was frightened, intimidated, and alone.

The second day of school got my mind off the morning's incident and it was just as wondrous as the first until school let out and we boarded the bus. Again Little Jr. and Big Jr., who were always together, sat behind me, and as before Sis and Dale were at the front of the bus. The morning scenario was repeated and I got off the bus crying. Sis and Dale asked what happened and I told them. They told me I was a sissy. When I got home no support came from there either. Little did I know that was what finding my own way was to be like. It was never clearer to me I was expected to make it on my own. There was no one to turn to for help. In the future I avoided sitting in front of the Anthonys.

As the first grade school year evolved, the sense of wonder did too. I was always curious, energetic, outgoing and active.

One day while in the high school study hall a group of juniors and seniors who had developed a country band were playing their musical instruments. There was a fiddle, guitar, drums and harmonica. The music lifted my spirits. The desks were moved back to clear some space. I got out in the middle of the floor and began clog dancing. We all had a great time laughing and listening to music. It seemed the entire school was in that study hall being entertained by that band and me. I had a great time and I thought I was a great clog dancer.

It was great until the bus ride home ended. We got off the bus and Sis and Dale collared me. "Where did you come off doing what you did?"

"What did I do?" I asked. I had no idea what they were talking about!

They tried to catch me to beat me up, but I ran home and told Mom what had happened. Sis and Dale came home and told her about my clog dancing and how horrible it was. While she did not give me any support she did not let them hurt me either. They said "Wait till Dad gets home, you'll get in big trouble." We always got home at 3:45 and Dad got home between 5:00 and 5:30. Those hours were filled with terror. What would he do to me?

When Dad got home he and Mother laughed. I complained about Dale and Sis harassing me, but Dad said, "Paul, what do you expect if you embarrass them? They aren't going to like it. Remember that." Although I didn't get support I was relieved Dad didn't whip me. I didn't understand what I had done that was bad, but Sis and Dale thought the world had come to an end, they said I had embarrassed the whole family by becoming a clog dancer! This day was the day I learned that not only did I have to make it on my own, I had to defend myself against my own sister and brother. Yet I had no way to defend myself.

Starting the second grade in school brought a great feeling of excitement and new fears. Excitement about going to school again and fear the ear flipping and taunting would start again.

I had avoided sitting in front of the Anthonys until the first day of school in the second grade. That first day of school Little Jr. flipped my ears at Big Jr.'s urging. I didn't say anything but I moved. When we got to school and Big Jr. left the area, I shoved Little Jr. and said, "If you ever, ever do that again I'm going to do something to you that you never heard of." The word spread, and from that day on no one flipped my ears. This could have been a learning experience showing me how to handle bullies in the future, but for some reason it wasn't.

Bob started first grade as I started the second, so he joined Sis and Dale in our daily walks to and from the bus stop.

Our second grade teacher, Mrs. Glyde Tayler, had a stern manner and a method of punishment feared by all. Her prior students graphically described all the various ways she induced physical pain. I was under her spell and in a state of fear before I ever encountered her.

No sooner had school started, and perhaps to set the stage for the year, the most feared ritual of punishment was given to Don Selby. Don made the mistake of talking back. Mrs. Tayler went to his desk and said, "Don, stick out your right hand, palm up." When his arm was fully extended and the hand was facing palm up, she took what appeared to be the world's largest ruler and struck his hand. We all watched him wince with pain at each blow. Finally, on the sixth blow, Don with reflex action punched her in the stomach with his left fist. When Mrs. Tayler recovered her composure, she sent Don to the principal's office. Then he was sent home by the principal. It took a miracle to get Don back into school. Don's father was a Pentecostal Preacher and most thought

God's hand had surely come into play to get Don back in school. The ruler although prominently exposed on Mrs. Tayler's desk never came out of its holster again that year.

The western band was still performing from time to time. Each day at noon, after eating our sandwiches, we would go to the high school study hall to watch them perform. I was invited to dance again, but being mindful of Sis and Dale's attitude declined each invitation. However, on this one day I had just acquired through a trade, a corn cob pipe with a yellow bowl. With that corn cob pipe in my mouth, my bib overalls, sack cloth shirt and clodhoppers, the spirit moved me to dance. I got out in the middle of that study hall and gave the performance of my life. The laughter and clapping were intoxicating. When it was over I went back to class, with my yellow bowl pipe placed where the hammers are usually carried in a pair of overalls. It never occurred to me to put tobacco or anything else in that pipe, I didn't want to ruin it.

Apparently this time I went too far. Not only had I the audacity to perform, I had done so with a pipe in my mouth. We got home from the bus ride and I ran ahead of Sis and Dale.

My brother and sister couldn't wait to tell Dad about my "disgraceful behavior." Dad became so furious he took off his belt, bent me over and whipped me until welts rose. While whipping me Dad intoned, "I'll teach you to learn how to smoke. This is what you'll get every time I hear about your wanting to smoke!"

I didn't understand what I had done wrong, all I knew was that I was an embarrassment and a "disgrace" to the family. I couldn't fathom it. I didn't want to smoke, but if I wanted to why couldn't I? Dad chewed tobacco and Grandad smoked cigars and chewed. Almost all the high school boys smoked. What was wrong? Clog dancing, tap dancing or square dancing was done by everyone. So what was wrong? The lesson; don't embarrass your sis or brother or father. If you do something is wrong with you. The problem was, I didn't know what would embarrass them. When you're six years old you don't know what embarrassment is! I learned later in life, that childhood is a time of special innocence. Children tend to respond to the world with spontaneity and honesty. Their naivete and openness creates vulnerability to abuse that is most damaging when inflicted by other family members.

My next theatrical performance was an organized production in which the entire second grade performed. Our mothers made elf costumes by dying long handled underwear, the ones with a flap in the rear. They took socks and transformed them into elf shoes with pointed toes. Head gear was made for all but the lead in the "Jack Frost" winter production. The lead did not have to wear elf head gear because the title song "Jack Frost—Get Lost Get Lost" was to be sung. The head cover would have muffled the voice. I was selected to be the lead and performed to rave reviews, however I felt more ill at ease in this costume and singing that silly song than when I clog danced for the whole school. How can one thing seem so wrong while another appears to be okay? How can something else be so entirely right when others make it seem so wrong? It got lonelier finding my own way.

Grade school, and in the summer periods when church school was in session, was a time of learning fundamental rules. I was told what to do, how to do it and when to do it.

At grade school, church school and home everyone was telling me what to think, how to feel and what to say! I had no latitude to be an individual with individual thoughts, feelings or freedom in expressing them.

The hard work, discipline, lessons, and fear to which I was exposed in my grade school years however, did not completely thwart my spontaneity. Somehow I maintained a reservoir of curiosity, energy, childlike naivete, and I got into trouble with my family at every turn. I never had a problem with finding something to be ridiculed, laughed at, or punished for. My spirit pushed me to experiment with life, although I didn't call it that at the time.

Our pick-up truck was the family transportation. Dad, Mom and Sis always rode in the cab. Dale, Bob, Jerry and I always rode in the rear. The pick-up and livestock were a part of our lives. Because we hauled livestock with the pick-up truck from time to time, Dad had built a stock rack and mounted it on the truck bed. The stock rack was built in such a way that it looked like a jail cell. None of us boys liked to ride in it but we had no choice. As we peered between the cell bars, we thought people were making fun of us. Every time we went to town to get our mail, we parked on Main Street perpendicular to the store. The sidewalk was between the pick-up truck and the stores.

Mrs. Helmrich would come out of the Post Office and visit with us. She had heard me sing "Jack Frost" at school and "The Old Rugged Cross" at church and she offered me a penny to sing for her. To turn professional had not entered my mind. But I granted her request in exchange for the penny. I asked what song she wanted and she said the Jack Frost song would be fine. I sang it and she gave me the penny. I got permission to go into the drug store to spend it. I was not required to share my booty with Bob and Dale, so I didn't. For a couple of years after that Mrs. Helmrich asked me to sing, until one day she asked and I said I wouldn't for a penny, but would for a nickel, and she said okay. This time Dale and Bob wanted to join my singing and we sang "You Are My Sunshine." I had to split my booty with them. This helped me to realize that performing or striving can embarrass brothers and sisters unless money is involved, then self-interest alters the embarrassment enough for them to overcome it.

After that day Mrs. Helmrich no longer requested me to sing. I did not find until much later that I had priced myself out of the market. Even though the five cents got her a group performance it was not enough to sustain her interest.

Work is an important part of what rural folk teach their young. Dad told us, "People who don't work are lazy, worthless and I won't have worthless people in my house." Dad killed two birds with one stone by using free land from the Oil Company to have a garden for growing produce and run some animals on. At age six I had work assigned to me. Dad said it kept us busy and out of trouble. When we were big enough to do the work Dad bought some animals. We got to a point where we had a few head of hogs, cattle and chickens. We could have our own milk, eggs, butter, and meat. We occasionally sold an animal for profit. Our household budget was helped by producing some of our own food. As a family of seven it saved a lot of money.

Gardening was hard work. Not being farmers we didn't have the right equipment to make things easier. We planted and grew onions, cabbage, lettuce, corn, okra, tomatoes, watermelons, cantaloupe, plus many other items. At harvest time we canned many of the vegetables we grew for winter consumption. Mother did the canning with all the kids assisting.

I learned good values during this process of planting, caring for and harvesting. Rural people come to know the seasons in a close, personal way. But try to tell kids that when they are forced to labor, much like the old chain gang of the south. That's sort of the way we felt. Dad was a do-as-I-say-not-as-I-do kind of guy and was quick to back it up with his belt.

At early ages Dad made sure my brothers and I were busy all the time. He could invent more work to be done than anyone. He did not tolerate us in bed after 7:30 in the morning. He came and woke us, and if we didn't move quickly enough to suit him he pulled ears and inflicted verbal, as well as physical pain, until we were out of bed. Dad said, "You boys are lazy and I'm going to whip you if you don't get the jobs I've assigned you done."

He was almost impossible to please. We never worked fast enough or good enough. "Loud" worked in our house. When Dad raised his voice we all scattered. We knew what would happen!

The most severe fights I ever had with my brothers were while working on things Dad had us doing. Working under such conditions put us all in a bad mood.

Dad, Dale, Bob and I were working near the house one day when I was twelve years old. Something happened that caused Dale to become angry with me. He started chasing me and I ran to our car. I got in, slammed and locked the doors, before Dale could catch me. He started beating on the windows yelling, "I'll kill you, I'll kill you." I was scared! It seemed to go on forever until Dale finally went away. I avoided seeing him until supper that evening. I complained to Dad about Dale's aggressiveness, and Dad said, "Paul, don't give cause for Dale to hurt you and he won't." I never felt safe in my own family.

My memories of hard work began at age twelve. Dad did not lead us by example. I can't remember him working along side us. He told us what to do and watched us do it, or he came back and inspected our progress. The most wonderful feeling I would have ever had was for him to tell me, or us, we had done a good job. It never happened!

Butchering was always done in the fall, usually one hog and one calf, to last us through the winter. Chickens were butchered on an as needed basis. I found out pretty quick about the desire of an animal to live. A famous black hog with whiskers had become a pet to my brothers and me by the time it was large enough to be butchered. First we shot it in the head with a .22 rifle, then hit it in the center of the forehead with a ballpeen hammer and finally took a butcher knife, slit its throat and stuck the butcher knife down its throat to stick its heart. It must have thought we were serious, because it finally gave up. Chickens were worse. You could ring their heads off and they still flopped around on the ground.

The next step after an animal was killed was to gut it, skin it and do the final preparation for transportation to the meat locker in Skiatook. In rural Oklahoma, we didn't have refrigerators because we had no electricity. Only the bigger towns had meat lockers for rent. The meat locker personnel divided an animal into its various parts and packaged or wrapped it for our private meat locker.

Every Saturday we went to Skiatook for the meat we planned to use the next week, brought it home and placed it in an ice box. We bought ice by the twenty-five pound block in Skiatook. In later years, during the summer months, it was a real treat to go to the livestock auction in Collinsville, Saturday afternoons, then to Skiatook to the picture shows, then to the meat lockers before we went home. The picture

show was always a double feature. A "Western" starring
Roy Rogers or Gene Autry was usually shown, plus another
movie and a short comedy film. More often than not, the
Three Stooges.

After church on Sunday Dale, Bob and I would act out
with stick horses, masks (handkerchiefs) and Dad's old hats
the movie we had seen the previous night.

When we didn't have chores, and before we were
required to work for someone outside the family, we filled
the summer with Tom Sawyer types of episodes. We
explored hills, caves, visited the swimming hole, all the
while watching out for water moccasins, copperheads or rattle snakes. We seldom saw snakes, but our family pet dog
was pretty good at finding them. Dogs like to sniff things.
Snakes aren't creatures that liked to be sniffed. Nature was
cruel at times, snakes killed our pet dogs, sometimes a
chicken in the chicken coop.

Hunting and fishing were other activities we participated
in. My first was my last time to fish. I got the pole, cord,
bobber, hook and bait all set, threw the line in the water, and
sat there for three hours. The bobber only moved when the
wind moved it. There was no way I would like fishing so I've
never been again.

Hunting was another matter. We had several methods. In
the winter we hunted rabbits with a stick and a gunny sack.
We went to every oil well in the area. Each oil well had a
pipe, hollow and open at both ends. Rabbits built nests in
the pipe. One brother held the sack open around one end of
the pipe, the other brother used the stick to poke through
the pipe running any rabbits that happened to be there into
the sack. We used a shotgun for swamp rabbits, squirrel and
quail. Dale was the all-time best hunter and fisherman of the
family and still is. However, I did one-up him one day when I
was fourteen years old. We had just gotten a combination
410 gauge shotgun and 22 gauge rifle, called an over and
under. I took off to hunt anything I could find. I got no more
than 100 yards from the house and saw two squirrels. One
was crawling up the trunk of the tree and the other was out
on one of the limbs. I fired the shotgun at the squirrel on the

limb and the "22" at the one on the trunk of the tree. I killed them both and immediately went back to the house with my prizes. Dale, a competitive guy, talked about how lucky I was and how I would never be able to do that again. I didn't tell him or anyone else but killing those two squirrels really bothered me. I've never killed another one and haven't been hunting since. Hunting and fishing are not for me.

Despite the Tom Sawyer types of episodes and the normalcy, there was the ever present threat of physical violence if we didn't toe the line.

Floods were a part of our lives. On occasion lightning started fires. We were at the picture show in Skiatook one Saturday night in 1947 when Dad came in to get us, saying "Boys, we have to go home, our house is on fire." There was a severe lightning and rain storm going on and Ray Parks, our closest neighbor, had seen flames in the sky. When he went to see what was on fire and found it was our house, he kept going to Skiatook to find us. Neither Avant nor Skiatook had fire equipment, so once a fire started, it continued until it burned itself out.

We left Skiatook in a hurry, but when we got home, the house had caved in and was burning. The foundation was the only part intact. Before I tell how we found shelter, let me say something about my grandfather who was visiting us when the fire broke out.

Mom's dad and mother and youngest brother, Chuck, were visiting us from Holtville, California. Grandad Stephens was a great guy. Like my Dad he always had a cud of Redman tobacco in his mouth and, like my Dad, slept with it in his mouth. He always had a Folgers coffee can by his bed as spittoon to spit in during the night. Grandad occasionally smoked Roitan cigars, but mostly he chewed them. His mother always dipped snuff when he was growing up thus providing the role model that passed on from generation to generation.

Grandad was a crusty, coarse, swearing-every-other-word, old dude. He loved rodeos and wore snap button western shirts, Levis and a hat—felt in the winter, straw in the summer.

I loved him in a way indescribable for a young boy. Grandpa Stearns was okay. But Grandad Stephens was the greatest! I always seemed to matter to him, and he actually took up for me. He was a man's man and never took any crap from anybody, but on occasion gave it. I always felt safe and protected with him. I never had that feeling before he came to visit nor after he left. He was tough with his own kids, but with grandkids, he was tender. We didn't see him often but when we did it was the highlight, the crescendo. I came alive.

Tragedy had struck. Our house was gone. Because we had gone to Skiatook in Grandad's car, our car, which was parked too close to the house, was damaged too! The right front tire was destroyed and the fender paint burned. Minor damage, but it didn't seem minor that night in the dark. The lightning was still flashing in the distance and light rain still falling. We all kept asking, "Why, why couldn't the rain have been falling hard enough to put out the fire?" With no house, car or clothing, what were we to do? Except for the clothes on our backs, all we owned had been destroyed.

The tragedy was my first lesson in community spirit. People from miles around soon knew about the fire. Some friends in town took us in for the night. The next day we rented a house one mile southwest of Avant. People brought furniture, clothes, shoes and everything you might imagine to outfit the rented house. It was all old and used but we could still use it. They also brought an unconditional love born of compassion.

Over the next four months Dad found a permanent house to take up residence in. First it had to be moved across the holler from where our burned house was because the road system into the old house could not accommodate a truck with a house loaded on it. The new location was barely two hundred yards from the old one but required a different road and a new bus stop.

Memories of the old house faded, but never went away. Memories like becoming a shade tree mechanic, or at least a helper. Dad wanted my help to overhaul a '35 Ford. First the engine was pulled out of the car by throwing a chain over the biggest limb of the oak shade tree. My job was to fetch tools. I was ten years old and didn't know a socket wrench from an end wrench from a hammer, but that didn't matter, I was a mechanics helper. Everything went fine until Dad became frustrated with something. When I handed him a 3/8" socket instead of an end wrench, he said, "Paul, you're worthless, what's the matter with you, that's not the correct wrench, get your head screwed on straight and get me the end wrench." I got the wrong size, and he exploded saying, "You'll never be worth a dime." I ran into the house crying.

We moved into the new house as I started the fifth grade. We all helped put the finishing touches on the house. It was a family affair.

We salvaged and moved the old outdoor "john." Dale and I had dug a hole upon which it would sit. We had poured in some lye. After the "john" was set up we put a new coat of whitewash on it. The trees in the front yard were white-washed four feet off the ground to dress them up. A wash house was built and we placed mom's old gasoline engine Maytag washer in it.

The only remaining tie to the burned house location was our garden. The new house was bigger than the house that had burned. Our new house had two bedrooms, a living room and a room that contained the kitchen and dining area. It had cold running tap water, a gas mantle for lighting, a gas stove for heat and an ice box. We were still without electricity.

Dale, Bob and I slept three to a bed. Jerry slept in his own bed. Mom and Dad took the other bedroom and Sis slept in the living room. She couldn't go to bed until we all did.

It was in this house I learned to put my socks and shoes on before getting out of bed in the morning. Touching your bare feet to the floor in the winter time was not a good idea. With no heat in our bedroom and the wood floors covered with linoleum, the floors were extremely cold. Sub-zero was common.

Tom Sawyer's escapades were uneventful compared to ours. Our need to emulate our elders led to great experimentation and resulted in great discomfort when we got caught.

For example, smoking and chewing tobacco was something everyone seemed to participate in. When I was fifteen it looked good. I found some things to smoke that people had tried all the way back to the native Indians. Grape vine was porous and made good smoking, my tongue got beet red and awfully sore but that wasn't important. Corn silk and coffee grounds wrapped in newspaper made great smoking too, especially in a cave with a camp fire going and your friends at your side. I hadn't forgotten Dad whipping me for the corn cob pipe, but I didn't plan to get caught this time! The picnics around the camp fire in the caves included food preparations that made us feel like we were eating great dinners. Hot dogs, potatoes wrapped in tin foil and placed under the coals like the Indians of old did it.

Tobacco of all kinds was forbidden fruit. It was hard for a kid to understand why he was whipped for doing something his parents and everyone else did. Experimentation with forms other than smoking wasn't well received either. Dad's packages of "Red Man" chewing tobacco were always strewn around the house. His cud of tobacco in his cheek always looked so good. When you're a young kid you love your dad and you want to do everything he does.

Joe Dean Chambers, one year older than me, lived up the hill at the entrance to the dirt road that led to our place. A path we had made across the hills was a considerable short cut. We visited each other often and one day he suggested we take some of Dad's tobacco and go for a walk in the woods. We picked up a partial package and took off. We got out of sight of the house and placed a cud in our mouths. We chewed then spit and spit and spit. . .the saliva glands working triple duty. In an hour or so, I was getting sick to my stomach and it was getting dark so we started back to the house. Joe Dean went home; I went in the house. I did not eat supper. I was feeling woozy and sick to my stomach. I went to bed early. At breakfast the next morning guilt set in to such an extent that I had to confess my sin to Mom and Dad. I told them I had chewed tobacco and should be punished. They laughed saying Dad had told Mother the evening before he thought I had chewed tobacco and was experiencing its side effects. I avoided a beating because Mom told Dad that getting sick was punishment enough.

The most important fixture in our new house was a battery operated RCA radio. We sat enthralled listening to Jack Benny, George Burns and Gracie Allen, The Green Hornet, The Shadow or The Lone Ranger. Each evening this magical box transported us from those hills to new lands.

Exploring the woods near our home was great fun. Lewis and Clark did not see wonders more grand than those we saw. We saw fish swimming in the creek and when we were thirsty simply leaned over the clear water to get a drink. We walked across the swinging bridge, over Bird Creek. It was built by the oil field people to get more quickly from lease to lease. We placed our wart plagued hands into old dead tree stumps that retained rain water believing stump water would remove the wart. My warts did leave, but only after a doctor surgically removed them. Our walks involved picking hickory nuts, walnuts and wild greens for poke salads. Mountain climbing was always possible because the "holler" was about two hundred feet wide and seventy-five feet deep. It looked like a small grand canyon. We occasionally scaled the cliffs. The animals were as varied as could be and all had a purpose in our ecological system. Hoot owls, swamp rabbits, squirrels, opossums, raccoons, birds of every description, had their roles. I came alive in those hills. I felt free in those hills.

The new house wasn't air tight. When we left in the winter, for safety we always turned off the open flame gas stoves. When we got home and lit the fires, it took forever to warm the house and sometimes it felt as if the house would never warm completely. The only thing to do was to stand directly in front of the fire, you got warm on one side and froze on the other. Getting into bed was particularly punishing, the cold bed sheets were very unpleasant. That was the only time sleeping three to a bed made any sense. Another indication that the house was not air tight occurred the morning we woke up and found a five foot black snake crawling up the wall.

For me grade school was an anxious time. It was all new

and I never knew what was going to happen next. Some of the things I did know were going to happen heightened my anxiety and fear. The seventh grade was one of those times.

Entering the seventh grade and witnessing the ninth graders entering high school was part of my anxiety. In two years I would be initiated and it became crystal clear that involved real pain. When we entered the ninth grade students were required to participate in two rituals as part of an overall initiation. Both were carried out the first day of school. The initation was for boys only. First hair was chopped using unimaginable instruments such as barber scissors, shears, knives, and the like. The haircut was uneven, butchered, and cropped looking. Once the hair was shorn, your pants were lowered and the pubic hair was clipped and shoe polish was used to paint the area where the pubic hair had been. After concluding these first two rites of passage all the upper classmen formed in two lines facing each other. They held their belts in their hands. Some had stainless steel tips, some were made out of old clothes line cord. Each freshman had to run the gamut, passing as many as forty boys, twenty on each side. As he passed each struck him, hitting his butt, legs, or back. Big welts were expected. Needless to say, speed getting through the "belt line" was crucial.

The initation rituals were never done on the school grounds. Most times they were done across the street from the school, sometimes downtown. As long as they were done off the school grounds the school officials had no authority to stop them.

Lucky for me a stop was put to these initiations before I had to pass the test. Invariably there was one boy who resisted and it took several fellows to cut his hair. That was part of the fun for the older boys. The year I entered eighth grade, a ninth grader knifed one of the upper classmen. The school took authority and decided the tradition had to end, and end it did. I had done all that worrying for nothing. I was just beginning to get good at looking ahead and anticipating pain that might lie there.

I was certainly getting old enough to see and understand

there were some things in the world which were intimidating.

Making money was important and occasionally selling animals or garden items showed me how money could be made. I started getting creative in supplying what I thought people might want and would pay for. The experience of making a penny and later a nickel every time I sang for the Post Mistress whetted my appetite for making money and buying things. The roots of my entrepreneurial yearnings started to take hold. They grew deeper throughout high school.

My first real entrepreneurial experience was ordering enough garden seed for our own use, and convincing Dad to get additional seed to sell to others. My market research wasn't good enough to tell me I didn't have a broad enough market. Within one and a half miles of our home we only had two neighbors. Even if they both bought from me, which they didn't, I still wouldn't have made enough money to pay for the excess seed we purchased. We planted all the left over seed, making a huge garden, making a bigger work load for us.

My bid to become a Grit newspaper carrier ended with the same result as the seeds venture. Just not enough customers. Grit was a publication distributed primarily to the rural population of America in those days.

My next venture showed my lack of experience in inventory control. I ordered, by mail, one hundred baby chicks. When they came to the Post Office, we picked them up and took them to their new home, an old oil tank made out of wooden stays, eight feet in diameter. With the help of Dad and Dale, "I" covered the top with tin. The night the baby chicks arrived a gully washer type rain came, the roof did not hold. All but twenty of the one hundred baby chicks were drowned. In frustration we raised the twenty baby chicks as fryers to be butchered instead of selling.

During the years I sold garden seed, Grit newspapers, and raised baby chickens I told the entire family one day I would be wealthy. It was clear to me money could solve some problems we had. They all thought that was funny.

The usual sarcasm was dished out, but in addition Dad said, "Paul, you'll end up like Leo Dhiel or Roe Little!" I asked, "What does that mean?" Dad explained that Leo Dhiel was a wealthy man who had owned several grocery stores. He was also an alcoholic, who died choking on his own vomit. Roe Little was wealthy, owned a furniture store and several ranches. He was a miser and screwed everybody he dealt with. He didn't have a friend on this earth. "Paul, is that the way you want to be, because that's what happens to wealthy people. You'll never be smart enough to succeed or make money anyway."

He didn't realize I wanted to make money to escape. It wasn't clear to me at the time, but obsessing about business began in those days. If my mind was on a business deal or a way to make money, then I didn't have to think of the pain I felt from being rejected. Dreaming allowed me to escape for a little while. I dreamed of a place where no one swung a belt, called names or made me feel I was insignificant.

Ray Parks now lived another mile down the road from us. Our new house was half way between his and the Skiatook Hill Road. He liked to drink and so did his many friends. We called them drunks because we didn't know what an alcoholic was. As Ray and his friends drove off the "Hill Road" onto our one lane dirt road they would finish a bottle of beer and throw the bottle out along the roadside. This happened for the entire two miles and they kept it up as long as Ray lived there. The empty bottles brought five cents each when redeemed at the store. I created the idea and solicited my brother's to help gather the bottles, take them to town and sell them to one of the stores. We began at our house and started up the hill to the main road. We then came back and gathered more bottles as we went to Ray Park's house. We were careful to look on both sides of the road. Pop bottles were okay because we got two cents for them, but beer bottles, at five cents, were what we were after. As we approached the house we noticed Ray was not at home. We continued right up to a shed where he always parked his pick-up. The trail of bottles led us into his shed where we found three more bottles. One was full and two were empty.

We didn't differentiate full or empty, we figured they were just laying around, Ray wouldn't want them. So we picked them up, emptied the full one and left with all three. Pouring out a full bottle for a nickel was not a problem to us. That day we hauled seventy beer bottles and ten pop bottles. Three dollars and seventy cents was all the money in the world to us.

All was well until two days later Dad came to us and said, "Boys, Ray Parks tells me he's missing a full bottle of beer. He thinks you boys took it, did you?"

We looked at each other and said, sheepishly, "Yes. We emptied it so we could sell the bottle."

Dad said, "Go give Ray twenty-five cents plus money to pay for the two empties you took. I also want you to tell him you're sorry."

Dad then continued the lesson in what stealing and honesty was. "You boys are going to be thieves are you?" he asked. I felt like a third rate thief. I wanted to hide!

Near beer was another matter. I never tasted anything that could look so good, yet taste so bad. I worked one summer for Fair King in his grocery store as a box boy and clean-up boy. One of my jobs was to re-stock shelves. For a twelve year old, a grocery store has wonderful, tempting merchandise. Temptation was everywhere and I desired much of the merchandise. All was forbidden fruit! Prince Albert tobacco and near beer. The Ray Parks episode was still fresh so stealing never entered my mind, but charging something to Dad's grocery bill was a major temptation

Near beer was non-alcoholic and kept with the pop in a regular pop box used as a cooler. Chunks of ice kept it all cold. People came in the store for pop breaks and drank pop and near beer while I worked. I was so thirsty I could taste that near beer. After working there for most of the week, I decided to charge a ten cent near beer (pop was five cents) to Dad's account. I started to drink it. It was so horrible it gagged me, and I couldn't finish it.

The end of the month came and Dad got his month end bill, saw the near beer and questioned us all. I confessed I had charged it. Dad hit the roof. It seemed his son had something wrong with him! He wanted to be an alcoholic. Dad didn't say anything about me charging it, but he said, "Paul, you're going to be an alcoholic, is that what you want?" My backside was sore for a few days as a result of the whipping I got.

In our family, each child was taught that physical work was important and something responsible people did. Those who didn't work were of no value. Dad made sure from the beginning that we always had something to do. If it wasn't picking up rocks it was mowing grass, or gardening. He went to great lengths to find us odd jobs or regular jobs with farmers, because the oil people wouldn't hire anyone under sixteen years of age.

When I was thirteen years old I worked two days for a neighbor. He was moving a house and had already done the foundation work and the house was in place on the foundation. My job was to backfill around the foundation and crawl under the house to hand tools to a plumber. The day began at 7 A.M. and ended at 7 P.M., with no lunch. At the end of the day the neighbor said, "Young man, I want you back tomorrow, how much do I owe you for today?"

I said, "Pay me tomorrow and I'll ask dad how much to charge and then you can pay me for both days."

The next day I was back at 7 A.M. carrying lunch. When the day ended, my boss said, "Thanks young man, how much do I owe you?"

I said, "Dad told me to tell you pay me what you think I'm worth." He handed me four dollars (two dollars for each day) and a black and white plaid flannel shirt with the pocket torn and dangling half off. The shirt was extra large and I wore a small.

I went home complaining, then showed Dad the four dollars and shirt. Dad said, "Well you must not have been worth more." I certainly felt like I was worth much more. I was angry but didn't dare show it. He knew I was a hard worker. I was angry with the man I worked for because I knew I was taken advantage of. At age thirteen I was big enough, strong enough and already doing a man's work. A man would have been paid more than two dollars per day and a junk shirt!

I was fourteen when I got my first steady summer job on the Oral Landis farm stacking hay. Dad had already placed Dale with another farmer and when he approached Landis, Oral said, "Sure, we'll be balin' hay on and off the whole summer. Tell Paul to come over and we'll give him a try. If he can do the job, we'll keep him until we're done." Dad said, "Okay Oral, Paul isn't worth much, so pay him what you think he's worth." I wondered why Did didn't consider how he made me feel when he said things like that, but I didn't have the nerve to ask.

Their farm wasn't mechanized but they did have a new John Deere tractor. All the other equipment was 19th century.

The close-knit family of eight plus an uncle from the extended family showed acceptance, love and affection for each other. It was an easy going environment where everyone trusted each other to perform his own role. Each had a role on the farm to play, but as they worked I noticed they were interconnected in a more meaningful way. I didn't understand it but I felt it. Perhaps it is the fact that farm families depended on nature for their living that gives them a different approach to life. They learn early in life to depend on each other, as well as nature. Farmers understand the concept of control being an illusion. Faith generally comes easier to people who realize they are dependent on nature.

The first day I reported to work we went directly to the hayfield. The whole Landis family was there, ready to go to work. Bill, Oral's oldest son was trusted with the tractor. Kenneth, another son, worked with a team of horses. Bill's job was to cut the hay, wind row it and get it ready for Kenneth to pick up. Kenneth brought the loose hay in and stacked it in a pile. Alberta blocked out a section of the hay going through the steam powered baler, Geraldine slipped the wire through, Norma Jean tied the section and it came out as a finished bale of hay. My work was to stack the hay. Mrs. Landis and daughters, Bonnie and Cheryl stayed at the house to prepare lunch. At twelve o'clock the dinner bell rang, everything was shut down and we headed for the house.

The dinner table was piled high with two types of meat from their smoke house. (The Landis' were one of the last farmers to use a smoke house.) Both pork and beef were on the table, as well as corn, okra, biscuits, honey, gravy and on and on. Dessert was both cake and pie! The quantity of food was unparalleled in my experience. After lunch, to go back to the field was tough. I was full!

The joyful banter I observed at the table was great. They talked about the problems of the day and had humor without hurting anyone. At my home seldom did a meal pass that someone didn't leave the table crying. Sarcasm, put downs, ridicule and tempers were the order of the day. The Landis family seemed to enjoy a serene life, while mine was always in a turbulent state. Meals in my house were where I developed emotional reactions which were a basis for some of my later problems.

The time I worked for the Landis family was great. I was envious of what I saw. They were naive, innocent, peaceful, harmonious and joyful people. I wanted part of what they had, but the longing I felt was not something I could express.

One of President Roosevelt's programs, the Rural Electrification Authority was a boon to rural America. In 1948 the R.E.A. brought electricity to the part of Oklahoma where we lived. It was significant to all who lived there. We now had electric lights and bought a refrigerator. The Landis' no longer needed their smoke house to preserve meat. Dairy farmers eliminated hand milking by purchasing electric milkers.

The end of the summer came and I felt wealthy with my pay from the Landis family. A ritual began that September that continued until I graduated from college. It was always the same: go to a dry goods store called Bayouths' and purchase three snap pocket western shirts, four pair of Levis, five pair of Hanes t-shirts and shorts, plus a pair of shoes.

School started in September and no sooner had it started, I was caught shooting paper wads and sent home. That was my punishment from school. The school principal knew that Dad had a policy at home to punish us there if we were punished at school.

I was scared to death. I wasn't looking forward to the beating I knew I was going to get. I remember the trip home vividly. I took the long way—railroad tracks along Bird Creek to the McBride Power House, walked across two open farms and then crossed a swinging bridge over Bird Creek— through the rock quarry, to the power house where Dad worked. It took a couple of hours. I never gave a thought to the longer it took the more time I had to worry about the whipping I was going to get!

I met Dad at the power house and told him what happened. He said "Paul, what are you going to be? Worthless all your life! Go on to the house! You ain't even worth whipping." He didn't whip me. This inconsistent behavior made it hard for me. I got whipped for things I never thought would bring a whipping, and didn't get whipped when I thought I deserved it!

In November the eighth grade class planned a bonfire and wiener roast on the banks of Bird Creek. My good friends, Smokey McLaughlin and Little Jr Anthony and I went to the wiener roast. By the time we arrived the whole class was there. So was Floyd Street the grade school bully. I was getting a little attention from the girls and Floyd came over to bully me. He taunted and taunted and taunted me. It occurred to me the only way to stop him was to hit him. I reared back and drove my fist into his nose. Splat—the blood went everywhere. Floyd hit the ground flat on his back. He never got up. That was good, because I was so scared I could not have gone on. I looked around. All the boys in the class came over, slapped me on the back, while Floyd lay on the ground holding his nose. I was a hero, I did what they all had been wanting to do since fifth grade. None of us ever had trouble with Floyd again. He became my friend, as well as a friend to all of us.

School was our contact with community, but the church was the centerpiece of our family. Church helped define what was wrong with me. It taught me that something was inherently wrong with me. It was drummed into me that basically I was neither good nor worthwhile; unless I was saved I was headed to hell. I couldn't figure out a way to do that. I didn't feel the way they told me to feel, although I tried. I never felt safe in church.

Dad's family was very religious. His sisters, Aunt Mary and Edith were missionaries in Africa and India, both serving over twenty-five years. They were married and worked in teams with their husbands. Every five years they came back to the United States to visit relatives and always came to see us. Everywhere they went they were asked to give presentations and show photographs about their experiences. After each presentation the church took up a collection to help them with their work.

Aunt Mary's and Edith's visits came at different times, but it was as if they were the same person. Both were stern, serious, tough and righteous. They had the answers to everything. Their job was to seek converts in Africa and India. I noted religious people were unwavering, yet I was not moved and stimulated in a positive way by what they said.

I winced when I heard them refer to the Africans as stupid niggers. They said it was common to punish them for their transgressions with whips. They also said they had to be taught the right way to think and be punished until they got it right. They preached the fear of hell fire and damnation. Their preaching made the vengefulness of God awesome to behold. When you are ten, eleven, twelve or thirteen, your imagination becomes active when vivid descriptions of God's wrath are described by fundamentalists.

The church picnic or socials took on an air of gaiety, and helped distract me from the fear of dying before I found out how to be saved. Unfortunately they weren't held frequently enough to wipe out the fear completely.

Most of our ministers were not trained at seminary. They were men who had felt the word, had a calling, and on the strength of that became ministers. What they told us was seldom good theology, but generation after generation passed it down without checking it out.

During my sixth grade, the cause of one of my most significant anxieties came from my Father. He did not attribute what he told me to the Bible, but the inference was there. "Paul," he said, "I'm worried about your brother Bob, I think he's going crazy."

Well, he had my attention. I asked, "Why, what has happened, is there anything we can do?"

Dad nodded. "Paul, he's been playing with himself, and going crazy is what happens when you do that."

I didn't figure out for some years that I was at the age of puberty and his true concern was for me. He seemed sincere in wanting to make sure his boys didn't go crazy.

Robert Bly, in the *Naive Male* wrote "In our culture we are often betrayed by our parents—the very ones who love us. They betray us in two ways, the first is by (example) saying 'Johnny, you asked where does the sun go at night'. Johnny says, 'Yes, daddy where does it go?' 'Well, Johnny,' his dad says, 'the sun goes down behind that barn for a rest. It will be rested tomorrow and will come back out.' Bly goes on to say that you might tell a four year old that, but to continue to tell him as an eighteen year old it is a lie and that's a betrayal. The second way Bly talks about betrayal is that our parents don't always tell us how tough it is out in the world. That too is betrayal.

I must have started playing with myself the same day Bob's dilemma was announced to me. If I didn't start then it was certainly on my mind. The exact opposite of what Dad wanted. I think of that incident when Garrison Kieller of *The Prairie Home Companion* said his religion stressed sex as a sin. Taught that way and as a forbidden fruit, he started thinking about it "only at least one thousand times per day."

Masturbation became a release of sorts for me. I remember that on occasion feelings and moods came over me that I thought would never pass. These feelings and moods stemmed from being oppressed and to release them I would go off to the woods, hide behind a tree and masturbate. It was a release of sorts but as soon as I was done, guilt would wash over me to bring back the anxieties I had been feeling.

In our church as you got older a more concerted effort

was made to save you! Reverend Hinckly was still preaching hell, fire and damnation. I reached an age where my fear reached a peak. At the end of each sermon, the pianist played the most tear-jerking old Methodist hymns to arouse people emotionally. After the first stanza, Reverend Hinckly stopped the music and made an appeal to sinners who should be saved. He was always most aggressive on Sunday night. He shouted, "Do you want to go to hell? Do you want to burn? What if you die in your sleep tonight and aren't saved? You'll go to hell." The piano began again and the congregation sang another stanza of *Just As I Am.*

lst Stanza

Just as I am without an plea but that thy blood was
Shed for me and that thou bidst me to come to thee,
O Lamb of God, I come, I come.

2nd Stanza

Just as I am though tossed about to rid my soul of one
dark blot, to thee whose blood can cleanse each spot,
O Lamb of God I come, I come.

Heady stuff during the years from seven to sixteen years old. On one Sunday night in 1951, Reverend Hinckly came back to a pew where Dad was sitting. I was standing beside him. While the singing was going on Reverend Hinckly said, "Kenneth, don't you want to be saved tonight? Will you come to the altar?"

Dad shook his head no. The Reverend went back to the pulpit and started another appeal to the congregation. "Don't you know what you're doing? Don't you know you're going straight to hell! It's not too late if you repent. Come now, come up here and repent your sins and meet Jesus! Tonight may be your last chance. You could die in your car on the way home tonight."

He then signaled to the pianist to start one more gut-wrenching verse of "Just As I Am." By now the emotion in the church ran high. It sure was in me. He left the pulpit and headed straight for me.

"Young man," he said, "Will you come forward and let God save your soul?"

Without a word, I started walking toward the altar. As sure as the hell he painted, I wasn't going to hell. I was willing to take out the insurance policy he was providing. I was baptized that night.

After the service a reception line formed to welcome me into the church. All the congregation filed by and shook my hand. I wasn't able to understand why they all thought I was so great, but they said I had been saved! There was still a problem though. I didn't feel saved. I felt humiliated, I felt afraid and scared, and at every service thereafter, I felt the same. That preacher had one clear cut ability and that was to scare the hell out of me every time he spoke. He never saved you once—he saved you every time he saw you. Dad never knew it, but I hated him for not protecting me that night. He could have made me feel safe! The preacher had used fear to cross my boundaries and I was helpless to do anything about it. All Dad needed to do was extend his arm and put it around my shoulder.

While school was active, so was the church. My being involved in the grade school play catapulted me into demand. Mrs. Higdon, the Methodist Church pianist, asked me to sing at the church some Sunday. It felt great to be in demand. I asked her what song she wanted me to sing and she said, "Let's sing Jack Frost because a number of people haven't heard you sing it, I believe the ones who did hear it want to hear it again." She had in mind a kid's song but I had in mind one of the old, great Methodist hymns. After negotiating, "The Old Rugged Cross" was selected and agreed upon. The designated Sunday morning service came and I belted out "The Old Rugged Cross!"

After the church service people said nice things about my singing, but did not praise me like they did when I performed in the grade school production. It was a let-down and I felt empty. I liked attention and needed lots of praise, but didn't get it on that day. However, when I got home I was ridiculed and humiliated for performing. When I got attention outside the home the rewards at home were sarcastic words and pain.

Christmas was the only good thing I associated with church. At home, even in the most difficult financial times, we always had home-made individual presents, usually some type of clothing. But what we always looked forward to was the community gift, the one gift Dad splurged to get us. One year a basketball, another a football, another a set of boxing gloves.

Christmas brought more rules. We were never allowed to open presents until Christmas morning. Since Santa wouldn't come in our small house 'til we were asleep,' we had to go to sleep at the same time. Since he never came until we went to sleep, the presents from Santa were never under the tree until Christmas morning. Mom and Dad put them out after we were asleep. Going to sleep was always hard because our excitement was great.

When the first person awoke, he awakened all the others, usually about 4 o'clock in the morning. We ran to Mom and Dad's room to get them up. Then we'd open the presents. Rock candy, candy canes, chocolate cookies and milk were in abundant supply—things we never had at any other time of the year. As soon as the community gift was unwrapped, we went outside. The gift, whether a basketball, football or boxing gloves was put to use. The entire day was devoted to using the gift, until boxing gloves came.

The Christmas when boxing gloves were the community gift was a black day. "Paul, I'll bet Dale can whip you" Dad said. Well, he sure did, he was three years older than me and inflicted more pain than I could handle or wanted. Dale whipped everyone who dared put on the gloves and go head to head with him. He was the "horse" as Dad put it. That meant he was the toughest. This Christmas, like many others, was destroyed for me. Christmas was always a time of high expectations and hope. It always ended with disappointment, frustration and unhappiness.

Dad measured his acceptance of us against a standard that revolved around how tough we were. I never seemed to measure up because I didn't feel tough. All of my life Dad pitted us kids against each other. He compared us to each other. He put us down and fostered an environment where we did the same to each other. Someone always won and someone always lost. A measurement of losing was how humiliated you were. Another measure of losing was to cry. That brought additional embarrassment and humiliation, because a sissy cries, a man doesn't. I can't remember a Christmas that didn't bring despair with it. Even after all these years I find Christmas time depressing. My feelings are hard to sort out, but the disappointment was hurtful to me.

One year was an exception and was a highlight. The gift of gifts over all those years was a basketball. Dad had secretly made a back board and had all the materials put together so it could be erected as soon as the ball was unwrapped. It took us an hour to get the hoop, back board, and pole put together and erected. It was still partially dark at 5 A.M. December 25th in rural Oklahoma, and the dead of winter. But on that morning in 1948 that was okay, because the Minneapolis Lakers weren't going to be able to beat the Stearns family at this sport. The basketball lasted for a long time and got more day to day use than any other gift we ever received!

Grade school graduation was the same basic ceremony as the high schools'. It was a big occasion, but for me some of the luster was dulled because Sis was graduating from high school. She was the first child in our family to graduate from high school. It was her big day! Her graduation bothered me immensely, not because there was a conflict with mine, but because I felt a little safer at school knowing she was there. I still didn't feel all that safe, but with her gone, what would I do? The idea bothered me, although no one else knew how I felt.

Aunt Edith and Uncle Harry returned from their missionary work in India and took a church pastorate in Johnson City, Kansas. They knew I was graduating from the eighth grade and asked if I might want to work the summer for a farmer friend of theirs in the area. I could start June 1st and stay until the end of August. The family decided it was a good idea so I agreed to go, but when the departure day came I had some misgivings. I didn't want to go but was expected so I couldn't say no.

Dad, Mom, Bob and Jerry took me to Johnson City, Kansas. We left Avant and drove to Liberal, Kansas, then stopped for directions to Johnson City. Then drove several more hours to Johnson City. The closer we got, the more I thought that God didn't know where the town was. It seemed as if we drove three weeks that one day. Aunt Edith and Uncle Harry were nice but no nonsense people. There was no laughter or joy in their house, only a "Fear of God" seriousness.

Aunt Edith and Uncle Harry took us to the farmer's house ten miles out across open land which was as flat as a pancake stretching to infinity, unbroken by trees or shrubs. We finally got there.

The farm house was fairly new. My folks, the farmer and his wife, their son and daughter-in-law, Aunt Edith and Uncle Harry visited for an hour or so while Bob, Jerry and I looked around the yard. Dad yelled, "Boys, we gotta go." We ran up to the people just as Dad said, "It was nice to meet you and I'm glad you've got a job for my boy," and they left.

There I was, fourteen years old, never away from home one night in my life, dropped off in the middle of nowhere. Aunt Edith and Uncle Harry were ten miles away, but frankly, they always scared the hell out of me.

The farm had two houses on the land, the original one and a new one built when the son married and started his family.

On the first night I was disoriented and homesick. I felt apprehensive and scared. My mind was so tormented I couldn't go to sleep. I was alone in a room above the detached garage, near the house. It was dark, so dark. When the breakfast bell rang the next morning I was still awake. I wanted to cry, but I didn't want to look like a sissy.

The son's wife, Mabel, yelled, "Paul, it's time to get up." I got up, looked at my watch, it said 4 A.M. I thought, my God, what is happening, our family had always been hard workers, but 4 A.M. was ridiculous!

I went across the driveway to the house and John, the

son said, "First we do the chores, we eat after we feed the animals." That took a half hour and by 4:45 we were at a breakfast table set for what I thought was fifteen people, but it was just for the three of us. Then I remembered the Landis family meals. Farmers are big eaters.

Before I left for Kansas the farmer had checked with my folks to make sure that I could drive, because I had to know how to drive a tractor. My folks told him I could drive, but that I had never driven a tractor. They said okay, they could teach me.

By 5:30 A.M. we were on the Massey Ferguson tractors, with fifteen-foot one-way plows mounted on the back. I had my own tractor to drive and started going around a section (640 acres) of land preparing it to plant wheat. By noon we had made one pass around that field. We went into the house, ate lunch and were back on the tractor until dark. By then we had made another pass around that field. I was following John alone on the tractor. I had a lot of time to think about my friends and family. The more I thought the lonelier I became. I was sure glad when we went into the house. We had supper, did the chores, took a bath, and went to bed. The next day was a repeat of the first. On Tuesday I said to John, "I have to go home, I can't handle this."

He said, "We're going to build a fence today because of the heavy rain last night. You think about it today and if you still want to we'll let you go home Saturday." We built the fence that day and that night we drove eighty miles to Liberal, Kansas, to go roller skating with a church party.

It helped a lot to work with John building the fence, some conversation distracted me. Being with other kids at the church party helped too! I was with people, I wasn't alone.

We had a good time and I met some kids my age. During the eighty mile trip back I thought maybe I could stick it out. But the next day we started those tractors around that field again and by noon I knew going home was the only solution. So John called my folks and said, "I'll bring Paul to Liberal Saturday to save you some time." Friday was a last day for me but Saturday morning we loaded a cow into a trailer. The cow had a cancer on her face, the open wound looked horrible. The farmer's son was taking her to Liberal to a sale. He had made arrangements to meet my parents there.

Five days away from home and I was going back, mission failed due to homesickness. We started for Liberal and I felt like the prodigal son, an abject failure. Anyone who's ever felt like a failure knows how I felt, however had I known the grief waiting at home I might not have gone.

When I got home that Saturday evening, the whole family started razzing, kidding, laughing at me. The badgering did not end until the next week, when I got a job paying $10 per day working eight A.M. to five P.M., five days per week. In Kansas the farmer was paying me $20 per week from four A.M. to seven P.M., six days a week.

The new job, my saving grace from failure, was cutting underbrush under the telephone lines strung mile after mile across the countryside. A company from Kansas City had the contract from the telephone company and hired local crews in the towns where they were working. I worked until the end of August and made more money than anyone else in the family. Once again I learned, to get praise and validation from work you earned a lot of money. I had no suspicion what a burden that would become.

We moved from the oil lease into Avant the summer before I began my freshman year of high school. Dad's company had sold the division he worked for and offered him a position in the wax refinery in Barnsdall. He was also offered a position with the acquiring company. After much thought he decided to go into the wax refinery. He had many years of seniority with the company and didn't want to start over with a new company. We now moved from the oil lease to town. We had bought an old junk house in Avant a year after we got there and rented it out. Now Dad asked them to move so we could move in. Dale, Bob, Dad and I remodeled the house. We put on new roofing, installed drywall, and applied paint. We brought it to like new condition. We also put in the plumbing for an indoor bathroom. The house had two bedrooms, a living room, dining room and kitchen. We had gas heat and electricity.

Freshmen at the high school were not being initiated

anymore, but were still considered trash and treated as such by the upper classmen. I competed and made the high school basketball team. It gave me some measure of respect, but I was in Dale's shadow. He was a gifted athlete in all sports, whether basketball, volleyball, hunting, fishing, horseshoe pitching it didn't matter, he excelled at them all. His shoes were impossible for me to fill, but I had become an over achiever and was game to try. He had been the junior basketball star of the school, but could not play his senior year because he had been injured in an automobile accident. It was a tragedy because the doctors never allowed him to play sports again.

My freshman year got off to a rocky start. Early in the fall I was driving our 1951 Chevrolet out in the country to the old place. Little Jr. Anthony, who had become a good friend, went with me. As we crossed Bird Creek Bridge, I saw Freddie Brown walking home and said, "Jr., let's give Freddie a thrill." I stopped and said, "Freddie, get in." I started spinning the tires on the gravel road and speed shifting the stick shift car. Our speed approached limits I had not driven before, but no matter, I was going to give Freddie a thrill. Little Jr. and I were sixteen, Freddie was eleven. The Hill Road surface had just been renewed with loose gravel and as we turned the third curve I lost control. The car went into a spin slid, hit the ditch at the side of the road and turned on its side. We sure had given Freddie a thrill! We got out to check the damage. I said, "I think we can turn the car up right if we all push."

We did and then we saw the damage all along the driver's side of the car. I got in the car, started it, and drove it home. When Dad came home from the wax plant I met him on the front porch crying. He looked at the car, looked at me and didn't say a word—another paradox. When I thought I was going to get killed, he didn't say anything; when I thought I was okay he kicked the hell out of me.

There was a family rule that after we were sixteen years old and had a driver's license, we could use the car one night a week. The hitch was that we had to be home by ten o'clock. Every week I got to drive it I paid for the gas to fill the tank out of own pocket. In the fall after school started, Dad bragged to everyone about how he hadn't purchased gas for the car for the entire summer. He never thanked me nor said anything to me. I figured that's as close to praise as I would ever get from him.

Avant was a class C school. There weren't enough students to field a team for conference football, so we played volleyball in its place, then followed the season with basketball. Although we had a regular conference schedule for volleyball, the real sport was basketball. Avant lived and died by its high school basketball team.

High school was a time of dating, going steady, playing basketball, and horseplay. But especially it was time for trying to grow up. Living in town was less attractive for folks accustomed to the vagaries of country life.

After school my friends and I went to Shorty Higdon's drug store. Most people smoked and the favorite thing to do was to chugalug bottles of Pepsi; the one who drank the most the quickest got his paid for by the others. Little Jr. Anthony who by this time weighed 250 pounds (the name Little Jr. was a contradiction in terms) could chugalug seven bottles in a row, a record I'm sure still stands. I wonder if he ever enjoyed any of those Pepsis?

At age sixteen, when I got my driver's license, dating became possible. Since I got the car only once a week I double dated with other boys so that I could go out more than one night each week. I took our family car one night and they took theirs on the other night. But we still had to get home by ten o'clock. We packed a lot into those evenings. The weather often altered our plans, particularly when it rained, because the floods made the highways impassable and mud made the hill roads impassable.

It's a good thing that in the fifties girls were not sexually promiscuous, at least the ones I knew. I never found one who was, although I was anxious to experiment. Based on what Dad said about masturbating and what the church said about sex, we thought we were lucky to be conceived! But the tacit approval to reproduce must have been there because there were plenty of kids.

My first experience with sex and booze came one night when we did not have dates. It was the summer after my junior year. Ron Selby had just graduated from school. His twin brother Don, born twelve minutes later had flunked a grade and was going to be a senior with Smokey McLaughlin and me. The Selbys dad was a Pentecostal revival preacher.

The Selbys were always wild and willing to experiment with anything. Ron bought a six pack of beer and announced, "Guys, I'm celebrating my graduation." I had never had a beer before but after the other three razzed me I opened one and took a few swigs. It tasted almost as bad as near beer, maybe worse. The fun and laughter began. Stearns was no longer a virgin, alcoholically speaking, now what about sex? The Selbys bragged they were sexually active and Smokey had too, although in the fifties, that was not very active, because girls rarely consented to sex. There was just too much taboo associated with it.

Someone said, "Let's go down to First Street in Tulsa and find a hooker," After much debate we headed for First Street. There was an old hotel with a flashing sign saying "Rooms $5.00" per night. Ron went into the desk clerk and found that some hookers had permanent rooms rented. He went up, stayed awhile and came back. He explained to Don what to do and Don left, and after a while came back. Smokey's turn came, he went and came back. Then it was up to me. Would I or wouldn't I? I did.

I walked in, passed the desk clerk, went upstairs to Room 6 and knocked. A hooker came to the door and said, "May I help you?" I stammered, "I don't know."

"Do you have $5.00?" she asked. I said "Yes" and she said, "Then I can help you."

She had on a sheer neglige with a black bra and panties. She took off the neglige, went over to the bed and laid down. She looked at me and said, "Come over here."

I was scared to death. Would the police come? Would I catch some disease? It was a terrifying time. She said, "Take off your pants and shorts." I did and she inspected my penis to detect any disease that might be visible.

Nothing happened! I could not get an erection. I was out

my five bucks. There was no way I could tell anyone. If I told the guys I would never live it down. If I told my family it wouldn't matter that I didn't do it. The fact that I had thought about it was enough. After that experience I concentrated on my basketball!

The Invitation Basketball tournament, held in Cleveland, Oklahoma, each year was a place for a basketball player to make a name for himself. A newspaper reporter, after seeing me play and score 35 points in a game, described me as the Avant Wheel Horse.

When I heard about the article I drove thirty-five miles to buy a copy of the newspaper. I read it and I felt good! God, I needed to be loved and accepted and the article gave me a little boost.

In our home basketball was always debated after each game. That began with Dale, continued with me, Bob and Jerry. Most of the time Dad went to the game, but by the time we got home he was in bed. We talked standing at the door to his bedroom. We debated, argued, cussed and discussed every play.

During the talks Dad would need to spit every so often. He slept with a cud of tobacco in his mouth. He would lean over and pick up his spittoon (a coffee can), spit, then set the spittoon down.

More often than not an argument occurred. I remember one night I scored forty points. I was on a high and really felt good when I got home. I was given lots of praise at the game and when I arrived home told Dad how good I felt. He became agitated and upset with me. He got up and lunged at me yelling, "I saw the game and you didn't play as good as you think. You hogged the ball and should have passed off to your team mates. Instead of being proud you should be ashamed of yourself. I never saw anybody so selfish. Tell us about the time you came home from Kansas with your tail between your legs if you want to tell us how big a man you are!"

What I wanted backfired. I hoped he would pat me on the back when I told him how good I felt.

The Team, as it came to be called, had been together

since the sixth grade. We played well together. There was even talk that we would go to the State Championships. It was an exciting time and we looked impressive with the Big "A" on our letter sweaters. It was important to file in and out of all the opposing gymnasiums as one. The previous year had been a good one and there was talk that we would go undefeated our final year.

The season started and week after week we won. Then we lost one, the 23rd game, then we lost a second, in the finals of an invitation tournament. Coach said, "That's okay, the district tournament starts next week, regionals the week after, state tournament the week after. We're still going to win the State Championship."

We started the district tournament with great hope, and weren't disappointed. We won. But in the regionals we lost the final game to Kaw City. They went on to State and won. We ended the season 30—3. High school was over for us though classes would not end for another month.

I graduated in May, 1955, during a period that later in the 80's would be called a vintage decade. Elvis Presley had just had his first hit. My classmates and I thought the world was our oyster.

That summer the Bareco Wax Refinery hired me into the maintenance gang. I worked there each summer till I graduated from college. Our maintenance gang cut grass, repaired leaking pipes and maintained the plant and equipment. The jobs I hated most were cleaning the settlings out of the big holding tanks. These tanks were fifty feet high and fifty feet in diameter. We opened an access panel on the sides and crawled in with an air hose and jackhammer. Sometimes the settlings inside were as hard as coal and could be five feet deep. Other times they were thick, like soft wet dirt and stuck to our tools like molasses. In any case, we used the jackhammer to loosen the material and throw it outside in chunks. In the summer the tank was 100 plus degrees inside. At its hottest we could only work inside for ten minute stretches. Our summer tans earned by shirtless, hard outdoor work, were gone in two days of working in those tanks. The perspiration bleached our skins.

My favorite job was digging ditches to bury new pipe. It was satisfying to see where I had been and what I had accomplished. I hated work that could not be measured with a beginning and an end or progress points in between.

Working at the wax refinery was hard work and we made $1.25 per hour. At the end of the summer in 1955 I was to start college at Central State Teachers College on a full basketball scholarship. I had been offered a full scholarship at Coffeyville Junior College and Oklahoma Baptist University as well, but selected Central State because Sis had graduated from there and Dale was a Junior there. It was becoming a family tradition.

In the Stearns family, college was an expected step; it was always assumed each of us would go on to college. Somehow the money for our education would be found. Although we grew up in poverty, we thought like middle class Americans and that meant college was important.

The preparation I received from my family and small town rural environment did little to prepare me for what I would face beyond those boundaries. It was presumed that most people in our town would stay, and most did. What we were taught and how we were taught by those folks influenced by the dust bowl and great depression years was wholly inadequate for someone leaving for college or a larger population center.

Life in those days was hard. In looking back I see the truth; the reality we understood in that place and that time was not the real truth. We lived in poverty, we suffered physical and mental abuse from our parents. It all seemed normal because most people used the same practices. Everyone participated so it was not as if someone knew about a different way to live. Ignorance was pervasive. The primary barrier to change was the deep seated insidious "dysfunctional family systems," which spawned the same cycles generation after generation. In retrospect the only hope for breaking the cycle was to be removed from the environment. But you still had to undergo a transformation. How can persons be transformed when the only known truth holds them in place? What was being passed down to my generation molded us to stay in line. The primary tools were religion, and what I later learned to call co-dependency.

FATHERS

Paul W. Stearns

Fathers conjure images
The Father of our country conjures images
Our Father conjures images
My Father conjures images
Fathers are originators, sources, prototypes
Some Fathers bring love and security
Some Fathers bring fear and pain
When I think of Fathers it is with strong emotion
Feelings come freely
Fear, pain, anger, grief, and yearning
My Father conjures all these feelings
Our Father conjures all these feelings
Biblical Fathers conjure images
Our Father and My Father are Old Testament prototypes
I was without Grace

COLLEGE YEARS

College was the turning point that took me out of my parent's sight and shelter. Although I had been on my own since first grade it had not seemed like it till now. I became increasingly fearful of finding my own way as I began college.

Central State Teachers College, in Edmond, Oklahoma, is an NCAA Division II School. It's only fourteen miles from Oklahoma City. Jim (Hog) Tyner was the assistant football coach and head basketball coach. Though his background had been football, he coached the basketball team.

Coach Tyner had heard about me. He knew I had better than a twenty-five point scoring average as a high school senior, but never saw me play. He asked me the previous spring to come to Edmond for a tryout. We met in his office in the gym. He was cordial, showed me where to dress, told me when I finished dressing to come back to the court and show him what I had. When I came on to the court Hog said, "Paul, don't be nervous, just give me the best you have."

In the next hour he put me through the paces to see how I worked the ball to the left and right, as well as how I handled the ball. When we finished he said, "You've got a full ride. Report to me as soon as you get to school in the fall."

In September, 1955 I arrived on campus, went to Thatcher Hall and checked in. Thatcher Hall was a men's dormitory and housed all the student athletes. Mother and Dad took me to school and while I was checking into the dormitory they went to visit Dale.

After checking into the dormitory I went over to the Athletic Office and saw Coach Tyner. He told me when basketball practice started and that part of my scholarship had to be earned by working part-time for the school. My job was to operate a grass mower! He introduced me to my boss and left. I spoke to my boss and went to register for classes. I enrolled for seventeen credit hours.

After enrolling I went to Dale's apartment, saw my parents off, had dinner with Dale and his wife, Lora. As Dad left he said, "How long will you stick this out Paul? Are you going to be a quitter here too?" With that vote of confidence I didn't go back to my dorm room until 11:00 P.M. I didn't tell anyone but the same feelings I'd had in Kansas came back. I was homesick, scared and desperate, and Dad's comment didn't help.

Dale, his wife, and their television were very much needed. For the next two months I clung to them for security and spent almost every night with them. Until then there were few times in my life I felt adequate, but I at this point never felt any more inadequate or afraid.

When I wasn't at Dale and Lora's I was with Jim Bowman and Jim Balkman in their dormitory room down the hall from me. Jim Balkman was a sophomore and Jim Bowman a junior and they both seemed to have it all together. The fact that they both drank a lot and did not associate with anyone else didn't give me a clue that anything was out of the ordinary. Who didn't drink a lot! I still had not had my first complete beer but that ended when I met Jim and Jim! They were fun and we had some good times, talks and visits. We were either in their room or mine, sometimes we watched television in the lobby of Thatcher Hall. That provided a few other people to cheer with us when sporting events were on.

The classroom was a scary place for me. There wasn't a day of that semester that I didn't worry excessively about flunking out. I worked hard not to fail. Much later in life I found that working hard, doing what you like, was working to succeed. That was fun, working hard not to fail is a killer.

When basketball practice started I met Big John Garrett. John was 6'10" tall. It was his scholarship Coach Tyner had given me. John had been kicked off the team the previous year and this year came out on probation without a scholarship.

I had been a center in high school but knew I had to switch to point guard in college. A 6'1" high school center could not compete with a 6'10" player in college. I also needed to perfect an outside shot to compete on the college level. I hoped someone could show me a technique for shooting outside or at the top of the key.

Basketball practice was hard for everyone. It was competitive, not like high school where all the players had been together since sixth grade. Coach Tyner spent all of his time with the starters.

When the season started I got a uniform and suited up with the team, even got to travel with the team. But when mid-year was two weeks away, Coach Tyner came to me and said "Paul, I'm going to have to pull your scholarship. I have to give it to John Garrett." He didn't say I had to leave the team, and I didn't ask. I said, "Okay coach."

What was I to do? I had failed. After some thought, and without consulting anyone nor telling anyone, I went to the telephone and called Jack Hartman, the coach at Coffeyville Junior College. He had offered me a scholarship at the beginning of school. I said, "Coach, remember me?"

He answered, "Yes, of course."

I paused before asking, "Coach does the offer still hold, I don't like it here and would like to come to Coffeyville."

He seemed delighted and replied, "Good, we'll start when you get here."

I waited until the first semester ended, and with my tail between my legs, I left. On that cold, winter day in December, I loaded my belongings on my back and hitch-hiked to Coffeyville, Kansas. It was sleeting and, as a result, a difficult day to travel.

It wasn't until three weeks later when my grades reached me, that I learned that I made fourteen hours of B+ and three hours of C. Doomsday had not happened. I was shocked! Of course with the state of mind I was in the success wasn't absorbed. I wrote it off to a fluke. I was already addicted to worry!

I later found that Hog Tyner always planned to give John Garrett his scholarship back at mid-semester. He was the starting center. If he hadn't given mine it would have been one of the other guys. At the time I took it personally, but over the intervening thirty-five years, I've learned that I was not emotionally or academically ready for college or to compete in college athletics.

Jack Hartman was glad to see me. He helped me enroll in

school and since the college didn't have dormitories got me into a rooming house across the street from the campus.

The season had started and the team had played a few games. Coach Hartman was pretty set in his game plan. I was new to my classes, and the scholarship consisted of a job at Karbe's Supermarket where I was a box boy. The school paid tuition and furnished books to scholarship athletes.

Coach Hartman was a tough task master. He had gone to Oklahoma A&M on a football scholarship but Henry "Hank" Iba was the head basketball coach and wanted him for basketball. I did not like Coach Hartman and never felt good about playing basketball for him, so at the end of the season decided I wouldn't come back the next year.

What I told the public for consumption was that basketball took too much time and hurt academics. The next fall I transferred to Oklahoma A&M and was going to concentrate on grades. I also told everyone Coach Hartman didn't know what he was doing and that he was a lousy coach. As a matter of fact he was so bad that in the seventies he took a Big Eight team from Kansas to the N.C.A.A. final four a couple of times! Ha! When you're hurting it's always tempting to tear someone else down to build yourself up. The real truth was I was neither good enough or emotionally mature enough at that time to compete on the college level. When my freshman year of college ended I thought I was darn lucky I had made it through. In retrospect, I did the best I could with what I had to work with at the time, but it wasn't enough for me to feel positive.

Summer found me back at the Petrolite Wax Refinery. It was no longer being called Bareco. The same workers—old hands and summer help—were there. The company had to have temporary help and hired the employees' sons as an additional company benefit. That helped many families to obtain more advanced educations for their children. Education they probably would not have gotten any other way.

Donald (Donnie) Claussen was back at Petrolite. We both were starting our second summer of work and both had been on the maintenance gang the previous summer. While I had completed my first year at college he had finished his second at Oklahoma A&M. He was a Lambda Chi Alpha fraternity member there.

The very first week of work Donnie started to do what he had done the entire previous summer. He started making me the butt end of jokes, razzing and playing practical jokes. It seems that wherever you find a group of men you always find an element who get their "jollies" preying on someone else's sensitivity.

The entire hourly work crew checked in at the gate house to punch a time clock prior to the start at 8:00 A.M. The gate house was also a place to gather for lunch and coffee, prior to the beginning of a shift. Since everyone began or ended at the same time there was always a crowd during punch in or punch out times. When the crowd was the biggest, Don Claussen would strike. He made sure his antics got everyone's attention and his subject was always the fool. And it was always me.

Some of the workers tried to promote a fight by saying, "Stearns, why do you take Claussen's crap, afraid he can whip your ass?" I always walked away with tail between my legs. I wondered if it was because that's what Christ would have done or if I really was a coward.

The situation reminded me of the grade school bully I fought at the wiener roast. Should I fight back? Maybe this time I would get hurt, but something had to be done.

The first week Claussen struck again! I had made up my mind I would not endure another summer as the butt end of a joke. We often worked on projects alone together and he was always a great guy under those circumstances—he was only a jerk when he had an audience. As soon as he and I got off by ourselves, out of sight of everyone, I grabbed him by the shirt lapels, pulled his face close to mine and growled, "Claussen, if you ever touch or ridicule me again, I'm going to whip your ass all over this plant." Then I let him go and walked on. He didn't say a word. The interesting thing was before the summer was over we became friends.

In September of 1956 I hitched a ride to Stillwater, Oklahoma home of Oklahoma A&M with Donnie Claussen. It was a land grant school and Division I in the NCAA. The college is located sixty-four miles north and slightly east of Oklahoma City. It was a town of about 25,000 population. We were called the Oklahoma Aggies. Later the college name changed to Oklahoma State University and became known as the Cowboys.

When we arrived on campus Donnie took me around and introduced me to people and invited me to the Lambda Chi Alpha house for dinner.

That first formal dinner at the Lambda Chi house was hard. I didn't own a suit. I wore a sport coat, a shirt and a tie. We sat down at the table and the president of the fraternity said grace. The only woman in the room was the house mother and everyone was respectful and deferential to her. I looked at the table and my place setting. I had never seen so much silverware. Big spoons, little spoons, big forks, little forks. At home we never had more than a plate, a knife, a fork and a spoon. I knew I was in trouble.

The dinner began and I watched what others did. They started with the salad so I was okay until the houseboy came and took the salad plates away. The plate and a fork was taken. When it was gone I noticed the little fork was at my place setting and the big fork was left at everyone else's. I don't know if anyone else noticed me using the salad fork for the main course or not.

I felt inadequate, awkward and stupid. That was not unusual because to always feel out of place was a pattern that had been well established. I just didn't know what to do about it. I wanted to join the Lambda Chi fraternity, but couldn't afford it.

I did not realize one of the purposes of fraternity life was to teach etiquette and social graces. After that night I decided to find out on my own to avoid future embarrassment. I read everything I could about how to dress, act, walk and talk!

Once enrolled at Oklahoma A&M I began to look for a part-time job. I still had to work because Dale was in his last year of college and Bob was starting as a freshman. Dad helped all he could but basically we had to earn our own way.

My first job was busing dishes in the West Bennett dormitory. I had applied to be a dormitory counselor but there weren't any openings. A counselor was responsible for keeping law and order for the section of the floor on which they lived. It was a very good job. In addition to a room, meals were furnished!

I bused dishes til mid-term when a counselor vacancy opened up in East Bennett Hall, an all male dormitory on the other end of the campus. I got a job on the fourth floor. With this job and my summer savings I could pay for all my own school expenses.

When I began my sophomore year at Oklahoma A&M I felt pretty good. There was no pressure to be a basketball star. I hated losing the extra money from the scholarship, but I did not miss basketball at all.

One of the reasons I felt good was that I had made enough money to buy clothes that looked as nice as everyone else's. I had Levis, snap button western shirts, street shoes and the greatest looking charcoal grey suede jacket you ever saw. It looked great and it looked greater on me.

Classes at Oklahoma A&M were tough. Central State and Coffeyville were like high school compared to Oklahoma A&M.

To me, the object of school was to get through it, if possible. I never had a class I didn't think I was going to flunk, except for a two hour photography class. It was understood if you showed up with a camera you got at least a "C".

The dormitory and my job as a counselor were great. Wayne Brewer and Jay Engelbach lived on my floor. The three of us were the same age and hit it off. They majored in accounting and helped me study for my accounting classes.

In my sophomore year my homesickness only lasted the first three or four weeks of school, but I was still scared all the time. My fear and inadequacy caused me to wonder how I could escape from classes and the general pressure of school. At the time it seemed normal, because I had always had anxiety.

The school year ended with me back at the Petrolite Wax Refinery. It was like old home week. The old hands were always glad to see the college kids come back.

That summer I started dating Peggy Jones on a steady basis. We had met in Barnsdall when I was a senior and she was a sophomore. Avant played each year at the Barnsdall Invitational basketball tournament. She was a cheerleader for the basketball team. Her family had moved to Skiatook when I went to college for my freshman year. She became a star on the girls basketball team and I went to some of her games when I came home from Stillwater on Friday nights. That summer she had graduated from high school and was planning to attend Northeastern State Teachers College in Tallequah, Oklahoma. That fall I returned to Oklahoma A&M for my junior year of college.

Peggy had the most beautiful blond hair I ever saw. She could have put Delilah to shame because she was a temptress and taunted me in ways no one else ever had. She was sexy and at the time lots of boys were sexually attracted to her, so was I. That summer the only thing that limited us was the fact I still only had Dad's car one night per week. Late in the summer I got a frantic call as soon as I got home from work at 5:30 P.M. She sobbed "Paul, I think I'm pregnant."

I came unglued. I left the house and told no one where I was going. I went directly to Skiatook. I never gave a thought to the fact that it was not my night for the car.

All the way to her house I was frantic rethinking my life, how was I going to face Peggy's parents? Mine too! When I arrived in Skiatook, Peggy met me on the front porch and announced she had started her menstrual cycle and she wasn't pregnant after all. I was relieved! If she made up the story and only one hour later changed it I'll never know. We ended the summer by her going off to Tallequah and me to Stillwater.

It's said distance makes the heart grow fonder. Well I'll tell you it does. I was in love. I couldn't resist beyond half way into the semester hitch-hiking all the way from Stillwater to Tallequah to spend a week-end. A friend of mine had an apartment there. He was going home for the week-end and let me use it. Peggy and I had sex that week-end, it was usual to have sex with her but this week-end was the first time we had slept together, sharing the night and the next morning. I proposed that we marry at mid-year, that she come back to Stillwater with me and get a job. I would finish school by going straight through the rest of that year and summer school. In addition, if I took four hours of correspondence credits I could be finished with school a year from that day. She said, "Okay, let's do it." I became excited!

Willie Jones, Peggy's father said it was okay for me to marry her so the plan I laid out was set. We scheduled the wedding at the Avant Methodist Church because the Jones didn't belong to any church. I was still three weeks away from my twenty-first birthday so Mom went with me to get a marriage license.

I was a marketing major and already looking ahead to employment. I knew I needed to add to my credentials so I joined the Mu Kappa Tau Marketing Club and the Young Democrats.

Peggy got a job at a library and, with the help Willie gave us, I went on studying.

During the last semester of school I made plans for employment and searched for a way to fulfill my military obligation without being drafted. I learned the Air National Guard had a program that allowed me to go through boot camp, then come back home and attend one week-end per month with two weeks summer camp each year. The six year enlistment with the Guard was a substitute for two years in the regular army. I joined and was able to defer going to boot camp until I was through with school in December.

Something radical happened at the Air National Guard physical examination! I passed the physical with flying colors, but when I got to the color test, the Sergeant brought out a book. He said, "These pages have numbers created by using hundreds of dots of different colors." I saw the sample page and the number 23 showed. I didn't know that the 23 was formatted so even a color blind person could see it. However, after the first page, it was all down hill. I didn't see another number.

The Sergeant said, "Son, you're color blind"!

I was shocked. "You must be wrong. I may be color ignorant but I can't be color blind."

We debated for a half hour before I accepted that I was color blind. That's also when I found my charcoal grey suede jacket was really dark green. No one had told me!

How could a person get through grade school, high school and four years of college and not know he was color blind? Since I had been embarrassed by Barbara Okerson in the first grade, I worked hard to cover up what I thought was an inability to learn my colors.

During my last semester of school several corporations such as Proctor & Gamble, Kroger, IBM and National Supply Corporation, then a subsidiary of Armco Steel, sent recruiters to the campus.

National Supply was an oil field supply company which manufactured oil field equipment and supplies. They wanted me, and offered me $428.00 per month. They wanted me to start as soon as boot camp ended.

They told me to report to their field store in Liberal, Kansas when I got back. I had experienced Kansas and wasn't thrilled. But they told me I had to be in their field store only six weeks, then I'd be reassigned. I thought for this great job I could spend six weeks in hell. It was the job of a lifetime. I had been raised in the oil fields and felt this job would be a real fit.

School ended late December, I finished in January, 1959. While school went well, Peggy and I fought almost every day. That seemed okay. I thought all married couples fought every day. Things were looking up. I was all set to get my military obligation handled and I had a great job offer.

I never liked Avant and wanted to escape. I never liked school and wanted to escape. Now I would be doing what I had been dreaming about since my first attempt to market chickens, Grit newspaper or garden seed. I was going to market real products for a real company and make real money.

I was out of school in January, however graduation was not official until May. Oklahoma A&M was changing its name to Oklahoma State University. I had a choice of either name on my degree. Nothing would do for a new graduate but a new name. I chose Oklahoma State University. Since then I have regretted not selecting Oklahoma A&M for nostalgic reasons.

To be out of school, a place that brought negative self worth, feelings of inadequacy, constant interacting with people who were better than I, needless to say, was a great relief. I wouldn't need to feel anxious, lonely, lost, uncertain and alienated anymore. Above all I wouldn't be uncertain anymore. Now I was going to work hard and make lots of money and buy all the things I had been deprived of while growing up.

CHAPTER FOUR

THE CORPORATE LADDER

FEAR

Paul W. Stearns

Memories before you are rather scant
As a matter of fact I can't
You distribute gifts of pain where ever you go
You came and for me, nothing has been the same
I don't remember how or when you arrived
Your movements are so subtle
You've become so familiar
Like an old friend
I've learned to give you my whole attention
You have followed me every place that I have been
You have become one of my most entrenched habits
I've watched you multiply as fast as rabbits
You keep everyone you visit in a constant tension
Symptoms of withdrawal set in when you become dis-
    tracted
That's when the pain becomes protracted
And your greatest enemy is love and self-acceptance
When love appears you go unattended
You know you have over stayed your welcome
Where is love for me?

Before heading for boot camp, I took Peggy back to Skiatook to stay with her parents while I was in San Antonio, Texas.

Dad had loaned Peggy and me a 1954 black and red stick shift Pontiac and I wanted to return it to him, but before I could I needed to buy a car. I went to Cecil Watson, the Ford dealer in Skiatook. He had known Dad for years and held our family in high esteem. I went to the dealership and said, "Mr. Watson, I just graduated from college and I need to buy a car."

He nodded, looked me over and said, "Paul, let's go back and look at what we have."

After checking several cars, I saw a light blue 1959 Custom 300 Ford, two door, stick shift with Over Drive. It had a radio, but no other accessories. "Put side rear-view mirrors on both doors and I'll buy it." I drove it off the lot.

Mr. Watson knew my job didn't start until after Air Force basic training sometime in March, so he did not ask for a down payment, nor did he require a payment until April, some four months later. I wasn't experienced enough to know that for the next four years until that car was paid for, I would owe more than what it could be sold for. Debt was something all rural folk knew. They assumed, like death and taxes, it was something to accept.

The next week I had my first ride on a train. I went from Tulsa to San Antonio, Texas to report to Lackland Air Force Base for basic training (boot-camp). My train ride gave me an opportunity to see the countryside in a way I'd never seen before. The experience of riding a train was thrilling, a sense of wonderment came over me.

Bootcamp was not fun. They cut off all my hair, outfitted me with military clothing and supplies, showed me my barracks, and I entered a world of non-stop harassment. For eight weeks we weren't allowed weekend passes or visitors. On the ninth weekend we were given a one day pass.

I remember that one-day pass because some of my buddies and I went to a bar in downtown San Antonio. I began drinking beer on an empty stomach. I had two beers, just two beers, got sick to my stomach and went into the restroom and vomited. My head was over a porcelain altar.

After I walked out of the restroom I realized my partial plate with one front tooth mounted on it had been vomited out and flushed along with my proverbial socks. The partial plate concealed the fact that one of my front teeth had been knocked out while I was a freshman in high school. I felt like a fool but was too sick to care.

At the end of ten weeks I got a full week-end pass. Peggy came down from Skiatook, and typical of our pattern, we fought. I was obsessed about her possibly seeing someone else while I was at bootcamp. Jealousy brought the uncertainty I intended to avoid after college.

When bootcamp ended in early April I went to the National Supply store in Liberal, Kansas. Peggy went too! We packed everything we owned in the 1959 Ford.

National Supply Corporation had a ten month Management Training Program for college graduates. I, with twenty others, was in the class. For the first six weeks each of us were assigned to work in field stores scattered across the country.

After our field store training we went to Pittsburgh, Pennsylvania. At the end of ten months we were to be assigned to full time jobs. So "working for the other man," (an Oklahoma expression), my first steady job had begun. The six weeks at Liberal, Kansas were uneventful.

Our trip to Pittsburgh was a real experience. I had never been East before. I was familiar with the geography of the plains of Kansas, Oklahoma and Texas, but I had never seen mountains, real mountains before.

The trip was long and tiring. We approached Pittsburgh at midnight and we were only a few miles from Pittsburgh when a tunnel loomed ahead of us. A tunnel going through a mountain was not the stuff an Oklahoman saw everyday so I was awed as we entered it. As we came out the other side, the sky was pitch black. No moon shown. What appeared to be giant fireflies appeared in the distance everywhere. I could not figure out what was happening. The next morning when I got up and went outside, I realized the fireflies were really lights on houses built in every conceivable position in and on the mountains surrounding us. I could not believe what I was seeing. How could people walk, drive, or move on the steep inclines? What did they do about snow and ice?

It was clear to me how Pygmies, who were born and lived in the rain forest felt when they were taken out of the forest. Frightened, the Pygmies went back into the rain forests and I felt like going back to Oklahoma. But I knew this time there was no going back.

I spent the next three months going to classes and training with the other twenty management trainees. We attended classes at the World Headquarters, in downtown Pittsburgh in the biggest office building I had ever seen.

We were at the National Headquarters for three weeks, then we went to steel mills in Etna and Ambridge, Pennsylvania for two additional months. I rented an apartment in what had been an old steel baron's house in Sewickly Heights, a suburb of Pittsburgh.

The National Supply Company training class of 1959–60 was convened by W.D. Senior, Director of Training. He had personally hired all twenty-one class members. All were college graduates. We met for the first time when we gathered together to begin the class. There were engineering, accounting, geology, finance and marketing disciplines represented. I was twenty-two. The average age of the class was 26. All but three were veterans of the military, all more experienced and traveled than I. At the time it never occurred to me I had been selected among a special group of people and the people who hired me looked on me as an equal. If I had it would have eliminated tremendous anxiety.

When the members of the class were hired we were told we could request specific jobs at the end of training but there was no assurance we would get what we wanted. Theoretically the accountants could be salesmen and marketing people wind up in accounting, but we all had faith we would get what we were after. The main thing was to be selected by National and start at $428 per month. In 1959 that was like dying and going to heaven.

When the class congregated my perceived inadequacies surfaced and became a problem. I was scared. I was sure my social graces and experience were no match with the others.

The class included some who had graduated Summa Cum Laude. There were some from wealthy families and some from New York City. All of them seemed savvy to the ways of the world. This was my first trip east of the Mississippi, except for a quick trip from Coffeyville, Kansas driving a Karbe's grocery truck to Milwaukee, Wisconsin.

One trainee with a degree in engineering had graduated with honors from Purdue. Purdue was a "Big Ten" school for God's sake! He had been in the navy and after discharge held jobs with two steel companies and three construction companies. He was 28. How could I compete with men like him? My wardrobe consisted of one suit, one sport coat, and two pairs of slacks. As in college, I asked questions. I watched everything and everyone. I tried to improve my social graces. It was during this period I worked on eliminating my Oklahoma twang! I consistently felt people were laughing at me. I didn't feel I was succeeding in hiding my awkwardness.

I was the youngest in the class, along with one other 22 year old. I was afraid of the 27 or 28 year olds and veterans.

During the next ten months I spent a lot of sleepless nights. Could I cut it? Could I graduate? Would I be kept on? All those things rolled through my mind the entire ten month training program. The other class members knew I was having trouble adjusting and I became the butt of some of their jokes. My naivety, curiosity, and energy left me wide open. Once again the six year old clog dancer was being ridiculed. The deep anguish and hurt, like a toothache wouldn't go away.

One day in class I raised my hand to speak and used the word "entrepreneur", a word that ultimately meant a lot to me later in my life, but after class that day most of other class members took me apart. "Stearns what did you say? Manure!" I was accused of being high fallutin' and razzed. It's too bad some people who razz others don't stop to consider what they're inflicting. I didn't figure out until much later they were impressed with the word and didn't know what it meant. It wasn't until years later that I learned they were as scared as I. In retrospect I see how we all create defenses built to protect ourselves, but which in fact deceive us. These defenses keep us from seeing how much we all have in common, however falsely we use them for protection.

After three weeks in the home office I spent the balance of my training traveling from Pittsburgh to Middletown, Ohio then to Redondo Beach, California, and Houston, Texas, where I ended my training and was given my assignment, as a production equipment clerk, in the Dallas, Texas division office. It was not something I was happy about, because I was supposed to be a salesman. They said I could be, but first I had to have further training.

In Dallas I worked for two different engineers, both of whom were near retirement age. There weren't any other male employees near my age there. I was there ten months and didn't like the work I was doing. I missed the companionship of people my own age.

After ten months as a clerk I went to the Division Manager and told him of my unhappiness. He said there was nothing he could do.

The same day I called Lowell Clark. Lowell was a Vice-President of Kerr McGee Oil, a corporation headquartered in Oklahoma City. I asked Lowell if he remembered me, and reminded him that he had offered me a job. Luckily Lowell remembered me and said, "Paul I have a job for you but you'll have to take a pay cut. You've just explained you started at $428.00 per month with National and are now making $458.00 per month. Our starting wage for Management Trainees is $400.00 per month. If you'll come I would love to have you and I'll guarantee you'll catch back up to where you are with National quickly and you'll make much more money with us in the long run."

I didn't hesitate. "Mr. Clark, I'll take it. When do I start?"

In January 1961 I moved to Oklahoma City to begin training. Peggy was happy to be returning to Oklahoma. I had told my Dad I was changing jobs. He didn't understand. "National Supply Corporation is a big company and a good company, and you're making good money. Why are you quitting? Why don't you ever finish anything you start?"

I explained, "Dad, I don't like the company and I don't like the job they've forced on me. I wanted sales, and look what they have me doing."

Dad still didn't understand. "You ought to feel lucky you have the job with National Supply."

My Creator was looking out for me, because Kerr McGee, the people and their program, gave me basics which I still use today. It provided a community where I developed and which was more like family to me.

Kerr McGee, a fully integrated, independent oil company, was founded by Robert S. Kerr and Dean McGee. Kerr McGee had 1,700 service stations in seventeen states. The marketing division was made up of two departments; company operated service stations and individually owned stations. There was no guarantee after training which department I would be permanently assigned to!

I was scared when I began my training working at a training service station in Oklahoma City. It was a standard three bay station with a classroom added. The training covered all aspects of servicing an automobile. It also covered all aspects of running a business day to day.

After the training center I was sent to the refineries to learn about product quality and how motor oil and gasoline were made. Next I moved on to each department of the marketing division to learn systems and procedures, from forms processing to service station construction. The whole idea was to give me a broad perspective regarding the business, the company, and then, specifically, the tools to run a retail or wholesale territory.

Lowell Clark was the Director of Training for Kerr McGee, as well as a Vice-President of the company. The fact that he was Senator Kerr's son-in-law helped him, but Lowell was good at his job and I was glad he took me under his wing. The benefit was mine, but testing because he took me out behind the shed a few times! That's what dads did when they disciplined a kid in Oklahoma in those days. Lowell treated me like a son!

After six months the training ended and I was assigned to a new retail territory in Lawton, Oklahoma. There were ten stations in place and three more under construction. It was a good territory, though small I could grow with it. At that point I felt inadequate but hoped the small territory would give me time to grow. Most territories had fifteen to twenty service stations. R.A. "Dick" Mooney, "Division Manager—Retail" was my boss. Dick was in his early forties and prematurely bald.

I was finally in a position to do what my favorite marketing professor suggested. Find a job you want to do, observe others doing it, then dress like them, talk like them, walk like them, act like them, and one day you'll be doing what they are. I emulated everything Dick Mooney did, tried to look like him. Except for his being bald, I did a pretty good job!

Kerr McGee had just purchased a chain of service stations from another company. One of them was to be a pitfall I almost fell into. The station in Cash, a small town, was owned by a big two hundred and sixty pound ex-rodeo steer wrestler. My orders were to go in and fire him. He didn't want to go. He had just invested several thousand dollars to buy the station. In actuality the prior company should have fired him, but the job was mine now. When I told him why I was there he became so angry I thought he was going to take me apart. He cursed at me, threatened me and I decided the best course of action was to leave. He followed me. There I stood (I weighed one hundred and thirty-five pounds and was scared to death) alongside a highway, traffic going 60 miles an hour on one side and the irate dealer screaming, "You ##))#), you're stealing from me and my family." "I'll kill you before I let that happen!"

I didn't respond, just stood there silently for an hour before he ran down. Then I left and went to a phone, called Dick Mooney and told him the story, ending with, "Dick, I'll never go back to that station, it's not worth it. You'll have to have someone else cover the location." He chuckled. "Paul, I wouldn't go back there either if I were you, at least not for a couple of days." Good old Dick knew how to diffuse a twenty-three old who had just had the scare of his life.

I did go back the next week and this time convinced the

dealer to leave. We took an inventory which Kerr McGee agreed to pay for. I still condemned myself for not accomplishing my mission the first time.

Dick was also helpful when I drove into Altus, Oklahoma, on a Wednesday morning, and the service station I supervised there was still closed at ten A.M. I walked around behind the station and saw some credit card invoices lying in the grass, and strewn all over the rear of the lot. Since they had been filled out and were good, I picked them up. The invoices totalled three hundred dollars so I was lucky to recover them. The departing dealer took all the cash, which we never did recover. Even though I saved money by recovering the invoices I felt I had failed because of the loss of cash. I was taught by my father I must be perfect and to me the loss of cash I saw as an imperfection!

I opened the station and started pumping gas, then called the newspaper to place a help wanted ad, which could not run until the next day. I continued to run the station until I could hire someone. Kerr McGee's policy was, a station never closes for any reason.

The next day I interviewed candidates but couldn't get someone to start until the following day. That meant I had to close at 11 P.M. two nights and open at 6 A.M. one morning. I was exhausted. I went to my motel to go to bed, unloaded my car, went in and fell on the bed. I didn't bother to undress. I slept until 5 A.M. the next morning. As I got up and was preparing to leave, I looked around. I could not find my company furnished Polaroid camera. I recalled that I laid it on top of the car as I unpacked the night before, and forgot it. I went to look for it. It was gone! Someone had taken it. I called Dick to confess my oversight and told him I would pay for it. He said okay, but never charged me.

The next week at a District Manager's meeting in Oklahoma City everyone gave me a rough time because I had volunteered to pay for the camera. Mooney had told them about my camera problem. "Stearns, what do you want to do, get us all in a situation where we have to pay for every mistake we make?" They were serious and I realized no one but me was concerned about the Polaroid camera.

I should have been overjoyed. Instead I found myself apprehensive. The problem dealer in Cash, Oklahoma, the dealer in Altus leaving with the money and losing the Polaroid camera brought pressure to me. I worried that my track record wasn't looking good. My Dad sure wouldn't let those things slide. Although Dick Mooney didn't seem concerned, I worried that he was.

Although I valued my association with Kerr McGee and the people I worked with, I felt out of step. The ideas I developed while in Avant and the opinions I expressed were not accepted. They weren't ridiculed but they weren't accepted. I started guarding what I said and what I did. My business and personal growth were stymied. Privately my life was hell. My fears and insecurities were getting more difficult to control every day. I was always in a high state of anxiety. Fear of not fitting in and fear of not being accepted and fear of getting fired haunted me.

Lowell Clark and Dick Mooney were interested in me. Of course they were interested in all of their employees, but I had special attention. I was out of the training program and everyone else in marketing either had been with the company for a long time or had been hired from another oil company. My assignment marked the establishment of a company policy to develop personnel from within. My success could prove the merits of a program they wanted to expand.

My territory assignment to Lawton was a challenge. To develop a new area was intimidating, but it was a challenge I was eager for. I went to work with gusto, evaluating each station, changing managers where needed. I also created an individual marketing program to enhance each station.

Fourteen months later my success was rewarded. I was offered the position of Advertising and Sales Promotion Assistant to G.W. "Bill" Williams, Jr., Manager of Advertising. It involved recognition and the continued salary improvement Lowell Clark had promised when I was hired. His promise had been contingent on performance, of course, and I was performing.

The promotion and move to Oklahoma City should have

brought joy and confidence, but instead each success drove me further into the labyrinth of despair.

Bill Williams didn't employ people, he adopted them. His "Golden Rule" approach to management was really pleasing to me. He made me want to go the extra mile to do whatever he wanted or needed. He was a meticulous manager who saw his role as serving and servicing the marketing department. Although I no longer reported directly to Mooney I came into regular contact with him because our departments serviced his needs.

I did have one problem. Air National Guard meetings weren't available in Lawton so I had to make arrangements to comply with my one week-end per month military obligation. I also was responsible for spending two weeks active duty in the summer. After checking, I found I could continue at Tinker Air Force Base in Oklahoma City. By this time I had been in the Air Force Reserves for two years and still had the same rank automatically awarded after boot camp. When I first went in the Air Force I was awarded the rank of Airman Basic. At the end of my boot camp I was automatically awarded the rank of Airman 3rd Class. I was still Airman 3rd Class, in part because I had attended meetings hit and miss while with National Supply and traveling all over the country. I had established a base in Texas while I was in Dallas but during the six months with Kerr McGee I was not able to attend meetings. The Air Force sent notice I would have to go on active duty for 45 days if I didn't start attending meetings at once. I started at once!

It was degrading to be Airman 3rd Class and, though I didn't want to be in the infantry, I decided to take the test to apply for Officer Candidate School in the Army Reserves. I could take the qualifying test and my college degree would help me get accepted. If accepted I could go to meetings on the week-ends and summer and within one year be a 2nd Lt. I passed the tests. But just as I did, I was promoted and transferred back to Oklahoma City. This caused me to decide to stay in the Air Force Reserves.

Going back to Oklahoma City was exciting because J.H. and Sue Engelbach, my good friends from Oklahoma State lived there. Jay was a C.P.A. with a regional accounting firm. Sue worked for the FAA in Oklahoma City. Peggy and I were able to pal around with them. My sister and her husband, Dick Rosebrook lived in Oklahoma City and the opportunity to see them more frequently was an attraction.

Simultaneously with the pressure I felt from work my relationship with Peggy was deteriorating. We had bought a house in Oklahoma City, some furniture and still were paying for the '59 Ford. We were up to our ears in debt. I was worried about losing my job, but that wasn't new.

I thought uncertainty would end after college as soon as I got a job. I had been with Kerr McGee 1 1/2 years, received raises in pay and a promotion, but I was still scared. I didn't tell anyone. I thought it was normal to worry about your work and work hard. I had watched my Dad do it all my life. Maybe it was normal but I had long since crossed the boundary of working hard and worrying about my work. I was in unhealthy territory, but didn't realize it.

All around me other persons in management positions, (not all mind you, but many) were pursuing sex, not relationships. Little did I know this behavior was symptomatic of the same problem I had. They needed to fill the holes in their souls too! What were we looking for?! Relief from pressure, sex or unconditional love and acceptance!

I started toying with the idea of pursuing sexual liaisons myself. My sex life with Peggy was active but not meaningful or satisfying. Each time we finished I still wanted more. I was still using sex to relieve the pressures that built up, but now is wasn't a release. It caused more pressure.

It began in Oklahoma City while at a sales meeting. One of the other district managers and I went to a bar after a late running sales meeting. We became friendly with two women. We picked them up and went for a ride. While on the ride my co-hort had sex with one of the girls in the back seat. I was driving and the other girl was sitting close to me. We knew what the two in the back seat were doing, but neither of us said a word. I didn't have sex with that lady, but that night was the beginning of attempts to relieve my stress and anxiety through sex with women other than Peggy.

From the first day we met my relationship with Peggy was born out of a mutual sexual attraction. She came from a family that treated her similarly to the way mine treated me. We were both in need of attention and someone to love and accept us.

In the beginning I was attracted to Peggy because she paid attention to me and pursued me. Association with the school basketball star enhanced her own image. Sometimes princesses want a prince who is not a frog. I was, as the sports writers called me, the Avant wheel horse, I was no frog. The truth of the matter was that I probably felt like a frog, because I didn't feel like a wheel horse.

We fought from the first day we met and the intensity picked up in that last year. In 1962 we had been married four years.

Peggy had worked since we were married, except while we traveled during the training program for National Supply. After that wherever we were transferred she always found a job.

Now in Oklahoma City she was working as a legal secretary. The lawyer she worked for was married, young and good looking. I accused Peggy of having an affair with him. She left the house in a huff and I thought she would be back in a little while. Time passed and some three hours later I called Peggy's Dad in Skiatook, Oklahoma. I needed to talk over some business with him. To my utter amazement Peggy answered the phone. The drive to Skiatook from Oklahoma City took two hours. It turned out she had driven around Oklahoma City for a while, then decided to leave and go home. While talking to her on the phone I became extremely frightened. I hung up, got in my car and drove to Skiatook. When I arrived it was midnight and everyone was in bed.

I wasn't looking forward to confronting Peggy and her family. My father-in-law answered my knock and seeing it was me went to wake Peggy. She came to the door and I began to talk. Everyone in the house could hear what was said. I took the entire blame for our problems and apologized. I cried and pleaded and begged Peggy to come back to me. After an hour or so of emotional talk we made up and went to bed. Our fights always concluded with sex and this night was no different.

The next day, we returned to Oklahoma City. I thought all was well. Little did I know this was the lull before the storm. Things seemed to go well until the following Thursday morning. Peggy left for work as usual. I was doing paper work at home when I heard a knock on the door. A legal process server handed me a supoena and a restraining order. I was being sued for divorce and restrained from going within 100 feet of Peggy, wherever she might be. She had convinced a judge I might harm her. She had no cause for the restraining order because I had never touched her in anger, but I was not able to tell anyone because I was not consulted. I had no way to control any of the events that occurred.

My payment for becoming vulnerable was betrayal and divorce. I knew that men crying and begging showed weakness and that was not accepted in our culture. But I was so desperate I did both.

What was I to do? I called Sis. She had a friend who was an attorney and suggested I call him. I did and he said he would handle the divorce for me.

Divorce was not accepted nor did it happen very often in 1962. I immediately went to my boss at Kerr McGee and explained my circumstances and asked how the divorce might affect my career. Bill said, "Paul, I don't know, but let me go talk to R.M. Dick Knox, the Vice-President of Marketing." Later Bill got back to me. "Paul, Knox said as long as you keep yourself clean you don't have to worry about your job." I didn't ask what "keep yourself clean" meant, but made assumptions and silently vowed; "you're darn right I'd keep myself clean."

The next several weeks were hell. Peggy didn't call me and my attorney advised me not to call her. He advised "Harassment could be alleged."

During the next several weeks I reached out for help and support. The first thing I did was to go to Avant and tell my folks.

I'll never forget being at home on the front porch crying, telling my Dad about how I had failed, "Dad, Peggy even said I never satisfied her once sexually during the five years we were married."

Dad looked at me in a strange way. "You know Paul, I always worried about whether I was going to enjoy sex and left it up to the woman to worry about herself."

Dad reacted to my divorce in a way I never expected. He showed, for an instant, an unconditional love for me which I had never felt before nor was I to feel again. My pain touched a nerve in him that allowed him to reach out to me. I did not think he would accept the divorce because the religion we practiced did not. The acceptance he showed was the only time I ever saw it.

The second way I reached out was to go to the church in Oklahoma City which I had been attending and volunteer to teach Sunday School. The guilt I felt motivated my volunteering. After three weeks I quit. How could I teach kids things I did not believe nor feel? I didn't know who I was or what I believed, so I quit teaching.

The third way I reached out was to go to a medical doctor. I had symptoms that told me I was ill and needed help. My stomach, legs, and head had various ailments. The doctor finally diagnosed hepatitis and checked me into the hospital. After three weeks my condition had not improved and he brought in a urologist. The urologist said I had a problem with the urethral seal to my bladder and needed surgery. Three weeks after surgery I was no better and this wise old country doctor looked me in the eye and said, "Stearns, there's nothing wrong with you. You have to go to someone you'll believe. I recommend you see a psychiatrist."

In 1962 it was unheard of for a regular person to see a psychiatrist. Shrinks were ridiculed and not someone you consulted. I did not believe my pain was psychosomatic any more than I had believed I was color blind. However I was desperate and decided to try going to a psychiatrist.

I went to see the psychiatrist. I entered his office foyer and detected that the building was designed so that no one could see you come in or leave. When I met the doctor I felt he was weird. I thought if this guy is sane, I must be crazy.

The initial interview lasted a half hour. He asked me to go to a psychologist for some testing. I took the Rorschach test. Some people see bears or cats or all sorts of things in the ink blots. Why couldn't I see what I thought everyone else could see? In every card or ink blotch I saw a woman's vagina. Well that confirmed it, I jumped to the conclusion I was crazy!

At the next session the doctor asked more questions and set up a plan to see me for what he called a 50 minute hour. In psychotherapy language we would talk for 50 minutes and I would get billed for one hour. The other ten minutes he would spend making or reviewing notes on our session.

The next session began with the doctor telling me he thought I might have a problem with sex. That was no surprise after being married to Peggy for five years. She and I had been having sex together for some time before we were married. I had sex with others during our marriage and although I don't know if Peggy had, I suspected it. Neither of us, in retrospect, could enjoy sex or have sex without a guilty conscience, because of the way we were taught.

The doctor asked if I had sex lately and I said, "not since my wife left and our divorce began," two months ago. I said I had been dating and there were a couple of women whose bones I would like to jump. "JUMP THEIR BONES!?!" he said in a shocked tone. I'm sure he was about to leap to the conclusion I was some kind of wacko guy until I explained I had a big desire to have sex with the two women I was dating. Explained that way he understood and it was okay. I only went to this psychiatrist for two months before I was transferred to Indianapolis.

Six months later the divorce was finalized. Peggy and her attorney were to come to my attorney's office. I was very nervous. How would I act? What would I say? What could I say? As it turned out Peggy and her attorney stayed in another office and I was kept in an office by myself. My attorney came in and out of the office carrying negotiating messages. I was there for final negotiations on property settlement matters. As he left my office the final time he said, "Can you think of anything we may have missed?"

I said, "No, I'm willing to give her whatever she asks for."

He had already informed me that in Oklahoma women get what they ask for in court so we might as well settle. Peggy wanted the car, which was now paid for. She also wanted all the furniture, which also was paid for. I was going to keep the house. It was going to be empty and I'd be saddled with the big mortgage. As my attorney turned to leave I blurted, "You asked if we had missed anything; tell her I want my name back!" He asked "Are you serious?" I said, "Yes." After a half hour he came back with all the paperwork signed. Peggy agreed to taking Peggy Jones back and release the right to be Peggy Stearns. A painful era ended. Or had it?

Three weeks later Peggy called and wanted to have lunch. I reluctantly agreed. The next week we went out for a tense, but fun, evening. When we got home, while still in the car, we kissed. It really felt great. She invited me in, but I knew if I accepted we would have sex and my sixth sense told me not to. This behavior was typical of Peggy, no word for six months, then the divorce, then contact. She always wanted what she couldn't have, and didn't want what she had.

That was the last time I saw Peggy. I knew if I saw her again it would be like taking the first smoke after quitting. If you smoke one you're back to a two-pack-a-day habit. Her erratic behavior would have made day to day living unpredictable. We had been married five years and it was over, yet the emotional upheaval was still in progress.

I've suffered severe loneliness in my life! The loneliness stemming from isolating myself from sharing and communication with others. The worst period for me, however, was the period after my divorce from Peggy. I felt like a complete failure. I couldn't satisfy her sexually, how could I feel like a man if I couldn't do that? My sense of loneliness, hurt and anguish didn't feel as if it would ever go away. They were like a bad toothache that goes on day after day, week after week, month after month. I was totally defeated as a human being.

The grieving process went on for several years before I reconciled to what had happened. To heal the wounds caused by a failed marriage took soul searching and personal growth.

Peggy and I had what is today called a co-dependent relationship, it was very unhealthy. Our incompatibility predated our marriage, but it was not helped by our individual behavior toward each other.

My fears always caused me to be insecure. Since my extra marital affairs had begun, the guilt they brought on bordered on paranoia. It exacerbated our problems. I could not give the marriage anything other than an agitated state of mind.

After thirteen months on the job in the Advertising Department, I felt I had learned what I could and was itchy to get back into the field. The field is where you could shine and where promotion opportunities were.

Theo Antonio, the retail Division Manager for the St. Louis division had been trying to get me to take a territory in Indianapolis, Indiana. There were nineteen stations in the territory and he had just lost the territory manager. I was afraid if I stayed in Oklahoma City I would be tempted to get back with Peggy, or at least try, so I decided to take the assignment in Indianapolis.

My life grew in each job I had and I began to see that luck played a large role in a corporate career. At Kerr McGee, Theo Antonio became my boss.

I had to report to Indianapolis the Monday following Thanksgiving so I drove to Avant from Oklahoma City and stayed with my parents through Thanksgiving Eve. Early Thanksgiving morning I started for Indianapolis, and thirteen hours later arrived at the Speedway Holiday Inn. It was about eight P.M. when I unloaded my car and checked in. It was not a good way to spend a Thanksgiving. I was lonely and the fear of the unknown was extreme.

I leased the house in Oklahoma City because I couldn't find a buyer. Since Peggy had gotten the furniture, car and

$500 in cash, I needed a car, so guess what I did? I bought a 1963 Super Sport Chevrolet. Red leather bucket seats and white exterior. You guessed it, no down payment and monthly payments that would go on forever. I didn't know any better. My father had always made payments on a car.

The next week I went to work and began to learn about my territory. Ben Mattingly, the Wholesale District Manager, lived in Indianapolis. He was my counterpart on the wholesale side of the business. He took me under his wing and tried to acquaint me with my territory. The territory man I replaced was gone and Theo Antonio was attending to other crises, so I was pretty much on my own. That was all right because I knew the ropes pretty well. I had toured all my stations and met all my managers.

The desk clerk at the Holiday Inn agreed to show me different apartment projects in Indianapolis. He was about my age and said he was thinking about a roommate and asked if I might like to see his place. I said that would be great.

After work the next day I picked up the desk clerk and we drove to four different apartment projects. After driving for four or five hours we went to the Huddle Restaurant for a hamburger and a glass of milk. Toward the end of the meal Harold became hyper and said "Let's go!" I didn't think too much about it but we left the Huddle to go to his apartment before going back to the Holiday Inn. As we walked up the driveway we met two guys coming out of the building. Both seemed nice enough, but they were very effeminate. I still didn't suspect anything. As we went in to his apartment Harold said, "Let me have your coat."

I hesitated before saying, "I really can't stay long so I'll keep my coat on." He became upset and insisted "let me have your coat!"

Because he had been nice to me I didn't want to offend him so I let him have my coat. He showed me around, his apartment was spotless. I couldn't believe how spotless, I had never seen a guy's apartment that decorative and well kept.

He sat down and asked, "Paul, do you know what it is to be gay?"

I sprang to my feet. "Yes I know what it is, give me my coat, I'm leaving!"

His face reddened. "I thought you knew I was gay, I'm very sorry."

I said, "Okay, I understand but I'm leaving."

He put his hand on my arm. "Please don't say anything at the Holiday Inn because I don't want to lose my job."

I mumbled "Don't worry, I won't," and left.

I couldn't believe my feelings. There was a side of me that wanted to go back in. That did it. "Stearns you're a homosexual." Just the thought was enough to condemn myself. Peggy said I wasn't any good at sex anyway. What I didn't know in those days is that the mind plays tricks on us and makes it difficult to ferret out true feelings in situations such as this.

The Oklahoma City psychiatrist advised me to go to a Dr. Robert O. Bill in Indianapolis. I went to him once a week for the next year, and although it was the most expensive thing I ever did, I started learning about what rural America, and more particularly Avant, people do to themselves. Things like thinking you'll go crazy if you masturbate. If you're told that from the time you are born you're going to worry about it until you learn otherwise.

I learned through working with Dr. Bill that I worried about being a sexual deviate because of Dad. He taught me I would go crazy if I masturbated, yet I masturbated. That was one reason, but another had to do with my attempts, during high school and college, to hug Dad. Every time I tried he would say, "Get away from me you queer!" and angrily shove me away. He made me think I might be a homosexual. The only time Dad ever touched me was in anger. Dr. Bill's help allowed me to learn I was not a sex deviate. What a relief!

I finally located a furnished apartment at 28th and Meridian and moved in that week-end. As I was doing so a long haired red head about 38 years old greeted me in the hallway. We introduced ourselves. She said, "You'll be tired at the end of the day and won't be feeling like fixing your dinner so why don't you come to my apartment and I'll fix you a hot meal."

I was surprised but jumped at the invitation. "Great, I'll be there at 8 P.M." It was Saturday and by 8 o'clock I was anxious to see the red haired lady again.

After dinner we had wine and were sitting on the floor relaxing when the urge to make love overcame both of us. The first thing I knew we were both stripped and ready to engage in sexual intercourse. I stopped and said I can't go through with this. I got up, dressed and left. She never spoke to me again, though I explained my problem. I told her I had gone through a divorce and was going to stay celibate until I remarried, that I had not had sex with anyone since the divorce proceedings had started. Since that time I figured out and understand why she became so upset. She had offered herself to me and I rejected her. She never understood my pain and confusion.

The first Sunday in Indianapolis, I went to church at the North Methodist Church at 38th and Meridian. Albert Cole was the Senior Minister and during the church service mentioned a single, young adult class which met each Sunday night. I attended and my life quickly began to revolve around the Single Young Adult Group.

At the Youth Group I met Libby Woodard and her roommate, Luanne Davis. I liked them both and wanted to date both, but instinctively knew that wouldn't work. One night I called intending to ask Luanne for a date. She wasn't home. but Libby was, so I asked her for a date. I didn't know it at the time but looking back that event proved to me that God does exist and was looking over and guiding my life. I'm sure if Luanne had been at home that night the last twenty six years that I've been married to Libby would not have happened. Looking back it's also clear to me that God played a substantial role in my asking for a transfer and taking the job in Indianapolis. I would never have thrown off some of my Oklahoma ignorance, had I not done that.

Jim Beck, a tall, lanky farm boy from Dana, Indiana, was teaching school in Indianapolis. Jim, a member of the Sunday Night Single Young Adult Group, was looking for a roommate. I was too, but after the homosexual incident I was cautious. After a few weeks of knowing Jim and asking around I determined Jim was straight. We agreed to find an apartment together.

After a couple of weeks we moved into a major apartment complex filled with single people and that's how I confirmed that Jim was not gay. He found more girl friends than I could imagine. Jim and I got along well, we had similar backgrounds and I learned that small town, rural Indiana wasn't much different than rural Oklahoma.

Looking back I see that Jim and I had similar views of life. We were taught hell, fire and brimstone, Old Testament fear. We often talked and nervously made fun of how the preachers saved someone during a church service, but it didn't stop there. Continued attempts were made to get people to get saved again. Jim didn't feel safe in church either! Sex was taboo, something unhealthy to do and to think about. We both thought sex and love were the same, and if we had sex we were being loved. We constantly looked for love because that is the one thing we both felt most deprived of.

Libby Woodard was a school teacher at the Crooked Creek Elementary School in Indianapolis, but was from Columbus, Ohio. Her red hair was gorgeous and her smile more so. After the near miss with Luanne Davis, Lib and I started dating regularly. I learned she had been in Indianapolis one year. Her dad was 50 and her mother was 48 when she was born, her older brother, John was 23 so she was pretty much raised as an only child.

When I met Lib she was 24. That was getting to be pretty old for a single lady. Heck, in Oklahoma if girls weren't married by the time they were eighteen, people started asking questions.

I found dating difficult. In the first five minutes of the date I felt compelled to tell a date I was divorced. I was scared to death it would cause them not to want to date me. Frankly I never felt adequate in dating. In college I never had a formal date. I asked a couple of times and got turned down, so I never bothered after that. On week-ends I dated girls I knew back home.

None of that mattered to Lib. She seemed to enjoy my company and I did hers. She was secretary-treasurer of the Sunday Night Single Young Adult Group and was very popular, a real leader too. I thought her serious dedication to kids, particularly the ones she taught, unusual. I continued to date other girls but to me Libby was special love, not someone to have sex with prior to marriage. You didn't try to have sex with someone you might marry. That was the Avant code.

Working for Kerr McGee was becoming a problem. Although my territory was running pretty well, each day I expected a calamity. It never came but I always thought it would. I was scared to death of getting fired.

Once a month I went to St. Louis for sales meetings and each time I did it seemed there were new faces everywhere. There was a lot of turn over in our division. The problem was our Division Manager. He was Theo's boss and Theo complained openly about him. When Theo called to say he and his boss were coming to inspect my territory, or at least the stations located in Indianapolis, I was sure I was going to get fired.

The next day they showed up and a proverbial white glove inspection began. I caught hell; in two of my stations a little oil was on a shelf. That wasn't okay with Theo's boss.

When he pointed it out in a caustic manner I got mad. "Look," I said, "I've been busting my tail. . .''

I don't think I would have had the confidence to behave in this manner if I hadn't already had a job offer from another company. My fears about being unemployed would have silenced my tongue.

The next day I wrote a letter of resignation and sent a copy to R.M. Knox in Oklahoma City. Theo tried to talk me out of leaving. I got the surprise of my life the next week. I got a call from Oklahoma City. "Dick Knox calling", a secretary said. Dick came on the phone. People at his level were like gods to me. I was shaking as I put the receiver to my ear. He said, "Paul I got your letter. I've been impressed with your performance first in Lawton, then in Oklahoma City and now for the last year in Indianapolis. You're not quitting this company. Get on a plane and come to Oklahoma City and tell me what the hell is going on in that St. Louis division!"

I was flabbergasted! "Mr. Knox, I've made up my mind to leave and I'm flattered you called, but I don't think it's my place to tell you what's going on in St. Louis."

The next day Dick Knox flew to St. Louis and fired the Division Manager. At the end of two weeks I was gone!

Ben Mattingly, the fellow who had helped me get indoctrinated in Indianapolis, was one of the people who already left. Ben called me to tell me of an opening with the company he had joined in Lafayette, Indiana. He was a sales representative for National Homes Corporation, the largest manufactured housing company in the United States. He was in the new Business Division, which was selling manufactured housing to home builders around the country on an unbranded basis. All National had done to that point was sell dealerships that had the National Home name.

I talked to Ben's boss, Frosty Winter and he offered me a job. I went to work for National Homes in late August of 1964.

Leaving Kerr McGee was very hard to do. Not only did I like the industry, I liked my job. I also very much liked the people I worked with. We did combat as fellow soldiers and developed a camaraderie. Looking back I can see, and I now know, why leaving was like mourning a loved one. I also remember how much fear I had and the panic I might get fired.

Libby and I had talked about getting married. I had been to her home in Columbus and she had been to my home in Avant.

In February I told Lib I wasn't going to date her anymore. I knew we were serious and decided I couldn't handle a relationship. Looking back now, I realize that I was afraid. I believe it boiled down to if I didn't get married again, I wouldn't fail again.

After three weeks of not seeing Lib I went to a party and

saw her there by accident. We talked for awhile. She looked terrible. She had lost weight and made it clear to me that what she felt for me and our breaking up was very bad for her. I was surprised—could it be someone really cared for me? I had never felt that way before, nor had anyone felt that way about me. We started dating again and in March I asked her to marry me.

I had been divorced for two years and though the scars were still fresh I decided that staying single the rest of my life was not an option. Asking Lib's father for her hand in marriage was tough. After all I was "damaged goods," but I felt it had to be done so we scheduled a trip to Columbus. Clancy was a 72 year old retired railroad engineer, and Melissa, 70 years old, had always been a housewife. As we drove in they met us in the driveway. After exchanging pleasantries Lib and her mother went inside. Her dad and I talked. I said, "Mr. Woodard I came to ask you for permission to marry your daughter." He looked at me with a stern look and said, "Young man, we'll have to talk about this." Then started to grin. As it turned out Lib had already warned her parents about our coming and the reason for the visit.

The next six months Lib and her mother were busy with planning and arranging for the wedding. Jim Beck agreed to be my best man. Despite my happiness up to, and including the day of the wedding, I contemplated how I could get out of it. We were standing in the church in our tuxedos and I turned to my best man. "Jim, I can't go through with this."

"Hoss," he answered, "You're going to do fine." The wedding went on without a hitch.

The honeymoon consisted of going to Cincinnati, Ohio for the week-end. Lib and I stayed at a motel that was a throw back to the dark ages, but it was cheap. I was so nervous I don't remember much about that week-end. It has been said we blank out painful memories. The damage done from my Oklahoma background and the five year marriage to Peggy kept me so vigilant I was anxious the whole week-end. I still hadn't gained the maturity to be sensitive to Lib's needs.

I do believe my marriage to Libby was providential! Little did I know that her sensitivity, faith in me, love for me, and constant reassurance would give me the help I needed to find and follow my bliss. She helped me move ahead against my fears.

When I left Kerr McGee, Lib kidded me about my paranoia. She liked to remind me of what a lousy job I was doing and how I was going to get fired, and then a vice-president called me to ask me to stay when I resigned. She had learned to sift through my paranoia. Theo tried every way he could to get me to stay. My image and reputation with Kerr McGee was very high. The problem was I didn't know and feel it. To be wanted felt good but that lasted about fifteen minutes. My low self-esteem took me back to negative feelings very quickly.

The mind is a secret place that can create great torment! I couldn't accept that I had value and really hadn't accepted that Libby could love me either. I felt lucky though and I wasn't going to tamper with that.

Now I was with National Homes Corporation, another company and in another training program. I was beginning to wonder if Dad was right, maybe I couldn't stick with anything. The good part was that the marketing approach of National Homes Corporation, National Supply Corporation and Kerr McGee were basically the same. My knowledge was transferable and what I really needed to learn was the difference in the industries and product knowledge.

Frosty and Ben helped me a lot in my transition in the first three weeks. Then a big bomb dropped. The new business division was disbanded. Ben and I were offered jobs as District Managers in the branded program of the company. Either I took over a territory in Michigan or I had no job. Lib and I talked about it and decided to go to Michigan. The company allowed us to select the city of our preference in Michigan. We selected Lansing because it was located in the center of the territory. This limited my overnight travel. The only time I was on the road overnight was when I went to the northern part of the state or made a factory trip back to Lafayette.

My job was to service the four or five existing accounts in Michigan and develop the state. The National Homes concept was to convince a stick builder, a builder who purchases raw materials from a lumber yard, builds the houses from scratch, to become a National Homes Branded builder. We supplied accounting systems, advertising and sales promotion materials, blue prints, and prefab packaged materials. The professional materials and business consulting we provided the builders enabled them to build homes more quickly than they could from scratch. The problem was, our costs were higher; the trick was to convince the builder our quality was worth the difference.

Frosty was my boss for only three weeks. I now reported to a new boss, but I got to see Frosty back at the factory with clients.

I was not happy with the surprise of the new business division being closed down. I felt betrayed and told Lib that someday I had to be in control of my own destiny. If I wanted control I had to become self-employed.

My training with National Homes lasted until October, so Lib and I moved into a furnished apartment near the one Jim Beck and I had been sharing. Wouldn't you know the very first night at dinner we were talking and I accidently called her Peggy. She looked at me and said, "Paul, you just called me Peggy!" The hurt look on her face stunned me. I apologized profusely.

Early in our marriage when Lib took the position she didn't like something I took the position she could leave. There were times she must have thought I was trying to drive her away. She didn't know that I was terrified of being hurt again. I thought if I kept her at a distance, and in the place I thought was safe, I wouldn't be as vulnerable to being hurt by her as I was by Peggy and my Father. At that point I was not going to expose myself in a way to hurt me again. To build trust was not easy for me. How she stood it I don't know.

The training ended. It was time to go to Lansing. Lib had a 1963 white, Chevrolet Nova station wagon and we loaded it to the hilt. I had a company station wagon, also fully loaded. I had sold the Super Sport and purchased a fifteen foot speed boat and pulled that to Michigan with us. It was October of 1964.

Before the move we went to Lansing on a couple of scouting trips and found an apartment. It was one bedroom, so small we couldn't cuss a cat without getting hair in our teeth (as we say in Oklahoma), but we didn't care. When we arrived at the apartment complex it was almost dark.

Ron and Wanda Roderick lived in one of the apartments and came out to introduce themselves. They had spotted our boat. It turned out they also had a boat and liked to water ski as much as we did. That was the beginning of a close, long lasting friendship. We've averaged having dinner together probably once a week since. The next spring, in order to water ski, Ron and I broke the ice on the Grand River, which runs through the center of Lansing.

During the next two years with National Homes Corporation Libby and I saved all the money we could to get a grub stake to start our own business. Libby had gotten a job at North Elementary School in Lansing so with both our incomes we were able to save $420 per month. We also were trying to get settled and acquainted with friends and find a church.

I worked long hours, traveling all over the state trying to convince home builders to become National Homes Dealers. The job was more that I bargained for. There were several problems. One was that after World War II housing was needed quickly and some builders, to expedite, bought and built National Homes in volume. They were cheap homes, poorly done and now, twenty years later, were dilapidated. Builders associated those homes with fire traps and didn't give National much credit. The second problem was that townships and cities had electrical codes and plumbing codes that hindered prefabricated housing. The third and biggest problem was trying to convince old line home builders there was another way to do business than stick built. We all resist change, but builders seem to be the worst.

The people at National Homes were different from any I had been around. They were rougher, coarser and faster living. After I went to work for National I learned that Frosty Winter was a recovering alcoholic. He was a millionaire by the time he was twenty-nine and lost it all.

One of the managers I reported to was an active alcoholic. He used to call and say, "Paul meet me in Detroit tomorrow at 11:00." I'd drive the hour and a half to Metro Airport to pick him up. "Paul, take me to the hotel and I'll get checked in." We talked business as we drove to the hotel. He would then say, "Paul take me back to the airport. I have to go to Columbus, Ohio. I'll be back at Metro Airport tomorrow. Pick me up at 10 A.M." I later found he had a girl friend in Columbus his wife and bosses didn't know about. I drove back to Lansing that evening and then back to Metro the next day. When I picked him up he ordered, "Paul take me to my hotel. I have to check out and get back to Lafayette." He was gone from Lafayette for two days and had interrupted me for two days. Neither of us did any work for those two days. On another occasion he came into Michigan to work Detroit with me. I set up some appointments with Detroit builders. We were to meet them at a combination bar and restaurant on Eight Mile Road. We had a two hour drinking luncheon. After it ended he spotted two blondes at the bar, went over to talk to them, came back and said, "Paul, you take the one on the left and I'll take the one on the right."

"I can't do that," I told him, "I don't run around on my wife. I've been married for six months and won't betray her." He didn't like that and let me know it.

Paul, what are you going to do? I asked myself. You've been on the job six months, your boss has been with the company since it began, he's the fair haired boy of the Chairman and founder, Jim Price. If you report him you don't have any creditability to get him fired; if you don't report him and continue to work for him he's not going to consider you for increases in pay or promotion, the way he will with the people who participate or condone his life style.

All through my years with big companies I was pushed to do things that compromised my values and I was tempted, but stood my ground. I've since wondered if Watergate would have occurred if people had stood their ground. It's hard to do, but although I thought I failed in many ways, this was not one of them.

My long term goal looked as if it were suddenly going up in smoke. My goal had always been to be the president of a company. Now with National Homes I was in an environment I couldn't tolerate. After debating with Lib I decided to keep my mouth shut and do my job as best as I could.

My conviction that self-employment was the only way out grew stronger. I saw employees of National Supply, Kerr McGee and now National Homes who gave their all to the company, and at the age of fifty or so were unexpectedly fired during cut-backs. The companies always called it early retirement, but when you're fifty to fifty-two years old, even if you're vested in a retirement plan it is not enough to retire on. I saw how big companies weeded out those people who would never reach the top to decrease their overhead.

I was also concerned about what I thought was immoral and unethical behavior. I could not adjust to it, but felt the pull to participate in it to get ahead. Working directly for people I felt superior to but who were connected politically showed me quickly that an employee's performance and individual capabilities, while important, were not the determining factor for rising to the top.

Life at National Homes was never secure. I felt like the odd man out. I didn't respect my boss. We dealt with the clients who dealt with a lot of money and where there is a lot of money there are always problems with alcohol, infidelity and fast track types of pressures. I certainly felt more comfortable with the service station dealers at Kerr McGee.

I worked long hours and drove over 40,000 miles per year covering the Michigan territory. I did hone my sales skills at National Homes and my ability to get appointments. Anytime you have a product that is hard to sell you get the opportunity to hone some skills. You either do it or fail and I certainly wasn't going to fail. But every day I felt as if I was failing. No matter how hard I tried, the feeling was there. Worry and insecurity pushed me to manipulate life to be the way I wanted it instead of the way it was.

Within two years of moving to Michigan, Lib and I saved $10,000. My job at National Homes became intolerable and I said, "Lib we have to make a move. I simply have to find some business I can own. If all I do is run a service station the rest of my life that's what I will do. I have to be in a position to do work where my talents bring rewards without the problems of company politics. I have to work at moral and ethical standards I set, not what someone else sets."

It's a good thing Lib's love for me was unconditional, because she was raised in a family where there was a pay check every two weeks. That meant stability and security. Going into business for ourselves certainly wouldn't be stable, and insecurity, not security, would be the watchword, until we got a start.

I used the sales skills I honed at National to convince Lib that self-employment was the answer and working for a big company wasn't. I said, "Lib, if you will support our effort for awhile longer by purchasing $25.00 dresses instead of $100 dresses, when we get our start you'll be able to buy $250 dresses." I really don't think my pitch helped much because Lib was not a materialistic person. None the less I made the pitch.

Lib smiled, "Okay, let's do it," and with that support I started looking for the right business opportunity.

My climb up the corporate ladder ended in 1965. I was twenty-eight years old with a $10,000 grub stake.

It was not apparent to me in 1965 that I was born to be an entrepreneur not a professional manager, but I was. I thought I was a quitter, and felt guilty leaving the companies that I left.

It wasn't morals, ethics, infidelity, or politics, that was my reason for leaving. It was that I didn't fit. I finally discovered I was an entrepreneur. I didn't fit, not because I wasn't good enough, or that I was a quitter, but because I wasn't cut out for the job. I had been trying to fit a round peg in a square hole and didn't know it.

I decided if I could find a business to get into I would use what I had learned working for big companies. One of the things I wanted was to make the rules. Until that point I had lived by everyone else's rules. If I broke rules I had to pay. I wanted to make my own rules and if anyone broke them I, and I alone, would sit in judgement.

CHAPTER FIVE

THE
ENTREPRENEUR

Jerry Lee was born in China. He was Chinese and spoke broken English. He came to Michigan to attend the Michigan State University Construction Management School. After graduation he started building houses and apartments in Lansing and for ten years had been a successful builder. In talking with him and trying to sell him the National Home concept, I told him I was going to start my own business. He said, "Paul, I've wanted to build scattered lot housing in the Lansing area for a long time. Why don't we form a corporation and do it together?"

After much discussion and negotiation we formed a company called LeMark Homes. I invested all of my $10,000 and got 49% of the stock. I was to run the company and had the title of General Manager. Jerry was the President.

It took me three months to learn about his business practices. While acceptable to some they simply weren't my standards. I thought about it for two weeks then, I decided to end the relationship. It took another three months to extricate myself. The courage to end the relationship was critical because I risked losing all that Lib and I took two years to save. Morally I thought I had no choice; I didn't want to operate the way Jerry was operating. I learned that with partners I still couldn't make the rules.

In the final negotiations I recovered $7,000 of my $10,000 and had worked six months at no salary. Needless to say if this was symptomatic of what my entrepreneurial success was to be I was in big trouble. I was devastated. I

117

could hear my Father saying, "I told you, you're too dumb to make money."

I didn't know that my experience with Jerry would one day reap big dividends, but I learned a tremendous amount. You couldn't buy experience like that, although I had! I was not ready to go back to work for a big company. My next step was to get on my feet and try again. After inventorying my skills, knowledge and bank account I felt that I could get into the gasoline distribution business. What I had learned at Kerr McGee gave me a good foundation to start a business without partners.

I began looking for vacant service station properties that were closed. I wanted to use my own brand name, find an oil company to supply me and start my own oil jobbership by breathing life into the closed station I found.

Luck, as I've said before, is important in a business career. My lucky break was to find a service station at Saginaw and Logan streets in Lansing. It was closed and had no markings on it. It wasn't for sale or for lease, but I went to city hall, and found out who owned it. I thought it was a great location, its attributes fit all the criteria I had been taught. I called the owner and said, "May I speak to Bruce Maguire, Jr. please." The receptionist said "Mr. Maguire, Jr. is on vacation, but Mr. Maguire, Sr. is here. Would you like to speak with him?" I said "Yes." I figured the father would know as much as the son.

It was 1966 when I said Mr. Maguire, "I'm a young man trying to get a start in the oil business and would like to lease a station your son owns at the corner of Saginaw and Logan."

He informed me, "That particular location is leased to Sinclair Oil Company until 1985." I thought that's unbelievable, he's leased an old junk piece of property to a major oil company for 20 years and he sits there clipping his coupons. Before I could respond he went on to say, "Mr. Stearns we have other properties and have worked with a half dozen men helping them start in business; why don't you come down and lets get acquainted. If we like each other maybe we can help each other." I asked in an excited voice "When?"

He said, "How about 10 A.M. tomorrow in my office?"

I went home and said, "Lib, this is our lucky day. I found our sugar daddy." Every young guy who ever dreamed of being in business always dreams of a wealthy person who will set him up! I didn't know it then but I found later that wealthy people are not looking for ways to put money in someone else's pocket. They are looking for ways to make more money for themselves.

The next day at 10 A.M. sharp I was ushered into Maguire's office and for the next two hours had the time of my life hearing his story. He was from Kansas and was 72 years old. In 1923 came to Kalamazoo, Michigan, moved there by an oil company. In 1924 he moved to Lansing and started in the service station business. Before the stock market crash in 1929 he sold this company to Cities Service Oil Company for over $400,000, the equivalent of several million dollars in today's money. In 1955 he started Wolverine Oil Corporation and leased all of his properties to Sinclair Oil Company. He changed the name of his company to Wolverine Development Corporation. When we met he was developing real estate. I was impressed. I told my story to Mr. Maguire who said, "Paul, all my friends call me Mac, why don't you?"

I thought, I've known him two hours and I'm this important man's friend already. I liked him a lot. He continued, "Paul, Bruce Jr. is due back in a couple of days. Why don't you come back, meet him and we'll talk again."

The next week I went in and met Bruce Jr. who was six years older than I. Mac did most of the talking. "Paul, I'd like you to meet Roy Isbister, an associate of ours, and President of Spartan Oil Corporation. It's an oil jobbership and has 13 service stations. They operate under the Bay brand name, Bay is a division of Dow Chemical Company. Spartan also operates a Kendall Motor Oil Distributorship."

Roy owned 50% of Spartan stock and Bruce Jr., with Moe Zoeller, owned the other 50%.

We went across the hall and met Roy. He was not very

cordial. It was apparent he was not happy with Mac about something. When we went back to Mac's office Mac said, "Paul, why don't you become a dealer for Spartan Oil, show us what you can do and while you're there look for an automobile dealership we can buy together. There's a lot of money to be made selling cars. They are a necessity in life. Transportation, food and shelter, are those basics that you want to be in as you start your career."

I was still hesitant and replied, "Mac, I'll consider that provided Mr. Isbister wants to talk to me further; I'll call him to find out."

I did call Roy and went to see him. He wasn't friendly nor did he come forward with a location for me to consider, but we did get better acquainted. I thanked him for his time and told him if he ever had anything open up, to give me a call. He said okay!

A few days later I called Mac and told him I hadn't had any luck leasing an unbranded service station, but that Mobil had a branded dealership location open at the corner of Jolly and Cedar and I was going to do a deal with them. All he said was, "Paul, don't sign anything until I get back to you tomorrow." He didn't explain why.

The next day I got a call from Roy Isbister saying he needed a dealer at his Willow and Comfort location, and would I meet him to talk about it. It was clear to me that Mac had convinced Roy to deal with me!

We met Sunday afternoon and after two hours we signed a contract. We shook hands and just before we parted Roy said, "Paul, I'm going to place this contract and lease in my desk drawer and this is the last time I ever expect to look at it."

I knew instantly he meant that we would have a relationship of trust and understanding and if we had a problem, we would talk it out, not resort to the courts to solve it. I said, "Mr. Isbister, okay, I'll do the same!"

I had learned by watching my Father in Oklahoma that with some people, you do business with just a handshake.

Monday morning Roy's operations manager and I met at the Willow and Comfort Service Station, took inventory and

I was the new dealer. Finally I was self-employed and I felt great.

The Willow Street Bay Station was good to me. By the time I ran it for 10 months I made enough money to save $10,000, to go with the $7,000 I had left after the Jerry Lee fiasco. Ten thousand in 10 months when it had taken two years to save the first $10,000. It really felt like an accomplishment. I had $17,000 saved. We were on a roll.

Mac came to see me at the Willow Street Bay Station the second day. We stood outside talking, our conversation was interrupted each time the driveway bell rang, indicating a customer had come in. During our conversation he said, "Paul, I still want you to consider researching the automobile dealership idea. I'd be interested in investing with you if the deal is right. Remember the Maguire family has helped at least six young men get started in business, Roy Isbister being one of them." I said, "Okay Mac, I'll start the research at once."

Over the next six months I contacted Ford, General Motors, and Chrysler, and met with them about dealerships for sale. I also talked with a number of dealership owners. Each time there was something to report, I called Mac. All of my research activities were in addition to running the Bay Station.

After six months and continual reports, along with recommendations, I felt Mac was playing me along. I finally said, "Mac, I'm angry with you. I've done all this research on my own time and expense. I've found several opportunities. You've shot all of them down and I think you're not for real. I think, for whatever reason, you're baiting me and you have no intention to deal with me. I don't have any more time to waste." I got up in a huff and walked out.

Mac followed me out to my service truck and said, "Paul, you're wrong and if you feel that way I'm sorry."

I got into my truck. "That's okay, Mac, but I don't plan to do any more of what I've been doing with you." I started my service truck and left.

The next day Roy Isbister came to inspect the station and I told him what had happened with Mac. I was so mad that I said, "Roy, if Bruce Maguire Jr. or Sr. come out here I'm going to ask them to get off my property!"

Roy smiled, and then really opened up with me. He told me why he had not been cordial to me and why when they were around he was always so cranky. It seemed when Roy bought the 50% interest in Spartan, he felt as if Mac had screwed him. From that day until the day of his death in 1989 Roy Isbister and I were special friends. Our relationship grew stronger as the years passed. He was no longer worried about me being a pawn of people he distrusted.

Mac did come out to see me a couple of times and I cooled down. Over time we became friends and mutual admirers. It became clear to me that Mac respected the fact that I was strong enough to tell him my feelings. I was surprised because I thought maybe I was too bold when I was in his office, dressed in my service station uniform, bow tie and hat with Bay emblems all over them. I arrived in my old beat up 1956 Chevrolet pick-up service vehicle, dinged up and rusted out, fenders flapping. Mac was a multimillionaire and he drove the biggest cars, Cadillacs and Lincolns.

Mac marveled that I drove that old, beat up service truck. He felt most people's egos wouldn't let them sacrifice in that way. I didn't know any better. It was all I could afford so I didn't think anything about it. During his visits to the station he also marveled when a customer came and I immediately left to go service the customer, even if I was talking to him. Not many people interrupted their visits with him for any reason. It never occurred to me that I could do anything but pay attention to my customers!

When Roy found I could not be controlled by the Maguires he became my mentor.

It became apparent that marrying Lib was good for me. Hard for her, but good for me. The residual pain from my first marriage and family of origin required assuaging and she supplied most of it. For the first two or three years of our marriage we laid awake most every night until midnight or one o'clock in the morning. She would listen as I talked about all the problems that occurred and the pain that I felt.

Gradually, with her care, love and support, some healing came.

Libby was pregnant when I took the Willow Street Bay Station. I started in the station in October, her school year was to begin in September. Being five months pregnant, she decided not to teach that year. She never went back.

Two months after taking over the station, Lib drove in one day and walked by the office window crying. She rapped on the window as she went on to the rest room. It scared me to death, but she told me later that her water had just broken so off to the hospital we went. December 8, 1966 was a great day! Scott was born. I bought cigars and gave them with a smile to any who would take them.

To watch Lib with Scott was special. She was born to be a mother. But her role as a wife was to save my life. Her belief in me gave me the courage to go on when I felt completely defeated.

Lib's ability to massage a penny and make a quarter out of it made it possible for us to save the $10,000 grub stake. At the beginning I was not able to control finances to save money. She clearly gets all the credit.

I figured my job was to make the money. Roy Isbister was to play a major role in my start. I was at the Willow Street Station for ten months when he came to see me. He told me he was having trouble at the Kalamazoo Street Station and knew I wanted to expand. He suggested, "Why don't you take over the Kalamazoo Station and see what you can do with it?" I didn't hesitate. Six months later I had both the Kalamazoo Street and Willow Street Bay stations operating successfully. Roy stopped by one day and after the usual amenities got to the reason for his visit. "Paul, I'm getting divorced, moving to Flint, Michigan and want to know if you would like to buy my ownership in Spartan Oil."

My initial reaction was to jump at the chance, but I controlled my first impulse and said, "Roy, you're uncomfortable with the Maguires. Knowing your uncomfortability and my failed partnership with Jerry Lee, why should I take on that misery again?"

He asked, "What if we can negotiate a contract for you to

purchase my 50% ownership and an agreement for you to run the company as if you owned it, except for misfeasance or malfeasance?'' I said that would do. He continued, ''Okay, find dealers to replace yourself, sell your dealerships to them and come into Spartan as my General Manager. Since I have to finance a portion of your purchase price I want to see what you can do and we need to show the Maguires you can run the company. They don't want anything to do with running it and never will but they care about having someone competent to run it.''

This made me hesitant. ''What if they won't agree to my taking it over? I'll be vulnerable. I will have sold my two dealerships and will be on your payroll.'' Roy offered me a solution. ''Paul, if by the end of ten months we haven't worked out an agreement all parties can agree to, both you and I will resign. You'll see, they'll agree, and we won't have to leave.''

I had trust in Roy and decided to gamble. I found two dealers, sold my interest in the stations and became his General Manager.

The first day I reported to the office Roy left for a three week vacation to Mexico. I didn't know at the time, but he wanted to see how I would react, what I would do and what would happen. He was not available to me, but unbeknown to me, he was in constant contact with his bookkeeper.

During the next ten months Roy became convinced I could handle the company and he would get paid if he financed me. During that time we had extended negotiations with the Maguires. They tried every way possible to keep Roy from leaving. I was still relatively green, they had come to respect and like me, but Roy Isbister was 53 years old and tested.

In the final analysis, it became apparent that Roy was leaving and I was going with him if we couldn't make a deal. They had two choices. They, and Roy, could hire a third party to run the company. The other choice was to sanction Roy's sale to me. They couldn't stop the sale, but with their 50% ownership they could stop me from becoming president of the company. They reluctantly accepted my buying

Roy out, and Bruce Jr. signed a contract with me. I gave Roy all the money I had saved to date, the balance I owed him would be paid off over the next five years.

It was 1968, half of an oil jobbership with 13 service stations, and a small Kendall Motor Oil Dealership was mine. I was scared but excited!

The Maguires were tough negotiators. They made the deal difficult and despite my hurt, I tried to understand their reasons. I did not feel real great about not being their first choice. I didn't care that when Roy took over the company had three service stations and very little motor oil business and he had built it to 13 service stations and a respectable motor oil business.

Once the Maguires made the decision to deal with me their attitude changed. I could not have asked for more support. I was adopted. Mac became my mentor and Bruce Jr., as an advisor and support person, shored up some of my insecurities. They gave me the confidence I needed. I had never had such support in my life. They made me feel as if I could walk on water.

I viewed Bruce Jr. like a partner because he always spoke for Moe Zoeller. Bruce owned a block of Spartan stock, Moe owned some too. I owned 50%. I viewed Mac as a friend and advisor but always talked to Bruce Jr. about company decisions.

The next five years were a whirlwind of growth and activity. We got rid of five dog service stations out of the thirteen and in the following five years we grew to 39 service stations, scattered over the central and western portion of the state. We also developed and expanded the Lube Oil and Industrial Oil Division. Our total dollar sales volume was 800% greater and our annual profits were unbelievable!

Lib and I purchased our first house a few months after taking over Spartan Oil in 1968 and in 1969 I bought my first Lincoln Continental as a company car. These were the first material rewards we received since we became self-employed. Those had been objectives for me to accomplish. When I grew up in the rural part of the country the biggest investment anyone ever made was a car, to have a Lincoln and buy a house was reaching the top of the heap! I could hear Dad say, "Paul, you're getting too big for your britches." Cars were always important to my father. As times got better he bought a new car every year. They were always the cheapest Ford or Chevrolet on the market and he financed them. Because of the interest he had to pay, the cars were always worth equal to or less than what he owed on them. I paid cash for my first Lincoln. From then on I paid cash for my cars.

Spartan was doing well in 1969! The Maguires encouraged me to become better known in the community, to join the Chamber of Commerce. They sponsored me in the Lansing Rotary Club.

Bruce Jr. was connected socially in the community and introduced me to the Lansing social community. Vera Maguire, Mac's wife, sponsored Lib's membership in the Junior League.

Our second son, Jeff, was born at 1:38 A.M. on July 11, 1970. His birth was scary. Lib's water broke early in the morning on July 10. We were concerned because he wasn't due for six more weeks. We worried through that day, until Jeff was delivered the next morning. When he was delivered he was placed in an incubator. His development was so rapid he came home three days after delivery. The doctors said he would be fine although he weighed five pounds at birth.

I dreamed of being a member of a country club. It wasn't clear to me whether I really wanted to join or whether I wanted to know I could join. But in 1970 it became clear I wanted to play golf and I decided to join the Walnut Hills Country Club. I purchased all the golfing equipment at the same time—shoes, socks, pants, golf shirts, sweaters, etc. The golf pro took me under his wing, gave me lessons and encouragement. All beginning golfers were automatically given a 36 handicap. With hard work, blisters and banging hundreds of golf balls and playing through that summer I lowered my handicap to 18, the second summer to 14 and the third to seven. The average country club member handicap was fifteen. Golf was a great challenge to me and gave me a diversion from business. I attacked golf in the same ferocious, energetic, dedicated way I had business. It was not a hobby, it was another job, and I loved it.

After four or five years of playing a lot of golf my interest waned. Playing golf as a hobby or for fun wasn't something I could do. I had to have a reason, objective or goal to shoot for! Some exciting things happened to me on the golf course, things like winning a couple of tournaments, two holes in one, some eagles and a double eagle. But it became clear I wasn't going to be good enough to turn pro and to win local tournaments wasn't enough. The challenge was gone.

I began going to Florida every year for a week of golf with three friends, Harry Schmidt, a local surgeon, Clyde Spencer, head of the Radiology Department at a local hospital and Ed Jones, who owned a chain of retail gift stores. We played 36 holes of golf every day for seven days. Other than making this trip for the camaraderie I only played golf four or five times per year after the first four or five years of trips. The trips continued for fourteen years, then we stopped going.

Lib and my relationship with the Maguires had become like family. One year Mac and Vera talked Lib and me into going on a trip to New York City with them. They wanted to educate and show us a life style we had never known. We were exposed to things I had heard about, read about, talked about all of my life. We experienced the finest restaurants, the theatre, Wall Street.

The trip to New York was scary. I was very intimidated. Coming from the country to the city was one of the most frightening experiences I ever had. I enjoyed the positives, but the negatives needed to be overcome.

My close relationship with Mac led to a relationship that caused me to greatly admire and respect him. I also grew to love him as a father, he built me up and accepted me in ways I had never known before. He made me feel safe and I felt lucky that he shared his wisdom with me.

After the first four years of running Spartan I began to be concerned about what the long term might be for oil jobbers. Oil companies were beginning to put the squeeze on small jobbers and I felt if we didn't diversify, in the long term, there would be a problem.

In addition to my concerns about the industry, I became more concerned about my relationship with Bruce Jr. I liked him a lot but didn't feel comfortable with him. He never came to work before 8:00 A.M. He always left by 5 P.M. and never worked week-ends. He seemed content to rest on his Dad's laurels and his Dad promoted it. I always felt Mac was afraid if Bruce did more than try to retain the family wealth, he would lose it. Also, although I liked Bruce, Jr., I didn't trust him. Roy Isbister had never trusted Bruce Jr. either.

It took fifteen more years, a major quest and a paradigm shift for me to learn that what Bruce Jr. did was his business. As a matter of fact, the corporate success he produced over that time frame vindicated him. During that time I learned it is not the number of hours you work, but the work you produce that matters. As far as trusting Bruce Jr., Roy and I always ran scared we didn't trust anybody including ourselves. I did not realize it at the time but this was the stage of my life when I crossed the boundary of living a reasonably healthy, day to day life. This was the period when the seeds for a later burn out were sown.

In 1972 we took our first real vacation. Lib, Scott, Jeff and I flew to Jamaica. The week was a disaster. I had a miserable time. I was out of my element and, since I wasn't working, decided I was unproductive. I kept hearing my Father scolding me for wasting time. I could hear him saying men work, they don't lollygag. Since I wasn't working I had to be lollygagging. The only way to gain respect was to stay on the treadmill of work, work, and more work. My mood was sour and I spewed my venom on my family.

I had an eight week hiatus between the Jamaica trip and my annual golf trip with Harry Schmidt, Clyde Spencer and Ed Jones. We headed for the golf school in Innisbrook, Florida to learn from the famous pro, Bob Toski. Every day I worked at learning and playing golf. Golf was work, not lollygagging. I worked at it so hard I knew my Dad would have approved. It never occurred to me to wonder how I could have such a good time with my friends and such a miserable one with my family.

My dream since becoming self employed was to build a

company and take it public. Spartan Oil Corporation as an Oil Jobber was not a business conducive to going public, so I developed the idea into the convenience food store business. At that time there weren't any service stations with convenience food, or any convenience food stores with gasoline in Michigan. I had seen the concept in the Southeastern and Southwestern parts of the United States. I traveled to both areas, did detailed research and as a result decided to build two prototype stores.

I presented the P.S. Food Store idea to Bruce Jr. and Mac. P.S. stood for post script; the market convenience food stores supplied. Mac and Bruce Jr. were not receptive to the idea, but when they saw how serious I was and how sure I was this opportunity would save the company from the big oil company pressures they agreed to go along with testing the idea.

I had been running Spartan successfully for four years. One year earlier, because of my fear of Mac and Bruce Jr., I acquired 1% of the company from Bruce, Jr. and that gave me controlling interest in the company. The reason I wanted control was I felt a little more secure with it. Earlier my fears had escalated to paranoia and I didn't want the Maguires in a position to control me. I could now force any management ideas I wanted but I had told them if they would sell me control I would consult with them on all major ideas. If I couldn't convince them I wouldn't do whatever it was I was recommending, however I reserved the right to resign and hire someone else to run the company. Then I would exercise all the power the 51% gave me.

The Spartan Development Corporation was formed on October 20, 1971. Two P.S. Food Stores opened the next spring.

My decision to develop Michigan's first convenience food stores in conjunction with gasoline was vindicated over the next several years. The concept spread in such a way that now you can rarely find a service station that doesn't sell food. It gives me a good deal of satisfaction to know I was the first in Michigan to spot the trend and implement it.

I became active in the Downtown Rotary Club, Chamber

of Commerce and the City Club. Bruce Jr. always introduced me as his associate, and people who didn't know me
thought I was his employee. It wasn't abnormal for people to
think I might be an employee of Bruces because the
Maguires had been in town for so long and were so successful. But it bothered me; my ego required people to think I
was an independent high flyer.

Lansing's business community at that time was composed primarily of second or third generation run companies, outside of the three primary employers of the community, which were Oldsmobile (Lansing is World
Headquarters), Michigan State Government and Michigan
State University.

My profile became visible in Lansing when I joined the
Rotary Club, Chamber of Commerce, Walnut Hills Country
Club and The City Club.

In 1973 I went to Bruce Jr. and said, "Bruce, I've had a
problem for a long time. I either want to buy you out or sell
to you or find someone to run the company that will report
to both of us."

Bruce was flabbergasted, and it didn't take long for Mac
to come to see me. He didn't understand. I explained I
wanted to be free to build a company and take it public, that
wasn't their interest, so let's end the relationship. I could not
tell them, that although I liked them both, I did not feel
comfortable with them and was tired of looking over my
shoulder. I still hadn't forgotten they tried to block my coming in and Roy's leaving. How could I tell them that I worried
if I got a company to the stage it could go public, they
wouldn't vote in the affirmative. I was between a rock and a
hard place and it was time to deal with the problem.

The negotiations were tough, both Mac and Bruce Jr. did
things during the negotiations which hurt me deeply. The
hard feelings resulting in ending our personal relationship,
as well as our business relationship. The negotiations
resulted in Bruce Jr. buying my interest out in late summer.

Neither Bruce Jr. nor I realized my prediction that the
big oil companies would squeeze little oil jobbers would
come true so soon, but three months after I sold to Bruce the

industry started to change. In the following year more changes occurred in the industry than had in the previous 70 years. Things were never the same for oil jobbers again. An era had ended. Selling out was lucky for me!

In 1973 I simultaneously was out of business and elected to be a Director of the Chamber of Commerce. I was 35 years old and ready to find a company I could breath life into and take public.

The goal of going public would be an accomplishment not even my Father could reject. It would be clear to him and everyone else that I was somebody and that I had talent. All the humiliation resulting from being made fun of all my life would end.

One goal was reached as I sold my interest in Spartan Oil. The position I attained, the trophies of big cars, memberships—the way I carried myself caused people to treat me with respect. There were no more bullies, no one telling me I was worthless. Women treated me differently now. I suddenly became popular!

The sale of Spartan Oil resulted in my feeling as if I had conquered the world. My confidence was never higher! At Spartan I had reached a goal that seemed to wipe out the failures of the past. I had a sense of having accomplished something for humanity and myself. I was euphoric.

I decided to take a three week family vacation, go to Washington, D.C., tour the Southeastern part of the U.S., and end up with a visit to my parents in Oklahoma. Lib agreed. She remembered I had complained that I was 35 years old and had been wishing my life away. I was always working for tomorrow. I needed to make one more dollar or buy one more service station or one more something. I had the feeling life was passing by too fast. I wanted to live more day to day and smell at least a flower, if not flowers.

Oklahoma wasn't a good place for me to visit. Oklahoma and my family, and the painful memories of my early years and from my divorce always made a trip there painful. But I had the yearning I always had for home. When we arrived in Oklahoma, Dad seemed glad to see us, but made it clear he had no interest in my life or what I was doing. We had been in Michigan for nine years. He had been there once and met Bruce Jr. and Mac. He didn't like them. He didn't like anybody who had money. Dad's attitude about money was strange to me. When I was growing up he often opened his wallet to show three one hundred dollar bills he carried. Yet he didn't like people who had money. He didn't like people who didn't earn money with their hands. I remember him being in my office during his visit to Michigan, Mac came over and told Dad how great I was and how lucky Dad was to have me for a son. Dad became very agitated and blurted out "I'm not any prouder of Paul than any of my kids. In some ways I'm prouder of them than I am of him!" Mac shut up instantly and the subject was changed. I felt like crawling in a hole.

We had been in Oklahoma for a couple of days before Bob, my brother, drove 300 miles to see me. I was flattered until he got me alone and asked, "How are you with the Lord?"

I said, "Fine."

Before he could respond his wife Velda said, "No Paul, how are you really doing with the Lord?"

I tried to be civil but put an end to the discussion by saying, "We're doing fine together." They didn't let it rest.

Bob said, "We were called to come here just to see you because we feel you aren't doing so well with the Lord."

At that point I snapped, "Bob, I'm not doing anything with your Lord. He and I don't talk the same language." I leaned over to him and said, "If you want to continue this conversation, let's go to the Hilltop Bar and finish it over a beer." My teetotaling brother was appalled and he shut up!

Almost every contact with my family resulted in an attempt to save me. They treated me the same way they always did. There was something wrong with me and they wanted it fixed. Their Lord would do the fixing. They felt you needed to be fixed every time they saw you. Hell! Anyone who made more than a pay check had to be fixed because he was doing something immoral. It was never said out loud but the undertone was that I was that "decadent, money grubbing Northerner" with the wife from Ohio and kids who didn't have a southern or Oklahoma twang.

While in Oklahoma Mother fell down a flight of stairs in a Tulsa office building. She thought her arm was broken, but after x-rays it was determined she had badly bruised it. When she got home she was black and blue all over. She told Dad she had fallen, but before she could tell him if she was hurt, Dad said, "Ruby, you're as awkward as a cow, don't you even know how to walk?" Mother cried uncontrollably.

I was glad to get back to Michigan. Three weeks off was hard for me. Since college I had not taken more than one week's vacation at a time and sometimes not even that. After this three week vacation I resumed my earlier pattern until 1989.

Every time I came back to Michigan from Oklahoma I felt bad for the first few weeks. My antidote was to work in a frenzy, as though someone was after me. After this trip I wanted to be a bigger somebody. I needed to find the company I would take public. My family and background weren't going to win. I would show them!

I began contacting C.P.A.'s, attorneys, Chamber of Commerce offices across the state and business consultants trying to find a new business in a new industry that I could build. I worked harder at looking for a business than I had running a business. After a few months I was negotiating several deals.

I became very frustrated. I had sold Spartan Oil almost a year ago and I didn't have a business. I'd find something I was interested in and inevitably negotiations would fall through. I became frustrated and began to wonder if I would ever find another business. For a young man in a hurry, I felt as if I was all dressed up with no place to go.

Lib constantly reassured me I had been successful and would continue to be, we would find another business. Other than her reassurance I isolated myself from others and wasn't getting any positive feed back until the day Jim Reutter called to ask Lib and me out to dinner with he and his wife Ann. At the dinner he opened the conversation. "Paul, the main reason I wanted to have dinner was to tell you how much I admire you. You may not remember, but six years ago I was having a beer at the Willow Street Bar with Dick Hacker. You came in with your Bay uniform on and Dick Hacker introduced us. You had just closed your service station and were having dinner. It was 10:30 P.M.! We asked you what your business plans were and you told us your dream to build a big oil jobbership. Now it's six years later and not only did you build it, but you've sold it. Not many people in life look and plan what they are going to do, much less tell in advance about it. He paused to take a drink. "Well Paul", he continued "Hacker and I laughed at you that night. We thought this guy is crazy, all those big ideas. My apologies for thinking what I did and I respect you, I wanted to have dinner and tell you this story."

I was dumbstruck. Jim Reutter was the President of the Chamber of Commerce, president of his own third generation company among many other accomplishments. In other words he was a "Big Wig" in the community, and made me feel good! When Lib and I left the Reutters she looked at me and smiled, saying, "You see Paul, lots of people have confidence in you, why don't you? You never pat yourself on the back, you just work harder. You've continued your fathers' role, you are very hard on yourself. We will find a business!"

The first negotiation to come to a conclusion was with a fellow Rotarian, Paul Hammond. Paul was dying of cancer and needed to sell his company. The Paul Hammond Company manufactured ventilation equipment for the recreational vehicle industry. Although the company had shrunk in sales volume and was only a portion of the size it had been, I still thought it was a pretty good opportunity. The company had reduced volume, because the recreational vehicle industry was depressed. The depression was caused by the oil embargo in 1974. Oil prices shot up so fast gasoline at the retail pump had gone from $.30 per gallon to $.55 per gallon. No one knew when gas prices would stop rising so automobile sales were hurt and R.V. sales were virtually nonexistent.

Curt Armbruster wanted to run The Paul Hammond

Company. While we were negotiating I had called Curt to see if he would be interested in investing and running a company. He had worked for me at Spartan Oil while he was in college. He went on to graduate from Michigan State University and was with the Burroughs Corporation. I always thought a lot of Curt and knew he had great talent.

We closed the deal and changed the name from The Paul Hammond Company to Hammond Mfg. Corporation. Curt became General Manager and was given the right to purchase 20% of the stock. I was President.

The company had eight employees and operated out of a 3,000 square foot building in Lansing. Curt and I worked very hard over the next six months at the end of which time he exercised his right to buy 20% ownership and I promoted him to President.

A few months later I ended a second negotiation with the acquisition of The Valley Farms Lumber Company in Lansing. Gary Chappel became the President and 20% shareholder. Gary had been my General Manager at Spartan Oil. Four months later we bought The Little Rock Lumber Yard in Alma, Michigan, merged and changed the names of both Valley Farms Lumber and Little Rock Lumber to Valley Building Centers, Inc.

I had been gone from Spartan Oil just under two years and just now felt we had another start. Hammond was beginning to show progress under Curt's leadership. Of the two lumber yards, Valley Farms was the youngest at 35 years in business, both were seasoned businesses. I felt pretty good about where we were, because Gary was an experienced manager I had trained.

Curt had worked for Gary at Spartan Oil. During a joint meeting we decided it made sense to consider building a business that would be consolidated into a conglomerate. It was decided to form a holding company and call it Ammond Corporation and Subsidiaries. Both Hammond Mfg. Corporation and Valley Building were the first two subsidiaries. Both companies grew and we acquired others.

In 1976 Valley Building Centers, Inc. formed a joint venture with Bob Neller to build some single family houses. A company called Nelco Construction was formed, which Bob Neller, a local builder, would run.

It was during this period that my political interest began. Curt worked hard and showed progress at Hammond while I helped Gary develop a couple of ideas.

In late 1976 Valley acquired Crawford Door Company and Raynor Door Company. We merged the door companies and hired a General Manager. This expansion was a natural because as a building center Valley was supplying residential and commercial builders all kinds of building supplies, adding doors was a natural.

As I was closing the negotiations on the Crawford and Raynor Door Companies Gary's division started losing money. Gary and I had several meetings and Curt was brought in. We decided I should become actively involved with Valley Building Center. I was to run the company directing Gary's activities until we got the company turned around. Gary didn't like the idea. Three months later he came in telling me he had decided to leave. We learned he had started looking for something else the day I took over. Curt and I wished him well and bought his interest in the company.

I began a search for Gary's replacement and found Phil Branstetter who had been working for Wicke's Lumber out of state. He came in as General Manager of Valley Building Centers Corporation.

Most of my time was used in politics. However when I was with Curt or Valley Building Center I dealt primarily with policy. Phil and I both worked hard to turn Valley around.

It was 1978. Curt developed a couple of new products for Hammond to sell, the R.V. industry was moving forward again and we were content with Hammond's growth curve. Curt wasn't too eager to acquire for growth, he preferred a steady progression of increased sales through internally induced growth.

There was a retail paneling store for sale next door to Valley. We decided to buy it. It was ideal. We bought and moved the lumber yard one block up the street into bigger facilities thereby consolidating both businesses.

By now I was spending 80% of my time in politics, but managed to take Lib, Scott and Jeff to Hawaii for ten days. We had a great time because Hawaii in the wintertime is terrific. Winter in Michigan with snow becomes very long. The last day of our vacation we arrived at the airport early, well in advance of flight time. We were in a gift shop when Lib said, "Paul, we need to move toward the plane or we'll miss it." "Lib," I said "How much have you flown?" She answered, "Not very much". I told her not to worry. "I've flown thousands of miles." I knew how the airlines worked. We continued to shop for a little longer, then went to the gate. Just as we arrived the door on the plane was closing. I went to the desk and said, "We need to get on that plane". The attendant was polite but adamant. "Sir, I am sorry but the door is closed and though the plane hasn't disembarked the airline policy is not to reopen the door once it's closed."

Let me tell you, at that moment Hawaii seemed like a foreign country. I knew we could not swim back to the Continental United States. I was the small town boy, not the world traveler I made out to be. Fortunately, I regained my senses, found another plane which was leaving in two hours and we caught it. Needless to say the boys and Lib, on all future flights, controlled our going and coming.

The trip to Hawaii gave me a chance to catch up on my reading, but I developed some headaches and decided to get my eyes checked. When we got home I went to see an optometrist, a fellow Rotarian.

As it turned out I needed glasses. Once more my sense of wonderment was pricked. Everything became bigger and sharper. I had needed glasses for a long time and didn't know it. I thought, why do I keep getting these surprises. I felt stupid that I hadn't known I needed glasses.

Scott became twelve years old. Lib and I (mostly me), had been worried that if I didn't start to develop a personal relationship with the boys by the time they were twelve I might lose my chance. I had worked long hours since Scott and Jeff were born. I always admired the Jewish tradition of

BarMitzvah, recognizing the boyhood to manhood growth progression. I told Scott that although we weren't Jewish I wanted to do something to highlight his passing from 12 to 13 years old. I said, "Lets you and me take a trip together, just the two of us. It will be for one week and we'll go where you want to and do what you want to do."

He made his choice. "Dad, I want to go to Jimmy Ballard's Golf School in Pell City, Alabama, this summer." We went and stayed in a motel together, ate together, took lessons together. As a result we began a personal relationship which continues to this day.

1978 ended with a bang! Our corporate fiscal year end required a corporate audit. When we took an inventory at the lumber yard we found a substantial shortage, which meant a loss of money that year. The General Manager's responsibility was to control inventories, and he had not. We talked and decided he would have to leave the company. I replaced him by promoting a manager who reported to him.

I bought the Building Center company with Gary Chappell in mind and was unhappy I had to take it over. Now he was gone and his replacement was gone too! I decided to sell. I talked to Curt and he agreed so within 90 days I found a buyer and Valley Building Center was sold.

Two years later the national energy crisis threw the R.V. industry into another tail spin and Hammond started losing $10,000 per month. After two months I went to Curt and said, "What are your plans? We have to do something."

Curt replied, "Paul, the market's going to turn around and we'll be okay, don't worry."

I shook my head. "Curt, I don't think so. It's going to take a while to solve the National problem and to continue taking this red ink won't work."

Thirty days later I called in a management consultant. I knew from experience what he would tell Curt, but I needed someone else to convince Curt because he wouldn't listen to me. Curt felt I had let him run the company in good times and now I should let him run it in bad times as well.

The consultant told Curt the same thing I had, and it was clear we had to diversify to save the company. Curt still didn't want to make changes, and by this time we had taken six months of red ink. I called a meeting and announced, "Curt, effective today I'm taking over the direction of the company. I want you to head up sales, and I'll handle all other duties until we get the company turned around."

Curt was reluctant. "Paul, I won't do that." I did the thing I knew had to be done. I asked, "Curt, how much notice will you give me to replace you?" Three weeks later Curt was gone. I was angry at Curt and resented his being so hard headed!

I was under pressure. Losing money to me was like going broke and nothing terrified me more, nothing motivated me more. Within three months I found a product line in Florida, I negotiated the deal and moved it from Ft. Lauderdale to Lansing. The product line was aluminum rear window louvers for cars. This product took us into a new industry, the automotive "aftermarket". It gave us some relief until the R.V. industry turned around.

The owner came to Lansing, and brought with him his plant manager. I had put one more fire out, but it didn't stay out.

It didn't take long to find out why the product line had been sold. The people I brought with it didn't have the talent to run a business. I kept the plant manager but terminated the original owner. My confidence was shaken by his failure. I wondered if my ability to pick people had left me. I was scared, but I couldn't quit! I was getting ready to run for public office, so I began looking for someone to run Hammond again.

I found a young man at General Motors. He was a Quality Control expert and had 300 employees reporting to him. We had about 100 employees so I figured this job would be duck soup for him. I hired him, ran for public office, and lost the election. It's a good thing I lost because in the six month interim he allowed the company to get in trouble, and I had to put out another fire. He stayed on but I ran the company. We had one problem after the other for the next three years. I never intended to run the company, but I was feeling like a failure, because I couldn't stabilize it. I obsessed that I was going to go broke. Selling was being a quitter, but I felt like I had no choice. It took me nine months to find a buyer and conclude the sale.

During those three years Hammond was very hard on me. Now, for the first time since college, I had nothing to do!

While traveling for Hammond I was exposed to Auto Care Centers and Automotive Service, a rapidly growing industry. Due to the 1974 oil embargo over 150,000 service stations had closed nationally and over 10,880 automobile dealerships closed. Automotive service became limited and where there is a need, a smart entrepreneur finds a way to fill it.

Chains of stores providing 10 minute oil changes came into being, chains of muffler shops, and chains of transmission shops started to develop. These companies were leasing space in Auto Care Centers which are strip shopping centers for automobile service. I researched the idea and decided if it proved out I would get into the real estate development business developing Auto Care Centers. By June of the next year my research was done and I started construction of my first Auto Care Center.

The decision to build Auto Care Centers was in part to defeat a personal defect. The defect was that every business I went into was great while I was getting into it, even building the business was fun and challenging but each time, at some point, I became obsessed about failure. Fear and paranoia set in. Suddenly the goal of building a big company became impossible and selling the business became a crusade. Each time I thought I might not get out without going broke. I tried, through psychiatry, to cure my problem. The problem was fear!

The real estate development business never really excited me, but it fit all the criteria I had established to defeat the fear and paranoia that had set into all my other ventures. It was the business that would help me defeat my defect.

When I sold Hammond I sold all its assets but the real estate. I kept the real estate and listed it for sale with a local realtor. There were three buildings in Lansing. After six months instead of selling I decided to rent out the real estate. This got a real estate development business started that was composed of leasing what I had and developing Auto Care Centers.

The first Auto Care Center was located in the Lansing area. Being a new concept meant it was a radical idea to the Lansing area. In Lansing radical ideas are never popular. It is a conservative, staid community.

A challenge came with selling a township planning commission, zoning board, and board of trustees that the township needed an Auto Care Center and that it was needed where I wanted it to go. The challenge continued with selling lending institutions that an Auto Care Center was a good idea and one that would be safe for them to lend on.

As the first Auto Care Center was near completion it was 100% pre-leased and it became apparent the concept was right so I decided to start two more in Lansing. This meant a bigger enterprise and I needed more help. I hired a secretary and an administrative assistant but I had to deal with leasing the manufacturing properties, leasing the Auto Care Center, and lending, as well as construction. I still needed more people.

A nephew in Oklahoma and his partner, were in financial trouble. They were doing real estate development when the oil economy took Oklahoma into a severe depression.

My nephew and his partner went out of business and were available. I had watched their activities and was impressed with what they had done. I felt if I could convince them to come to Michigan and if they would listen to me we could do some great things.

The partner came to Michigan and six months later my nephew followed. We completed the first Auto Care Center and started two more.

The next six months were hell. I had attracted two high flyers. We were going to build Auto Care Centers all over the world when, as it turned out, they did not have the basic skills the company needed them to have. I couldn't control them. I learned they had gone out of business, not because of the economy, but because they made some fundamentally bad business decisions. They were young and had not prepared themselves to be successful. Their aggressiveness and energy only served to get them into trouble. They did not want to listen or follow my direction. I finally decided to end the relationship. Because my nephew was involved it was a difficult decision to make and even more difficult to carry out.

I was a basket case! I had been dealing with real estate development for two years and it wasn't turning out to be the business to defeat my so called personal defect. Once again I became paranoid that I was going broke.

I had now completed and leased three Auto Care Centers in Lansing and started one in Jackson. These were the first Auto Care Centers in Michigan, Ohio or Indiana. It never occurred to me to pat myself on the back for spotting another trend and implementing it before others did. My centers were going well too!

All I ever saw was the down side, I never saw the good! My Father had taught me well. He never found anything good about what I did as I grew up! He always found a flaw or a fault. I now found myself finding flaws or faults, as well.

So it was on that November 12, 1987, I sat in a car with Mike Smith, outside my office, blurting out my state of despair. Soon I began reading materials that might give me some insight to my state of mind, and how to change it.

By March I wasn't feeling materially better so I went to a Psychologist. Maybe she would produce some answers. Maybe a new advisor or support system would help. The psychiatrist I had seen had died.

Barbara Andersen, a psychologist, was just starting to earn a reputation working with businessmen in Lansing. She was accepted to membership in the Lansing Rotary Club and although I had long since resigned, I respected the fact that she qualified to be a member.

We met once each week for an hour and within a month Barbara asked why I was so angry and why I needed anger. She asked me how I ever planned to retire along with a lot of other questions. She also began to try to get me to slow down. I was always in the fast lane doing 120 miles per hour.

Little did I know that it's hard to be in touch with anything, much less yourself, when you're moving fast all the time.

On June 1st I decided to start taking Wednesday afternoons plus Saturday and Sunday off for the summer months. Until that time I had worked 12 to 18 hour days plus Saturday and sometimes Sunday. When I didn't work on Sunday I was always thinking about it, plotting and strategizing.

Barbara Andersen recommended a trip and in September Lib and I decided to take a three week car trip out west. Jeff was going to college so Lib's schedule was free. I scheduled myself to leave Lansing for three weeks.

As we left Lansing we headed north through the Upper Peninsula of Michigan, then across Minnesota to North Dakota. This took us two days and during that time I wondered if I had completed the necessary details in order to leave. Reviewing in my mind all that I had done caused me to think about what had been left undone! After awhile mile after mile seemed to drone on. My mind, as we drove, continued to repeat the same thoughts over and over, obsessive thoughts about what I left undone in Lansing.

We left North Dakota heading to South Dakota, then due west again, through the Bad Lands into Wyoming, visiting Custer Park. We proceeded on north into Montana and back into the Wyoming portion of Yellowstone National Park.

Our second week on the road began as we arrived in Yellowstone. As we entered it seemed as if the entire park was burning. Forest fires, sparked by lightening, were causing debate in the national congress about how the fire should be handled. A portion of the park had been closed to tourists.

The second week I mentally shifted gears from thinking about what I left undone to what I would do when I went back. It was clear to me if I was unable to work, I might not be punished as harshly, if I thought about work maybe that would be considered working. I always felt guilty when I wasn't working.

We exited the park into Idaho, back through Wyoming,

Colorado and into Oklahoma. As we arrived to visit my Mother in Oklahoma our second week on the road ended.

The sites along the trip that first two weeks were wondrous to behold. Nature in all its glory was able to penetrate my obsessing. The third week I finally let go! Thoughts began to flow through my mind about events dating back to my childhood, things I hadn't thought about since I was fourteen years old. Until then my most vivid memories were of pain. Finally I remembered some happy moments! The wonder of nature, from the mountains of Colorado, through the Bad Lands and Yellowstone Park, nature had begun to free me. I allowed myself, I gave myself permission, to experience it all!

We left Mother's house, going through Missouri, Illinois, and Indiana in route back to Michigan. The three week trip came to an end as we drove into Lansing.

When we returned to Lansing I realized the value of both the work schedule cut back and the trip Barbara Andersen recommended. It was then that I began to make some slow progress toward recovery.

My road to recovery was composed of voracious reading and seeing Barbara Andersen once each week. That went on for most of the following year.

In the spring of 1990 I read about a course on self discovery offered at Michigan State University. More specifically, it was titled as a course on how to write an autobiography. When I looked further it was represented to be a way of going back in time and memory to view your life. Writing an autobiography was represented as being very therapeutic and would put life into perspective.

I decided to take the course and was fascinated with what I learned. The result, six weeks later, caused me to put my business affairs in order, I wanted to close my office and get completely on the sideline to give full attention to writing an autobiography.

I closed my office on October 1st, 1990 after selling some of my real estate holdings. What I didn't sell was turned over to a management company. I was free to start the book, and my hope was that in researching and writing the book I would find peace. I could then determine what I would do for the next step of my professional life.

Closing my office brought the same feelings I had each time I sold a business and began looking at new possibilities. The in-between time brought more feelings of uncertainty, anxiety and fear. This time I hoped to find solutions. But would I?

CHAPTER SIX

THE CITIZTICIAN

At the same time I was an entrepreneur I became involved as a citiztician. Citiztician was a word I coined when I went into politics.

It was important to me not to be called a politician because of its negative connotation. What I was doing was more than an ordinary citizen would do, so I came up with a hybrid word, Citiztician. A cross between politician and citizen.

I defined the word as "An individual who is taking a responsibility to have an impact on government. He gets involved, not because he wants to, but because he has learned the value of disciplining himself to do many things he does not want to do in life."

For the next two years Citiztician was our rallying cry. Large numbers of people who had never been involved before got involved in the political process.

I sold my interest in Spartan Oil Corporation and for several months looked for business opportunities. Several prospective corporate acquisition candidates had been identified and I was in the negotiating process. While waiting for the pot to boil during the negotiations I had some spare time.

During the waiting I wondered if there wasn't someway I could make a contribution to society. It seemed to be a good time to look at some kind of civic involvement. Some kind of activity that would be selfless. An activity to which I could give some time and energy, without thought of recompense.

All through my corporate years I had carried a quote by an unknown author in my wallet.

"I shall pass through this world but once.
Any good therefore that I can do,
Or any kindness that I can show to any human being,
Let me do it now,
Let me not defer or neglect it
for I shall not pass this way again."

I carried the quote to remind me always to practice its spirit. but was never sure I was living up to it to the extent I could, or should.

The corporate activity I created generated jobs and taxes. The corporation therefore made a contribution to society and I felt that was a high calling. However, I was never sure it was selfless. I always felt people who had achieved economic success owed some duty to the community as a whole. That commitment could be to the town, city, state or nation. I was thinking more about the City of Lansing. That's why I agreed earlier to serve on the Board of the Lansing Chamber of Commerce. However I didn't find the Board of the Chamber of Commerce fulfilling. I felt that it was a do-nothing board and was composed mostly of people looking for community positions to salve their ego. I served the last year of someone's term and when time came to fill a full term I declined.

I searched for a way to fill a role where I could be of some value. The opportunity came when Charles Chamberlain, a Republican U.S. Congressman, decided to retire. Chuck had served eighteen years.

I knew Congressman Chamberlain. Every year he chartered a plane to Washington, D.C. and businessmen from the district purchased tickets, paying prices in excess of normal air travel. The congressman called our annual trip "a businessman's day in Washington." I had been on five or six of these trips. The schedule always included briefings from key cabinet officials, as well as senators and congressmen. Most briefings were in the White House.

Two candidates on the Republican side surfaced to challenge in a primary for the right to run against Bob Carr, the Democrat candidate. Bill Ballenger, a successful, incumbent state senator and Clifford Taylor, a young attorney, were the challengers on the Republican side. The Lansing establishment had lined up behind Senator Ballenger.

I was invited to a meeting by Jim Anderton. Jim's father, along with Harry Guyselman, both leaders of the local establishment, had been Congressman Chamberlain backers for all the years he was in Congress. They made things happen!

Jim called a meeting at the Old's Plaza Hotel to decide how they would make Bill Ballenger the next congressman. There were several local businessmen present. Most were either second or third generation businessmen. Jim went around the room and said we need each of you to raise or give $5,000 to Ballenger's campaign. "Paul" he asked, "Will you raise or give $1,500?"

Apparently I wasn't considered on par with the others. I said, "Sure Jim, if I decide to support Senator Ballenger. To help me with the decision would it be possible for me to get a copy of his voting record?"

Jim was taken back, no one else had asked any questions. Suddenly I felt uncomfortable, but Jim finally responded by saying, "Sure Paul, I'll get that information to you."

The same evening of the meeting I was watching the 6 o'clock news and saw Cliff Taylor being interviewed. He was bright, articulate and good looking. I said, "Lib, I think I'll call him and see if he'll meet me to explain where he stands on the issues." I immediately got his telephone number and called. I introduced myself and said, "Cliff, I'm a businessman here in Lansing. I'm going to get involved in the 6th District Congressional race on some basis. Would you meet with me and tell me why I should support you?" There was a pause. Then Cliff said, "Paul, this the most exciting thing I have had happen in our campaign. Can you meet tomorrow?" I said yes, and we set a time. We met at the City Club, located in the Olds Plaza. Cliff brought Spencer Abraham, his Campaign Manager. Spence was a Senior at Michigan State University.

At the meeting I said, "Fellas, I've been invited to work for Bill Ballenger, but before I made a decision I wanted to meet with you. I've never been involved in politics before, but want to work for a candidate I can believe in and who has a chance to win! I don't want to waste my time fighting windmills."

Cliff and Spence responded in an articulate, informed and convincing way. It appeared to me they were highly talented and gifted. I liked them both and although I didn't know if they had a chance I decided I wanted another meeting to help make a determination.

Two days later we met. Both Cliff and Spence went over their campaign outline with me. I had heard enough. I was so impressed I said "Fellas, if I support you what would you like for me to do?"

They said money is the mother's milk of a politician and it was their critical need! Will you raise money, because we can do the rest? Though I still did not have Ballenger's voting record, I decided to support Cliff.

I called Anderton and said, "Jim, thanks for thinking of me in the group you put together but I've decided to support Cliff Taylor." Jim said "That's okay Paul" and hung up. He wasn't worried. All the money and the polls showed Ballenger would win.

Being a novice, I had no idea where to start raising money for Cliff's campaign! At first I was lost, but as I went to work I got more focused, although I did begin to wonder what I had gotten into.

The idea came to call every Rotarian and Walnut Hills Country Club member and every Lansing Country Club member and City Club member. I introduced myself to those who didn't know me, and asked if he or she had decided who to support for the up coming congressional race. Because it was so early most said no! I then asked, "Would you like to come to a meeting to hear a candidate to help you make up their mind who to support?"

Almost everyone I called said yes, but finding a time for the meetings turned out to be a problem. It seemed that busy people all have meetings that run into the evening on week days. They hold their week-ends open for family. We tried a couple of evenings and not many people showed up. That was a disappointment to Cliff, Spence and myself.

Within a couple of weeks I discovered breakfast was the one time people couldn't tell me they had another engagement so I went back and recalled those I had spoken to before and started calling everyone else. I told each one, "We're having a breakfast meeting, Cliff Taylor will be there and speak. Come and hear him, no obligation, all it will cost you if you don't support him is your breakfast. What morning can you come?" If someone said Monday, I said okay, if someone said Tuesday, I said okay. The first thing I knew I had some people for every morning during the week. The breakfast meetings went over great. A lot of people showed up! Cliff's talks were compelling and each time I closed the meetings saying, "If you like what you've heard and you want this man as your congressman we need your support— give us one, two, or three hundred dollars today!"

From March until the August primary voting date we raised the money Cliff and Spence needed to fund the campaign. Bill Ballenger was defeated and Cliff won the right to run against Bob Carr in the General Election.

I had told Cliff and Spence I was available only during the primary. Ten days after the primary Cliff called and asked to see me. When we met he said, "Paul, we're in trouble. We need someone to raise money for us. The establishment won't come on board. They have no interest in helping us defeat Bob Carr. Will you please come back and help?"

I told him I'd have to get back to him. I still hadn't gotten a business started, and Lib and I had just bought a new house. I said, "Let me think about it."

I talked it over with Lib, called Cliff the next day and told him I would help. As it worked out I was just consummating the purchase of the Paul Hammond Company and Curt Armburster was going to run it.

The August primary win gave us some momentum.

There hadn't been a campaign like the one Cliff ran for years. We raised record amounts of money and had knocked off a very popular state senator no one thought could be beaten.

I went back to work raising money to fuel the general election. In addition my job was to help Cliff bring leaders of the establishment into the campaign.

The general election came one week too soon. We lost by four hundred votes. We felt if we had only one more week we would have won. Everyone was devastated.

One week after the congressional campaign ended Cliff and Spence came to me saying, "Paul we want to manage a campaign to get you elected as Chairman of the Ingham County Republican Party. We'd like you to rebuild the party, strengthen it so Cliff can run against Bob Carr again two years from now. I was flattered, but stunned! Also interested!

I thought as County Chairman I could impact the politics of one congressional seat, three state representative seats, one state senate seat, twenty-one county commissioner seats and five county elected officials seats. I thought I could make a real difference. I decided I could give my civic contribution all at once, then go back and devote full time to the business. I talked to Lib about it and she agreed.

I told Cliff and Spence to throw my hat in the ring. By January I was County Chairman! Spence went on to Harvard Law School. Cliff went back to his legal practice.

My life was going pretty well when my parents told us they were coming to see us. It was the second time in ten years. I was glad to hear they were coming and anxious to show them what I was accomplishing financially and politically. It was going to be good to see them.

The very first night Mom and Dad arrived I filled them in about all I was involved in. I also told them some exciting news I received that day. As I finished Dad blurted in an angry, loud voice, "Paul, I'll always be prouder of Dale than I will be of you. If you believed like Dale then I could have some respect for you! He visits old people in nursing homes on Sundays while all you do is make money." My jaw dropped. That was the last thing I ever expected. I felt as if a fist had slammed me in the stomach!

Dale was my older brother and as we were growing up Dad had always pitted us against each other and he was still doing it.

The rest of Mom and Dad's stay was not very pleasant. I decided to work long hours to avoid being with them. Lib was furious with Dad. But neither of us said anything about Dad's outburst nor did we show our hurt.

I learned politics was a tough business. Jim Anderton barely spoke to me and old line Republican establishment leaders were miffed at me because Taylor had beaten Ballenger. They reluctantly came on board, very slowly, to help rebuild the party. It was clear to me I had a big job to do and needed something to get everyones attention. I had to come up with an idea or way of getting everyone to come together. An idea to give us a common dream or goal to work for.

My major corporation experience had taught me more about politics than I realized.

I put committees together to study ways to rebuild the party and selected some of the people whose noses had been bloodied to chair these committees. We started the machinery to breath life back into the party.

We needed a permanent office but lacked the money to open it. I approached a friend who owned The Lansing Office Equipment Company and he donated office furniture and equipment to outfit new offices. I hired James Digby as a full time Executive Director for the party. Those two moves brought party volunteers back into the fold. These were all good moves but still weren't the big idea I was looking for. It was March and precious time was passing.

I was to deliver a speech to a large group of people on campus at Michigan State University. Speeches were hard for me and this was my first big one. I had, over the years, given prayers at Rotary Club but had never spoken publicly. I laboriously prepared my speech. I rehearsed and rehearsed. When the appointed time came I wanted to flee from the scene. I went so far as to ask Jim Olson, a fellow Rotarian friend of mine, to take my place. He said, "Paul, you don't need me to take over for you. You'll do fine. Just envision you're talking to me, and only me. When you begin don't think there is anyone else in the room."

Jim Olson empowered me. The speech went okay and each passing speech became easier and better. However, I never fully got over stage fright.

If you want to get attention in politics, money always does it. I finally conceived my big idea. I developed a major fund raiser idea. The featured star attraction was to be ex-Secretary of the Treasury, John Connally. He had been Governor of Texas while I lived in Oklahoma. He was a Democrat as Governor of Texas, but later converted to the Republican Party and I had been a member of the Young Democrats at Oklahoma State University and now was a Republican party official. We had some things in common, maybe that's why I liked him.

However there were some serious problems. The first—could I get John Connally to Michigan? I located the phone number of Governor Connally's law office in Houston, Texas. I called and told his secretary what I wanted. She said she'd talk to Governor Connally and get back to me. The next week she called and said the Governor would like to come if the dates could be worked out. I said, "You tell him to pick the date". He picked November 11, 1975!

You talk about ecstatic—happy—jubilant! John Connally was coming to my fund raiser! Now I had to convince eleven other County Chairmen to buy into the plan. I wanted the eleven additional counties involved to make the event a big one. To my great amazement they did. It was March and we had five months to make the event the biggest of its kind!

Lib and I invited Republican leaders from all over the state, about 100 people, to our home for a cocktail party preceding the dinner.

I arranged to pick Governor Connally up at the airport in a limousine. The Ingham County Sheriff supplied two off duty detectives to escort the limo. John Connally came to Lansing alone. When we met him at the airport, he asked to go directly to the hotel. He said he needed to make a couple of phone calls. I accompanied the Governor to the Presidential Suite at the Hilton Hotel. Within ten minutes he called people both in South America and Argentina. I was really impressed.

We left the hotel within an hour and headed for my house, where the Republican leaders from around the state were waiting, including the Lt. Governor and State Party Chairman. The Governor of Michigan had been invited but sent his regrets.

Lib was very nervous. She had never entertained that many people at one time and certainly had not entertained any big name dignitaries before.

After the party we went to Longs Convention Center for the dinner. Over 1,000 people showed up. As Master of Ceremonies I introduced Governor Connally. During my introduction I had the chance to share a belief I held high. It was written by an anonymous author and it goes like this:

"One Man Can Move The World?"

It is true one man acting alone can do little—
But one man interacting creatively with others,
Can move the world.
He affects others, who in turn effects others.
You and I can make the hope for a better tomorrow a
    reality!

Local media gave the dinner broad and expansive coverage and telegrams of congratulations poured in. We raised over $150,000 at one event. That was never done at an event of this type before.

I was pleased. All I had hoped to accomplish had come together. We raised the money we targeted, gained the recognition we needed, and the local party leaders came on board.

To further involve the business community I spoke at every service club in the city. Each time I gave examples from my past which underlined my understanding of their problems.

Unexpected side benefits began to develop. I started getting invitations to attend meetings at the Governor's residence. I also received an invitation to introduce the Governor at a State Convention in Grand Rapids.

Over 1,800 delegates attended the State Convention, and my introduction lasted three minutes. I prepared as if it was a State of the Nation speech. I gave the introduction and worried about how well it had gone. What came next was a great surprise! As I sat down, the Governor came to the microphone and stood there for what seemed like fifteen minutes as the ovation to greet him rocked the hall. When the crowd of 1,800 delegates quieted the Governor bellowed into the microphone, "PAUL STEARNS, remember that name. He has a great future in Michigan politics." I had been anointed!

Looking back, the high public praise I received from the Governor was like a heroin fix must be for a drug addict. I was given praise and adopted in a way I never before had experienced!

As my experience broadened I learned two things. Once a governor embraces you, it is like wearing a brand. "Paul is my boy." In many ways it was beneficial, but it didn't help me with those opposed to the Governor. The second thing was the Governor was attempting to get me on his side to help him in his future effort.

The John Connally Fund Raiser gave me respect in my home county and a name across the state. I was on a roll! The State Party Chairman started inviting me to meetings he called for party leaders. The Republican Leader in the State House of Representatives invited me to meetings. Some local establishment leaders, who had been foes in the congressional race, began dealing with me again, welcome to Michigan Politics Paul! I had a fleeting thought—for a guy that was going to give some time and move on, I was in pretty deep!

The National Republican Convention was held in August of 1976 in Kansas City. I was elected to be a delegate to it.

During the same period President Ford scheduled a campaign train to come through Lansing. Betty Ford, in a separate trip, was coming to Lansing on a campaign trip too! Because of my profile and reputation I was asked to help plan the activities of both the President and First Lady's trips. In this interim I experienced activities that people who work a life time in politics don't. A benefit for me was to see the President and his wife and find they are people just like the rest of us. It helped me to see the inadequate feelings I had were not real.

If you've ever felt inadequate, intimidated or as if you were where you didn't belong, then you know how I felt for the two years I was County Chairman. My need to win approval pushed me to deal with people of rank, title, position and/or status and left my head swimming. True I acted as if I belonged, but all the while I felt out of place, not good enough.

The National Republican Convention was fun, particularly when at one key point of the convention the C.B.S. television camera crew focused on me with a close up. My face was shown all over the United States. It happened the first day of the convention and was used as a film bite three more times during the convention. When we got back to Michigan it was fun to get phone calls from friends all over the U.S. telling me they had seen me on T.V. In Lansing we had fun because the local people kidded me about being a celebrity.

It was interesting to feel the acceptance that people demonstrated toward me. They were drawn to me but I was guarded toward them!

My term as County Chairman lasted two years and ended with my decision not to run again. Our success at the polls was not good. It was a Democrat year. Ford was defeated, in part for giving Richard Nixon a pardon. We did not win the races we targeted. I was devastated.

Our Governor wrote me a letter that helped to salve my wounds! He said he knew we had run a text book two years, set records in all categories by which you could measure political success. I appreciated the letter but I didn't feel much better.

Spence Abraham was back from Harvard to run Cliff Taylor's second congressional race and they lost again. In 1977 I was out of politics for what I thought was for good. I had looked at the prospect of running for State Party Chairmanship but couldn't get the Governor to make a decision to support me at the convention. He was staying neutral, so his liaison people said, but it was common knowledge he already had a candidate in mind. I decided not to run. It is rare that a Governor of a state can't have the chairman he wants and our Governor did not seem to want me!

Lib and I bought a cottage on Coldwater Lake, near Coldwater, an hour and fifteen minutes south of Lansing. Most people in Michigan go North to purchase cottages. We went south! At the same time we bought a 19' Century TRV 200 speed and ski boat.

We also joined the Coldwater Country Club. Scott liked to play golf and I liked playing with him, so once in a while we played at the Coldwater Club.

Within three weeks the Governor asked me to come to his office. He wanted to talk about, and get my advice on, a small business council he wanted to form.

The small business community had become a thorn in the Governor's side due to a tax consolidation the Governor had gotten the legislature to pass. The small business community thought the law was harmful to its interests and was giving the Governor a rough time.

I was briefed before I got to his office by his Administrative Assistant so I developed some recommendations on how the council could be formed. I told the Governor it should consist of fifteen different geographic regions with a chairperson for each region. Each regional chairperson should select a minimum of fifteen other businessmen from his area who would meet monthly to discuss current public policy issues, deliberate and give the Governor advice regarding public policy. The regional chairpersons would then come together and meet with the Governor once a month to pass along their group thoughts and recommendations.

When I finished presenting my recommendations the Governor said, "Paul, that's good and that's what I want to do. I want you to Chair the group and put it together."

I was surprised and flattered! "Governor, I'll help put it together but I'll have to think about being the Chair. That's a big job and unless I can give it full attention I won't do it. Let me get back to you next week."

I talked to Lib and my business associates and decided that maybe I should take the time to do what the Governor wanted. I knew I had said I was going back to business but duty called once again. The next week I made an appointment with the Governor.

The Governor was happy to see me. I got right to the subject. "Governor, I'll chair the Small Business Council and put it together on one condition." He nodded and I continued, telling him I did not want the council to become a political tool or football. I said, "I can't be successful unless I can tell my suspicious business friends the group will be a legitimate policy advisory council." The Governor agreed to my conditions.

Running the Council became a full time job. It took three months to get fifteen qualified chairmen and 325 council members to agree to serve! The whole group came to Lansing and met with the Governor. He told them what he wanted and expected to accomplish over the next year. The following month the fifteen chairpeople came back to Lansing and met with the Governor again in his office, however after six months it became apparent to the group that we were being used as a political football. The Governor promised it wouldn't happen, but it did. I felt betrayed and resigned in protest. Within two months the Small Business Council was disbanded. The 1976 election defeat and disappointment, and now the 1977 disappointment with the Small Business Council were too much. I wasn't on a roll any longer.

At this point I believed I had neutered myself and if I wanted a political future my path was blocked! I had lost an election and a governor was unhappy that I resigned from his service.

March 9, 1977 I got up and went to the front porch to get the morning newspaper. I saw a light flashing and went outside to see what it was. A big flashing reader board sign read—"Paul Stearns claims to be an Okie—But is now 40 and Pokey." Welcome to mid-life Paul!

Bob Hughes, a good friend, had gotten together a group of people, rented the sign, hired a truck to deliver it to my front yard at 5 A.M. Later that day they gave me a big party. To have friends do special things helps your spirits! This really was a spirit boost!

In 1978 Scott was playing Little League Basketball and Jeff was in Indian Guides with me. Their lives were going well. Lib had been, to this point, a key player with me in politics, but she never forgot being a mother and wife came first. We took a family vacation to Acapulco, Mexico that winter and went to our cottage every week-end during the summer.

I helped raise some money for some political candidates and became a board member of the Capital Area Political Committee. I continued to be politically active through 1979 but decided to sit out the 1980 elections. I was tired and unsure of what future role, if any, I wanted to play in politics.

My profile in the Lansing area was such that I was asked to be a board member or leader in several organizations. Although I was flattered I refused. I had my reasons. One, I felt I was expected to be a member, but not a meaningful participant and anytime I gave my time, I committed myself or didn't participate. The second reason was my sense of inadequacy. I'm sure at that time few people believed the second reason. My aggressiveness was not read by some as insecurity but as a big ego at work!

I did accept one board seat as a member of my church Council of Elders. Peoples Church is an Interdenominational Church affiliated with four denominations, the United Church of Christ, Methodist, Baptist and Presbyterian. Our senior minister retired after serving the church for eighteen years and we had gone through several ministers without success. Replacing a long time senior minister is always a problem, and our church was no exception. They asked me to organize and chair a search committee to find and bring a new senior minister to the church.

My attention was diverted when my Father died after a long illness resulting from a stroke the previous year. I went to Oklahoma for the funeral. Although I felt the natural feelings of love for my Father I hated what he had done to me. Going to the funeral did nothing to abate that feeling.

After interviewing candidates for seven months we made a final offer to Richard Devor, the Senior Methodist Minister at Central Methodist Church in downtown Detroit. Dick was a great pulpit preacher, and politically liberal. He had been one of the early marchers with Martin-Luther King in Alabama. He accepted our offer.

I thought of re-entering politics. I had been on the "sidelines" for a year and a half. I was still frustrated with what I considered my failure in party politics and tired of being called by everyone to raise money. I felt I was thought of as merely a fund raiser. I asked Dick Devor's advice about considering the State Party Chairman office. What I asked was if he thought a Christian could be called to politics. He said yes, he felt there was no higher calling than politics.

I felt, in my heart, I could make a contribution to our system of government, that's why I had gotten involved. After my experience I began to wonder if I was in politics for the wrong reason. Was I involved for ego gratification only? My personality seemed to invite that allegation. That's why I had gone to Dick for an independent view. I wanted someone whom I respected and trusted to advise me.

When my soul searching and conversations with Dick came to an end my thoughts about getting involved in politics were different. I made up my mind and decided to become a candidate for public office. It was time to start thinking about the election coming up in 1982.

I hadn't had too much success helping people getting elected, but when successful, inevitably I became disappointed. I found most ran for office saying one thing and, after they were elected, did another.

After talking with Lib and my business associates I decided I would run for State Representative. The election was twelve months away and if I began in January, 1982 I had ten months to mount an effective campaign.

Geographically the 59th House Seat covered Michigan State University and the East Lansing area. It was considered a liberal seat. My opponent, Lynn Jondahl, was a twelve year Democratic incumbent. Before entering politics he had been a professional minister. I was a business man with no name recognition. The combination of republican ideology and lack of recognition were big hurdles to overcome in the 59th district.

I was well rested in January of 1982 as I started the campaign. My business affairs were run by others and the Search Committee assignment had concluded. I was able to devote full time to campaigning. Our race started slow but with each passing month the momentum built. The "Citiztician" was on the move again! None of the political experts thought I had a chance to win but, like all candidates, I didn't see how I could lose. That feeling must be a virus you catch!

The support I got was breath taking. We worked from sun up to midnight going door to door, giving speeches to any group or anyone who would listen. My Campaign Manager, Denise Haugen and her staff ran a picture perfect campaign. Three weeks before the election we were ahead of Jondahl by thirteen points in the polls. We all felt euphoric. We thought "we're going to win," but what about events you can't control? The same day the poll came out our Republican Gubernatorial candidate was quoted as saying women needed to know their place. Having babies and staying in the kitchen were their jobs. He was a Mormon. Well in the eighties, even if you're Mormon and feel that way, it was suicidal in politics to say it. Women all over the state, both Republican and Democrat were angry with all Republicans now. An event I couldn't control made them mad and it became clear it hurt our campaign.

Election night was long. When the polls closed the results started to come in and with each tally it showed the race close. We were slightly ahead until 4 A.M. in the morning when the tide turned and Jondahl was ahead by about

800 votes. It was clear with a 450 vote swing we would have won. Instead we lost! The next day we considered a recount, but after discussing it I decided to call Lynn and congratulate his win. No one knows what it feels like to lose an election unless it's happened to them, a deep sense of pain and anguish set in.

The next few weeks brought letters, phone calls and telegrams congratulating us on the campaign, even though I lost! Everyone wanted to know our plans to start the next campaign!

Our Republican State Convention was coming up and I was approached to run for State Chairman of the Party again. This would make three times I had considered running. I really wanted to run for State Chairman. I felt I had the executive and managerial skills needed, but the timing and support never met my expectations. Maybe you just run anyway and see what develops. It was a good thought but I was too practical to do that.

I didn't run because I had just lost an election. I didn't want to be rejected again! It hurt too much.

Spence Abraham graduated from Harvard Law School, came back to the state and taught at Cooley Law School. Spence came to me and said, "Paul, I understand you are thinking again about running for State Chairman." When I told him I was, he said, "I would like for you to consider stepping aside and supporting me. I would appreciate your support!"

I was peeved at his audacity. Why wasn't he coming to me saying I support you in your thoughts about running Paul. I didn't voice my feelings. What I said was, "Spence, let me think it over and I'll get back to you."

At a second meeting I asked, "Spence, if you want me to consider your request, you need to tell me in more specific terms why I should support you." I finally stepped aside and Spence was elected. He did a great job and later went on to an important job at the White House. I never regretted supporting him.

It took until January to close my campaign headquarters. When the final day arrived Jeff reminded me we had not taken our trip together. Over the years I had been too busy to take him on his twelfth birthday and still too busy on his thirteenth. Now at fourteen he insisted we go! I knew he was right. Had I fallen into the same pattern of ignoring my son as my Father had me? Was I only available when discipline was needed? Guilt washed over me and I said, "Okay Jeff, where do you want to go?" I figured it would be like my golf trip with Scott. I was wrong.

Jeff said, "Dad, I want to go to a martial arts school to study Ninjitsu." Before I could respond he said, "It's oriental martial arts, Ninjitsu is a form of it that was practiced by the Japanese in the 1400's and 1500's." Can you imagine my thirteen year old telling me that?

"Steven Hayes, the only American who ever became a master teacher of Ninjitsu, is teaching the course on the campus of the University of California, Irvine Campus and I want us to go!" I was dumbfounded! Suddenly the trips with the boys didn't seem like a good idea! I was neither physically nor mentally ready for what lay ahead, but I would do anything for my son—right?!

Jeff and I arrived at the Los Angeles airport on a Sunday, rented a car and drove to the campus. We checked into a dormitory with bedrooms that had bunk beds. I took the top bunk which gave no more than 24 inches between the bed and the ceiling. Remember, in California it gets hot and heat rises. Our room had no air conditioning. I climbed a ladder to get into bed.

After we inspected and moved into our living quarters we went to eat. When we returned to the dorm, one of our roommates had arrived. He introduced himself and said he had been told the other fellow wouldn't be coming.

As soon as Jeff and I were alone I said, "Jeff, do you know our roommate is homosexual?" He said, "Sure Dad, what's wrong with that?" I was pleased with his response, the result of Lib handling most of the basic education for the boys. He wasn't being judgemental about a different life style, and that fit what his mother taught him. I didn't either, but having been, at one time, a red neck from Oklahoma, I wasn't too sure!

Ninjitsu's mysteries began to unravel during our training. As I look back, my quest was enhanced by my experience on this trip with Jeff. I learned a lot about being one with all and all with one. The martial arts are about self-defense, but cover a much broader spectrum including self-awareness, the awareness of nature, and how we humans should flow with nature.

Jeff and I had a great week together, developing some memories that to this day are wonderful to talk about.

I was also busy with some statewide political issues. I had told everyone I expected to run again two years later and expected to win the second time.

In January I devoted full time to business for the first time in eight years. It was a good time to do it because my business was in trouble! Too much attention to politics and not enough to my business. At the same time I found that my negative feelings resulting from losing the election, were continuing and wouldn't go away, I also had moods of being depressed. The public had rejected me. I had failed again! Dad was right. I couldn't finish anything I started.

It seemed that the reservoir of confidence and success that I had at Spartan Oil Corporation was all used up. I was now feeling the way I did when I was rejected by my father and Peggy!

WORK

Paul W. Stearns

Work must accomplish something
Something for the minds eye
The minds eye depends on conditioning
To some work is produced by mental labor
To some work is produced by physical labor
To some physical labor is demeaning
I came from one and became the other
Work can come from the inner or the outer
    Work   Work
Work must accomplish something
Work requires exertion of strength or faculties
To some work is not work—my work was my play
My work kept me regenerated
My work was not work, it came from the inner
It brought me attention, praise and validation
I worked for play
     Work   Work   Work
Work must accomplish something
Some like attention, praise and validation
They bring feelings of control
What if what you accomplish is addictive
Work becomes work when you don't want to do it
When you're addicted you have to do it
Work becomes work when it comes from the outer
Work brings burn out and pain when you don't want to do
    it
I feel empty now, I feel out of control now
Work can lead to de-generation
I worked for attention, praise and validation
    I worked for pay

PART II

THE INWARD JOURNEY

CHAPTER SEVEN

THE QUEST AND THE PARADIGM SHIFT

THE QUEST
Paul W. Stearns

To some life is but a Quest,
What is it to all the rest?
Who calls us to the Quest,
This journey we make?
To where we go we do not know
To some Don Quixote is an archetype
To some life is a Chinese finger puzzle.
To some a pedestrian journey will suffice.
I began with an inquiry, I was merely seeking
It became an investigation
In hot pursuit, it became a search
A search for self-knowledge
A search for liberation and freedom
There were lots of questions, lots of analysis
I had to learn the trail
I had to learn the language
I had to find the key
Is this no more than a test -
Just like all the rest?
What awakenings will befall me?
What voices will I hear?
Who will my rabbis be?
Who will be my alchemist?
I am but a pilgrim.

BODY LANGUAGE
Paul W. Stearns

The body talks to all
The body talks in loud voices to some
The body's language is pain
When the body talks it talks with pain
Pain caused by the internal
Pain caused by the external
It can talk any time
Don't have to be 40 you see—don't have to be 53
Psychosomatic pain is a language hard to understand
It's the only kind that requires transformation of the mind
When the body starts to talk—it talks with pain
Chiropractors may help symptoms of pain
Osteopaths may help symptoms of pain
Medical doctors may help symptoms of pain
Transformation of the mind is the only cure for pain from
   the internal
Psychosomatic body language is hard to understand.

A brand new power. Could it be possible?
Some of my gifts as a child, were curiosity, enthusiasm,
energy, endurance, drive and creativity. In my earliest memories I used these gifts in work. My Father made sure of that,
even if he invented work. When I was twelve I began creat-
ing projects I liked instead of the farm work or physical work
my Father had us doing. After high school and college I used
my gifts in other ways; money, status, position travel and
power. Each led to an insatiable desire for more. I established a pattern of going just so far and starting over. Thus in
25 years I went full circle four times. Each time I started a
business, I brought it to fruition. Each time at a crucial
moment my fears made me sell it. Each time I started once
again. I hit an emotional bottom! To deal with the despair
and its symptoms I tried psychiatry, medical doctors, osteo-
pathic doctors, chiropractors, and massage therapists.
It seemed there was no way to fill the longing inside me.

Throughout my life a thirst I couldn't describe always pro-pelled me forward. I couldn't find a way to fill an ever present, empty space within me. I couldn't stop the fear. I tried religion, but going to church and the Bible didn't help. If anything both made matters worse.

I read Matthew 7:7 "Ask and it will be given to you, seek and you will find; knock and the door will open to you." I thought, what a bunch of crap! No one sought or knocked more than I had and the result was always the same. Noth-ing!

I tried self-examination with a psychiatrist named Byron Casey. But that wasn't the answer. I lived a moral and ethi-cal life. These were values I reluctantly thanked my Father for, but in some ways, when others weren't returning those values, I felt as if I were on a one way street.

Mike Smith and I had our lunch and I was reading *Conscious Contact, A Partnership With A Higher Power*. As I read I felt a slight re-generation and a little more energy. I wondered, had I missed something in my search? Was it possible? Could it be that Benjamin Disareli's quote "To be conscious you are ignorant of the facts is a great step toward knowledge" might apply to me. In case it might be true I wondered if I should keep trying. I remembered a "Wall Street Journal" article entitled "Don't Be Afraid to Fail."

DON'T BE AFRAID TO FAIL

You've failed
many times,
although you may not
remember.
You fell down
the first time
you tried to walk.
You almost drowned
the first time
you tried to

swim, didn't you?
Did you hit the
ball the first time
you swung a bat?
Heavy hitters,
the ones who hit the
most home runs,
also strike
out a lot.
R.H. Macy
failed seven
times before his
store in New York
caught on.
English novelist
John Creasey got
753 rejection slips
before he published
564 books.
Babe Ruth struck out
1,330 times,
but he also hit
714 home runs.
Don't worry about failure.
Worry about the
chances you miss
when you don't even try.

*A message as published in the Wall Street Journal by
United Technologies Corporation, Hartford, Connecticut
06101

Epiphanies don't come on command! At different times
in my life, I'd think aha! this is it, I've got the answer. Then
I'd encounter another unexpected Epiphany. Usually the
more I argued in defense of some long-held belief or conviction the bigger the surprise and the surprise was a revelation
which would cause me to take a turn in my road of life. A

deeper meaning or hidden truth, changed an accepted reality.

I've always been amazed at people who, without questioning are content to accept what their sisters, brothers, parents and society pass on to them. Some even die for these passed down truths. I believe some people accept these "truths" because it's easier than encountering the uncertainty which comes from challenging a myth and throwing it up in the air for debate or discussion.

My energy and curiosity pushed me forward, took me to deeper truths, though at the time I did not recognize what was happening. As I moved from Avant to the Midwest I noticed a gulf between Midwesterners and me. That gulf had to be crossed if I were to catch up. As I caught up, the conflict that prodded me didn't stop.

I decided not to let fear stop me and to begin again. I started by eliminating cigars and initiating a three day per week physical conditioning routine. From past experience I knew if I didn't do physical exercise as I stopped smoking, a sudden weight gain would be a problem. Instead I decided to lose the thirteen pounds I had been intending to lose. My quest had begun!

Roy Isbister, my mentor from Spartan Oil Corporation, played a role in my quest. After retiring he had moved to California. When he visited me in the summer of 1987 I noted he had lost a great deal of weight. More important, he didn't want to play golf. I knew if Roy didn't want to play golf, something was wrong.

Yet I was unprepared for his phone call the following November. "Paul," he said, "I wanted you to know. I've been diagnosed as having cancer in my pancreas and it's terminal. I only have a few weeks to live."

It took me a moment to compose myself. We had talked weekly and this was the first idea I had of his illness. I brought myself under control and said, "Roy, I'm coming out."

He protested. "I don't think that's a good idea."

His words shocked me, but I wouldn't be put off. "Roy, I'm coming. I can't force you to see me but I intend to camp on your doorstep and someone will have to tell me you won't see me."

He paused, then in a quiet voice said, "I wanted to spare you. I warn you, I don't look like the same person you know."

I fought back tears and answered, "Roy, I love you and always have. I'm on my way."

Though he didn't say so, I heard the relief in his voice. "Okay, since it's so close to Christmas and both my son and daughter will be here why don't you wait until the first week of January to come."

I needed a miracle. I was having personal problems and now a person I loved was dying. I was really down. I bought a copy of a book entitled, *Love, Medicine and Miracles* by Bernie Siegel and read it. The book opened my eyes in ways I never expected. I knew it would be helpful to Roy so I asked to have Dolores, his wife, buy a copy for him. She did and Roy read it before I arrived to see him.

I arrived at Roy's the first week in January.

Roy had always been a nervous, on the go type of business executive. He was gruff on the exterior but gentle under the surface. He was 6'4" and usually weighed two hundred twenty to two hundred thirty pounds. When I arrived he weighed 150 pounds. He was as relaxed as I had ever seen him, serene because he had accepted his condition. He told me how wonderful the Siegel book was. We spent two wonderful days reminiscing. We talked of the old days, of our early years together. We also talked about what it was like to be terminally ill, to realize that we are allotted so much time on this earth, to realize that although we live like it will be forever, life does end for us all.

Over the next several weeks Roy's cancer went into remission. He lived another year and a half before the cancer recurred.

I am convinced the Siegel work, *Love, Medicine and Miracles* gave Roy the miracle of one and a half additional years of life. A better quality of life than he had ever known. He used the year to repair relationships with members of his family. He also paved the way to a peaceful culmination of a full life. I saw a man accept life on its own terms who all the years I had known him had been in a constant state of anxiety. That last year he was a totally different personality. We talked once each week by telephone until his death. We both knew his past behavior had much to do with his health problems. I felt it shortened Roy's life unnecessarily. The anxiety Roy always knew probably brought us closer over the years, because we had that in common. Of course we had it in common with most of our peers, but among men that is something that is seldom talked about. Roy's death gave me added incentive to unravel the reasons for, and hopefully end of, my anxiety. I knew if it continued my immune system could break down as Roy's had, allowing disease to set in.

I made one more trip to see Roy and our conversations were intimate. I am blessed that Roy and I had the two visits. It was a great gift to me to have shared life with him and see him through his illness.

The experience with Roy, reading and reflecting on Siegel's book, plus the reading materials Mike Smith shared with me gave me the stimulus I needed. A "major quest" was underway and with it the energy and courage to go on.

My quest took on a radical flavor! The hope of unraveling the mysteries to my problems took a quantum leap. Somehow I intuitively knew that what had brought me to this stage of my life would not carry me the rest of the way. The life style I had been practicing simply wasn't working anymore. My state of understanding was in need of a shift. Much of my experience was invalid. Why else did I keep coming full circle each time? I started a new project or activity, always thinking of making linear progress but instead went 360 degrees.

From November until the following May I read thirty-eight books on self-help, psychology, mythology, religion and spirituality. I read books on life changes and transitions too!

In March of 1988 Lib and I went to the Island of St. Croix. Wanda and Ron Roderick owned a house there and encouraged us to visit. They knew of my quest. When we returned from St. Croix I felt the reading I had been doing was helpful but not accomplishing what I needed. I felt I was benefiting intellectually but my emotions were lagging behind. My feelings weren't changing as fast as I wanted and the lack of speed in my progress was frustrating. A friend commented, "Paul, all change is not growth and all movement is not forward." I agreed!

I decided to go to a psychotherapist. A friend recommended Barbara Andersen. Barbara agreed to meet with me once each week. We began in May, and shortly after she asked me to consider slowing down my work pace. "What will you ever do when you retire" she asked.

"I don't plan on retiring Barb, a small business owner doesn't have to" I replied.

Then she said, "For purposes of our working together I want you to try and slow down, to put some energy in what we'll be trying to accomplish." I reluctantly agreed and asked, "What do you want me to do?"

She said, "Take every Wednesday afternoon as well as Saturday and Sunday off. Block out that time as time you absolutely will not work. Do that from June to the end of August and then take a three week vacation in the fall."

I was astounded. "I don't know if I can do that, but I'll try."

I did exactly what she asked me to do, continuing to see her once each week over the months. Lib and I discussed and planned the three week vacation, now it was September and time to go. I had been gone from Lansing once before, but it was a combination business and vacation trip. This time, vacation only, no calling my office, no business. During the summer months I felt I knew and understood some things but still wasn't re-generated.

Throughout the rest of 1988 I was completing a major fund raising project for the local community college, and continued to read. I also was completing a couple of business projects. In January and February of 1989 I was still completing the college and business projects and trying to live day to day. I continued to see Barb Andersen.

I approached our minister about starting a book review

group that would also be a support group. He liked the idea and advertised the group in the church portal. Ten people came and the group began in March. A book was selected, we each agreed read to it, then during the meetings discuss how it pertained to our lives. We started with *Making Sense Out of Life's Transitions* by William Bridges.

The book helped me identify and cope with the critical changes in my life. His writing took me step by step through the transitional process, offering skills, suggestions, and advice for negotiating each of these perilous passages.

Through William Bridges I confirmed that the passages Gail Sheehy talked about are real. The transitions from passage to passage can be identified and rather than fighting each one, managed as a normal process of change. Change and transitions are necessary to our humanness.

At this point my quest had included suffering with Roy Isbister, reading voraciously, meetings with a psychotherapist, plus taking some time off. I was beginning to feel again. In retrospect, I was stunned that my feelings had been so numbed. Without realizing it I had numbed my feelings to avoid pain.

The balance of 1989 brought some major decisions. The first was to resign from the Country Club after twenty-one years. Golf had become a major frustration and was incompatible with my perfectionist approach to life. Lib and I rarely used the club socially, except for Scott playing some golf (and he was now gone) and Jeff's occasional use of the swimming pool we didn't use the club much. We also decided it was time to look for a place in the country and fulfill a life-long dream. Lib and I had dreamed of having a farm or ranch some day. We always said we would do it but something always got in the way.

The first decision was to see Barbara Andersen and the second decision came in January, 1989. It was to sell part of my business holdings and place the balance with a property management firm. My objective was to select a broker to sell the properties I wanted to sell and select a management firm. They could take until the next fall to get me in a position to close my office by October of 1989. At that time I planned to take a six month period off.

The selection of a management firm was made by August 31st, 1990. I was still struggling with the concept of letting go, but I was determined. I always had strived for control, not to let go of it. It would be a test!

When September, 1990 came the real estate broker I had selected had sold the properties we'd hired him to sell. I signed a contract with Hamco Management Company to manage the rest of my properties, closed my office, and stored all of my office furniture.

It was my hope I could get some answers to my questions by broadening my education.

That same month Scott Peck gave a one day seminar in Detroit based on his book, *The Road Less Traveled.*

In the book he provides a foundation to recapture spiritual growth and development, reach higher levels of meaning, confront personal problems and enhance personal and professional effectiveness. He lays this foundation by dissecting discipline, love, personal growth, religion and grace.

At his seminar, "A Day Along The Road Less Traveled" he spoke to issues of human nature and spirituality.

He said the essential characteristic of human nature is that individuals have the capacity to transform themselves for better or worse. Transformation, he believed can best be discussed by talking about the four stages of spiritual development. In addition, he considered the role of conscious choice.

Peck said the nature of humans is to have a thirst for spiritual fulfillment. He stated, "Addictive personalities use addictive agents as a false substitute for a higher power." That sure made sense to me!

Conscious choice was discussed in the context of effective problem solving both personally and organizationally.

1. Social and personal costs of poor problem solving.
2. The true complexity of problems and solutions.
3. Integrity and individual responsibility for change.

Through Dr. Peck I listened to another voice that brought clarity to my own human nature. I heard and read material that spoke to my own experience in such a way that I now knew my instincts were okay and that my early socialization was wrong.

I learned that recovery comes when spirituality and self-awareness are practiced in community. The healing can free one to love.

The beginning of 1990 saw the pace of my quest go to another level. While my properties were being sold I was getting the rest of my affairs ready to close my office. I also scheduled some university continuing education courses, plus seminars and work shops.

In April I enrolled at Michigan State University to take a course on how to write an autobiography. The class was scheduled to meet one night a week for six weeks and was advertised as a course of "self-discovery."

May brought my willingness to experiment with attending meetings of Co-Dependents Anonymous and Emotions Anonymous. I had been reading about twelve step programs and wondered if there might be something there for me.

May also brought Bernie Siegel for a repeat performance in Detroit. I went to hear more about his work. In his new book he confronted time honored perceptions, eloquently explaining the link between mind and body. He showed how people can become exceptional patients and be survivors.

Siegel is a general surgeon in New Haven, Connecticut. He conducts experiential workshops around the theme of his book, *Love, Medicine and Miracles* and shares his therapeutic approach to illness. It is aimed at integrating the body, mind, and spirit. Participants explore the role of hope, love, spirituality and unconscious beliefs in the healing process.

In the course of the workshop he discussed imagery to interpret the symbolic and hidden aspect of conflict and illness in our lives. Dr. Siegel teaches the importance of resolving conflict and the need for unconditional love to direct all our energy toward healing. He says the removal of conflict can be like a 10,000 pound weight lifted from your shoulder.

This gives unbelievable energy to put toward healing. Unconditional love can give that kind of release. I could relate because Lib's unconditional love and acceptance for me had helped heal some of the rejection I felt from my family of origin and my marriage to Peggy. I had experienced some of the release Siegel talked about.

According to Siegel, illness can be a gift because pain and illness can cause re-direction in our lives. He suggests you ask yourself why you need the illness. The answer leads to an understanding that can facilitate change.

Loving, caring and sharing with others fosters unconditional love. The mirroring process of ourselves in a loving way to others bring healing.

By June my business affairs came together well enough for me to volunteer one afternoon a week to work with chronically and terminally ill patients at a local hospital. I soon learned I had problems, but I wasn't dying. I didn't have problems like the people I worked with had. My view of my own plight changed after seeing, and visiting with people who were terminally ill.

Two important lessons came very quickly as I worked with the terminally ill. The first was my obsessing about my own plight didn't exist while I was trying to help others in need. The second was the mirroring process Siegel talked about. Sharing feelings and emotions with the terminally ill gave them, and me, a healing.

During the spring and summer Bill Moyers did some programs on PBS television with mythology as the subject. He presented six, one hour programs with Joseph Campbell, the comparative mythologist.

Campbell's work, stemming from his comparative studies of mythologies throughout time and history, did more to release me than any other subject I studied.

He slanted his study toward what all myths throughout time had in common; how they were similar.

His writings scorned theologians. He condemned them for interpreting myths literally and historically rather than symbolically and psychologically, and he came to the point of berating them for interpreting myths at all.

Campbell's view was that myths express raw, unfiltered experience, which he felt theologians artificially interpret. They imposed interpretations to fit the convictions of their specific religions.

Campbell took the position that the true meaning of myth is psychological, metaphysical, and mystical, but that also the true meaning of myth was true. Mythology was not a lie, it was the penultimate truth only because the ultimate cannot be put in words.

To Campbell, myth represented a collective bible for all of humanity. It alone contained the wisdom necessary for what amounts to salvation. He felt myths give one message and that message is the oneness of all things. Myths don't assume but preach mysticism. The true meaning of myth to Campbell was the oneness of all things, and that all things are truly one. Myth discloses the deepest truth about reality. Campbell died in 1987. Through him I learned once and for all, fundamentalism, as taught to me in Oklahoma was flawed and I could finally let it go. I was free to find the religion or spirituality that spoke to my true nature.

In August my 35th high school reunion was being held in Tulsa. I wanted to attend, particularly because while taking the course on how to write an autobiography I was going back in time and memory.

There was a potential of fourteen graduates attending; one was deceased. Nine of us showed up. We reminisced from 6 P.M. until 2 A.M. the next morning. All but one had gone from first grade through twelfth grade in Avant.

Going back to Avant caused me to think about the course I took on how to write an autobiography. During the course I decided to research and write mine. Being in Avant for the reunion gave me an opportunity to do some research. During the course it was said "often the way forward is the road back." The road along time and memory. It was my hope that the way out of my labyrinth would be found in writing the book.

When it was time to start writing my autobiography Lib and I decided to go to another city for a portion of the time it was going to take. We decided on Columbus, Ohio because that is where she grew up. While I was doing my writing she could visit with family and friends.

We leased a furnished condominium in Columbus for the months of October and November. I rented a trailer big enough to take my desk and credenza, as well as our clothes, and we headed to Columbus.

I also wanted to go away from Lansing to break my routine. I decided that I wanted to do things differently, and try to break some old habits. For example, my hair was cut by the same barber for the past twenty-six years. The first week we were in Columbus I went to a stylist and said, "I'm in your hands, style my hair the way you think it would look nice." She did and I've worn it that way since. Always in the past I directed and controlled the precise way my hair was cut. This was my start at trying to release control.

During our stay in Columbus I was scheduled to attend a one week grief workshop sponsored by Elizabeth Kubler Ross. The workshop was at Stoney Point, New York. I read the book *On Death and Dying* written by Dr. Kubler-Ross, which discussed what the dying have to teach doctors, nurses, clergy and their families. The book explores the fear of death and attitudes toward death and dying. She identified five stages dying people go through:

1. Denial and Isolation
2. Anger
3. Bargaining
4. Depression
5. Acceptance.

At the workshop we discussed death and dying. We talked about the importance of placing death and dying in perspective. We also talked about the importance of living fully until we die.

Kubler-Ross teaches that we develop and pick up negativity over our life time. She calls this "phoney baloney". The grief workshop I attended helped me get rid of this "phoney baloney." The workshop was aimed at bringing the proper balance into four areas of life: spiritual, physical, intellectual and emotional. The healing that came from my beginning to achieve this harmonious balance freed me to give and receive unconditional love.

I learned to reach into the recesses of myself to ferret out all the emotional pain I felt and surface the reasons for it. An example is that I learned something about my being a "people pleaser" and why! Early in my life I became a people pleaser for self-protection. In church my fears were used against me. I was told that I would go to hell if I didn't do this or that. Dad told me if I didn't toe the line he would whip me. I was whipped so much that I would do anything to avoid being hit. My older brother coerced me into doing what he wanted by using physical intimidation.

I was vulnerable and without protection. Mother stood by and did nothing. No one took up for me. When I cried I was told I was a sissy. When I fought back the punishment intensified. When I ran I was caught. The only way out was to try and anticipate their moods and reactions. The need to survive caused me to do things to please. I played the games Dale wanted to play and did the things he wanted. I volunteered to rub Dad's neck and back, as well as pick his toes. They were degrading jobs, but better than the alternative I knew existed.

There never was a "calm before a storm." The storm was in constant motion. The only thing that varied was its intensity.

I felt a lot of shame, fear and rage, but showing any of it was grounds for more punishment, therefore I wasn't allowed to surface these feelings.

There were times I thought I would explode, but didn't understand why. I sought relief in masturbation, but that brought more guilt. I sought relief through fantasizing making money to escape, but that brought allegations I would be an alcoholic or a miser and more guilt!

At the Kubler-Ross workshop, I was provided a safe place to surface these long hidden, suppressed reasons for being a people pleaser. I was allowed to grieve what had happened and I cried uncontrollably, as a child would. I learned that when I cry I'm experiencing parts of me which were neglected as a child. As a child, nature gave me the gift of being able to feel my feelings. These feelings of anger, fear, grief, sadness or even happiness are expressed when I cry. I found that although these feelings are okay, in my family of origin, they were cause for punishment.

Another example is that I learned as a child I was like an empty vessel. My vessel was filled with too much negativity—you'll never be worth anything, you're no good, you're an embarrassment, you'll be an alcoholic, you're a quitter, you're lazy and always will be, etc., etc. These, and all the rest of the non-acceptance, the rejection, caused conflicts to develop, which led to self-defeating behaviors.

If you don't face these feelings, you will hang on to self-defeating behaviors. Only when you're willing to face shame, fear and rage can you start to heal. For me it was scary and painful to face the experience that I had suppressed for so long, however, not facing the pain earlier was far worse. My painful existence of denial had been comparable to a living hell.

Dad taught me to believe I was being conceited, selfish and shameless if I liked myself. I could excel at sports, work and life in general, but not give myself any credit. I didn't know until I got into recovery that this attitude led to self-rejection. I became unacceptable and disliked myself. The clog dancer was abused and rejected every time he performed. I learned that I had picked up the habit my family had and continued abusing and rejecting myself without knowing it. In recovery I learned that I had to be free of this attitude if I was to have emotional health. Peace of mind began to develop as I began to accept and love myself.

Somewhere along the line I became caught in a vicious cycle. Although I was successful and excelled at sports, work and life in general it was never good enough. I had to get better, I had to get more. I tried harder but never got fulfilled. It was never good enough and I beat myself up!

First I came to understand I needed to accept full responsibility for my feelings, thoughts, actions and choices. Secondly I was provided a safe place to release the negative emotions that I repressed in the past. Doing these steps allowed me to release blaming others, including my father for my plight. I now felt able to change the way I responded to the negative feelings and thoughts I had. It became immediately evident I now could make good choices and take actions that would accomplish a free, happy and loving life. One where I would be at peace with myself and others. The release I felt brought feelings that I hadn't felt since childhood. The wonderment of being in touch with that side of me again I learned to call the "Wonderchild."

Through Kubler-Ross I've learned how to live better until I die. She showed me how life is a process that can be lived harmoniously with some joy and peace. With her help I also removed the fear of death and for that I will always be grateful.

I attended a three day Common Boundaries Conference in Washington, D.C. The common boundary between spirituality and psychotherapy is the boundary they refer to. This conference included workshops on several topics. I attended three; Imagery in Healing, Minding the Body—Mending the Mind, plus Living An Inspired Life. The theme running through all the workshops was the common boundary spirituality has with psychotherapy.

Scott Peck was back in Detroit doing a one day workshop on Nature and Addiction, which I attended.

All during 1990 revelations came from everywhere like shooting stars. Matthew 7:7 came to life for me. Prior to this "Ask and it will be given to you, seek and you will find, knock and the door will be open to you" meant nothing. Now it meant everything. What had happened, how had it happened? It seemed that each step I took led to the next. What I seemed to need came!

THE PARADIGM SHIFT

Paradigms are your basic assumptions about how you live your life. They can help you to digest new information, evaluate and quickly organize it. At the same time paradigms can be so ingrained and so deeply rooted they become barriers to your growth and development. It's like being locked in a room with open doors!

While the perspectives and unwritten rules you take for granted—the paradigms—can bring joy and peace, they can also be harbingers of emotional and physical distress. They can be seeds of disharmony in your relationships.

Paradigms, like trees, have roots. For every growth upward and outward the roots deepen and widen. There are species of deciduous trees for example, that have a tap root. It extends downward and stabilizes the tree at the center. It reaches the deepest source of water. The root system then branches out equally to provide balance and draw nourishment from the soil. Our paradigms go deeper with persecution like tree roots do in hostile climates. My paradigms came from my background. Oklahomans, steeped in the traditions of the frontier spirit and the Bible Belt, exhibit deeply rooted paradigms. The ones I was exposed to grew to radical proportions.

Radical as defined by Webster means to proceed from the root, original, fundamental, reaching to the center of ultimate source. Rooting out paradigms requires a radical approach, a willingness to do whatever it takes. To do this unconscious issues must be made conscious. Intellectual awareness by itself won't do the job, because your emotions very often lag far behind. Most of us resist acknowledging intellectually uncommon issues, and overcoming this resistance is your first step.

I learned by overcoming my resistance that I had been in denial for years. I had been unwilling to identify Dad's mental abuse as the ultimate source of the suffering. Rooting out the unwritten rules I lived by brought the pain I wanted to avoid. In the past I would approach some answers and then stop because of the pain. This time the break-through showed me I shamed myself. I self-induced fear and guilt rather than positiveness and trust. I subliminally imitated my Father's behavior. The shame, fear and guilt Dad taught me were so deeply rooted I continued them. It took great patience and hard work to ferret out the reasons. Of course, in this process it became apparent that Dad passed on what he had been taught.

Psychologists have found that all change, wanted or not, brings stress and resistance to change multiplies stress and the transition time becomes more protracted. Your willingness to change determines how teachable you are!

Some people change just enough to avoid some pain, but the change is superficial and is a band-aid approach. It depends on what the root of the pain is whether a band-aid will do the job.

Dr. Carl Simonton in *Getting Well Again* published a "Social Readjustment Ratings Scale." It was the Rahe and Holmes Stress Scale.

SOCIAL READJUSTMENT RATINGS SCALE

EVENT	VALUE
Death of spouse	100
Divorce	73
Marital separation	65
Jail term	63
Death of close family member	63
Personal injury or illness	53
Marriage	50
Fired from work	47
Marital reconciliation	45
Retirement	45
Change in family member's health	44
Pregnancy	40
Sex difficulties	39
Addition to family	39
Business readjustment	39
Change in financial status	38
Death of close friend	37
Change to different line of work	36

Marital arguments	36
Change in number of marital arguments	36
Mortgage or loan over $10,000	31
Foreclosure of mortgage or loan	30
Change in work responsibilities	29
Son or daughter leaving home	29
Trouble with in-laws	28
Spouse begins or stops work	26
Starting or finishing school	26
Change in living conditions	25
Revision of personal habits	24
Trouble with boss	23
Change in work hours, conditions	20
Change in residence	20
Change in schools	20
Change in recreational habits	19
Change in church activities	19
Change in social activities	18
Mortgage or loan under $10,000	17
Change in sleeping habits	16
Change in number of family gatherings	15
Change in eating habits	15
Vacation	13
Christmas season	12
Minor violation of the law	11

Using these objective measurements of the amount of observable changes in people's lives, one is able to predict illness with a high level of statistical accuracy. Forty-nine percent of the people who accumulated scores of 300+ points within twelve months on the scale reported illness during the period of the study, while only 9 percent of those with scores below 200 reported illness during the same period. A following twelve month study of those who participated indicated that people with total point scores in the top third reported 90% more illness than those in the bottom third.

Although using this scale makes it possible to predict the probability of illness based on the number of stressful events in a person's life, it is not possible to predict how an individual will react to stressful situations; in the study Dr. Simonton published, 51% of the individuals with scores of 300 did not get sick during the period. While stress may predispose to illness, the significant factor is how the individual copes with it.

When you acknowledge and have emotional distaste for an issue at hand you can truly move on to a lasting behavioral change. Resistance, if balanced, is acceptable to some people, however generally extreme resistance does not allow healthy change. This resistance brings you pain, agony and despair. I had been an expert at resisting!

Our Western Culture hinders our willingness, and therefore our ability to evaluate individual paradigms.

In my own case the pride I had taken in my ability to endure helped in my undoing. In Chess, physical and mental stamina are crucial, but they were a handicap when I needed to identify and let go of old paradigms. I was told, "Paul, you don't have any problems, be a man."

We are caught up in being "individualists," "Be strong, you can do anything in the world if you just work hard enough" is one of our maxims. A bumper sticker on a garbage truck in our town reads, "God said it, I believe it and that does it." How can you argue with that?

At a party I was discussing some of my reading. The President of the Lansing Chamber of Commerce looked at me and asked, "Why didn't you read one book and say this is all there is and be done with it?" The conversation stopped abruptly. It was clear to me that my questioning raised problems and feelings of discomfort some people didn't want to deal with. It brought memories of my Father, I always got in trouble when I asked too many questions. He would say, "Paul, things are the way they are and you had better go along with it or I'll whip you!"

I had to hit an emotional bottom to be able to let go, surrender, yield, admit I was powerless over my emotions and my life was unmanageable. For sometime my body told me I needed to do something, but what? I felt alcoholics had an advantage over me. Their enemy was visible! Other people have heart attacks or ulcers to give themselves permission to make changes.

What paradigms did I need to look at? Which ones did I need to modify? My quest exposed me to psychiatry, mythology, religion, spirituality, the twelve step programs and giving myself to others in volunteering. These exposures, in large measure, were new to me and if they weren't new, I was exposed in a new way. Now my receptivity or ability to see was working. The fact is I slowed to a pace that allowed understanding!

My paradigms were below the surface and they began to surface slowly. Going back in time and memory helped to identify some paradigms. Going back reminded me how I found out I was partially color blind and how being color blind caused me to form some unwritten rules.

It was at my 35th high school reunion that Barbara Okerson reminded me of the incident.

"The day you and the others laughed," I told her, "was the day I decided no one would ever laugh at me for that reason again. I decided to cover up what was a learning disability. After that embarrassment I devised an elaborate scheme to prevent people from knowing I didn't know my colors. This behavior on my part continued until I was 21 and took an Air Force color test."

My second experience with identifying unconsciously held paradigms came during a trip to New York and shopping for a new pair of shoes. I went into Sak's Fifth Avenue shoe department and told the salesman I wanted to see what he had in a 12C shoe size. He measured my feet and went out to the store room. As we started to try the first pair on I noted they were size 13C. I said, "Sir, these are 13C. That is not my size."

He said, "Sir, I have several shoes in a size 12C and if you insist I'll get them, but it's the wrong thing to do."

I was indignant. "I've been wearing a 12C shoe size since college and I know what size my feet are!" He didn't budge, asked me if I had noticed any tightness in some 12C sizes. I said, "Yes, as a matter of fact I have. Two pair at home in my closet are too tight." But I told him, "The manufacturer has changed the last they use to make the shoe and I can't wear a shoe with that last."

The salesman then explained the arch in peoples' feet falls sometime around middle age. Their feet require one full shoe size more because the feet spread. He went on to say, "I'll sell you what you want but I'm convinced the bunion on your right foot is from wearing the wrong shoe size."

He convinced me I'd better go back to fundamentals, the root of the problem and have my feet measured each time I buy shoes and try each pair on before I buy them to make sure of the fit. It never occurred to me before that my shoe size could change after high school. When I got home I threw out all my size 12C shoes and purchased new shoes that fit. I learned it sometimes is costly to let go of the old to birth the new!

The third experience of a hidden paradigm was discovering the reason for my habit of putting my socks and shoes on before any other clothing. My boys kidded me about this practice, which seemed weird to them.

The reason for it was identified as I did research to write this book. I heard the question asked, "What personal myths are you living your life by?" In my case one of them is that bedroom floors aren't heated and are always cold. The ritual resulting from the myth was for me to put on my socks and shoes before my feet touched the floor. This produced a habit of my socks and shoes being put on before any other clothing. This habit continued though my house has central heat and carpeted floors. The habit formed all those years ago, when I lived in a house with no heat in the bedroom and linoleum on the floors.

The reasons for not recognizing and accepting color blindness, wrong shoe size, and putting my shoes and socks on first were only three of the revelations that came as a result of my new found receptivity.

In part, my new found receptivity came from learning about what Kevin Truedeau, of the American Memory Institute, calls our teachability quotient or index. It has two aspects, one he calls our willingness to learn. He asks you, on a scale of 0 to 10, to rate yourself. The second aspect is your willingness to change. Again you rate yourself on a scale of 0 to 10. I always thought I had an open mind and was willing to learn. I also thought I was willing to change. I deluded myself for too many years, to change I had to let go of control, and until now, I wouldn't.

I began to reflect and evaluate my past addiction to ciga- rettes and after a ten year interlude of not smoking, an addiction to cigars. I began looking at what had happened at Spartan Oil Corporation, Crawford and Raynor Door Com- panies, Valley Building Centers, Inc. and Hammond Manu- facturing Corporation. Those were all in my past, but now I was in real estate development and suffering the same symptoms. Fear was causing me to sell out!

Each time I created an idea and started to build the idea to a vision, I became paranoid with fear, afraid I would go broke. That fear motivated me to sell out—but why? What was the central misunderstanding, the central paradigm that always brought me back to the point of the beginning? A path of 360 degrees! Could it be the fear my Father implanted in me when he talked about Roe Little and Leo Dhiel? If I became too successful would I die in my vomit like Leo had?

The self-centeredness the twelve step programs talk about and that I developed kept me from looking at myself objectively. My self-centeredness protected me. Self- centered people seldom look at their behavior and if they have a deep self-centeredness, they are blind to it.

The real shift from looking to the outer and looking at the inner began. Jesus said "The kingdom is within" and I began to understand what He meant.

Through reading and attending twelve step programs I heard other people talk about themselves. Their pain, prob- lems and ways of dealing with life mirrored my own pain, problems and way of dealing with life. Through them I saw a mirror image of my behavior.

I learned that all family systems have some degree of dysfunction, some more severe than others. And when there is a severe case those who suffer from it develop methods of self protection. I learned that people who suffered from severe abusive systems adopt controlling behavior to control their circumstances. They try to salve their pain with addictive agents such as work, food, sex, alcohol, exercise or dependent relationships.

In my own case, I developed a central paradigm to take "control" and I salved my pain with obsessive thoughts about sex which began at a very early age. Later in life, to salve the pain of low self esteem and inferiority I became an overachiever, a workaholic.

I learned that all of us are addicted to something and have addictive behavior. Addiction cycles are perpetuated when you deny problems or have a greater fear of withdrawal than you do of the problem. The real fear, for me, was the emotional fear of losing control. Control is an addiction and like others, the addiction says use more of me—you have a high tolerance! Use more of me—you can handle it!

Yes, from a very early age I asked questions, was curious and was impatient with people who were not. What I didn't know was that if you are always in control the questions you ask may not be the right ones. If anything my questions were phrased in a way not to be open, but to control. I had to learn to ask the right questions to let go of control.

The need for control is as old as creation, so it is a human tendency, but the trick is to learn that human beings will never gain control. Control for us is an illusion.

The paradox for me was that when I began to surrender my addiction to control I was led back to a healthy state. My surrender, at first, was hour to hour because I took control back repeatedly! I didn't trust letting it go.

I came to a point where I learned I was powerless and what that meant. I learned to let things go down to the most trivial of issues such as trying to hurry a traffic light. Truly fortunate people come to the point in their lives when they realize it is not possible to control the circumstances in their lives. These people are fortunate because they come to the end of themselves. Self-centeredness isn't necessary. As I said before it is human nature to want to be, and believe we are, in complete control of our circumstances and lives.

I learned to be careful not to substitute new addictions or transfer obsessions. Admitting "I am powerless" was the antidote.

When I admitted powerlessness, I didn't realize instead of being defeated by my admission, I had placed myself in the strongest position to surrender trying to manage things and be free to partake of my higher powers of unlimited resources. I became vulnerable and learned that vulnerability has a strength of its own.

The problem with paradigms for most of us from dysfunctional families is that the roots are so deep they seem to bar any hope of growth and development. To be able to identify dysfunction, accept it, and let our pain be a gift is to be blessed. We then learn that people from dysfunctional families don't have some necessary skills and must begin the process of learning them.

I learned that once I developed a means to look at my behavior objectively then Epiphanies started to come. I started to make forward progress when I began a holistic approach involving the mind, body and soul!

CHAPTER EIGHT

PSYCHIATRY: DREAM INTERPRETATION, MEDITATION, IMAGERY

RADICAL IDEAS
Paul W. Stearns

You pull an onion from its roots
You pull pain from its roots
You can peel pain away to its core
Sometimes you cry when you peel an onion
Sometimes you cry when you peel pain away
Peeling an onion is easy to do
Peeling away pain is hard to do
It takes strength to pull an onion from its roots
It takes mindfulness to pull pain from its roots
It takes a radical approach to eliminate pain
Most people search wide and far looking to the outer
Some people explore the inner, finding the kingdom
    within
Finding the true self can eliminate pain
God can eliminate pain
For some that's a radical idea

Western culture tends to discredit anything it does not understand or has not been scientifically proven. For that reason psychiatry was slow to be accepted. People who sought psychiatric help were condemned and criticized as being defective.

I first went to see a psychiatrist in 1962. To see a "shrink", as the psychiatrist was commonly called then, was a major decision. I took the step with great trepidation, I knew society norms dictated self-sufficiency and self-management. It was thought people who did not adhere to these norms were defective.

In addition to societal pressure, I had an unconscious fear there really was something wrong with me. The message I received from my family, then my ex-wife, was, "There is something wrong with you." It never occurred to me people often treat other people that way because of their own short comings, and maybe they are the problems! I had to learn the skill of interpreting my family and ex-wife's messages.

My doctor said there wasn't anything wrong with me and a psychiatrist confirmed it. What did they know? My family had rank over some doctors I didn't know well and my family said there was something wrong!

For many years I kept the fact I had been to a psychiatrist a secret fearing what people might think. When I ran for public office it was in the back of my mind that if the newspapers wrote about it I would be destroyed politically. Over the years political candidates careers suffered when it surfaced that they saw a psychiatrist.

The first psychiatrist I saw was in Oklahoma City. He explained there wasn't anything wrong with me, but that I might benefit from psychotherapy to help me deal with my anxiety. He noted I seemed anxious and that meeting with him once each week might disclose why. If I knew why maybe I wouldn't need to be anxious. He said the divorce was the biggest problem.

Three months later I was transferred to Indianapolis, Indiana. I requested the psychological test results be sent to

Robert O. Bill, a psychiatrist in Indianapolis whom I decided to see.

The Oklahoma City psychotherapy experience was beneficial to me only in the sense it got me over the hump of doing something new and frightening. Frightening because of the uncertainty and my ignorance.

In retrospect I did not benefit as much as I could have. Like the root of a big deciduous tree, my tap root of insecurity and inferiority had gone deep. The persecution I felt taught me not to talk, trust or feel. To maximize my benefit I needed to do what I couldn't at that time—feel, trust, and talk.

When the psychologists tell us all change, welcome or unwelcome, creates stress I know what they mean! I also know that resistance to change added to my stress level, thus my difficult transition time was prolonged.

I couldn't move freely into the future unless I left behind the past. I found we can only leave behind the past by raising unconscious issues to the conscious level. My family of origin background did not prepare me for change. They all fought change!

I went to see Robert O. Bill every week without fail for one year. He provided two significant contributions to me. The first was education.

The second contribution was he gave me support and reassurance. That is something I never had before, and it was a wonderful feeling!

Dr. Bill, in effect, became my mentor, he began re-parenting me to help me change some of my understandings.

Through him I began to learn about how people are socialized. My sons were taught about this in their school system, but in Avant—they didn't acknowledge psychotherapy and never heard the term socialization.

The reading materials Dr. Bill exposed me to were designed to help me clear up and develop healthy understandings about sex and religion.

The year that I went to Dr. Bill was hard and painful. I learned that much of what I had been taught was wrong.

That was hard for me. It was even more difficult to meet the demands of my new knowledge and allow behavioral changes to occur. An example—new realities about sex. My obsessing about sex could stop now, however it didn't.

I moved to Lansing and Dr. Bill referred me to Byron Casey. He didn't think I needed to see another psychiatrist but told me that Dr. Casey was available in case I needed him. I did go see Dr. Casey regularly during my transition to Lansing and continued seeing him sporadically through many years. I didn't realize it at the time, but Casey represented moral support during the insecurity created by moving.

The psychiatrists I saw were from the Freudian theory of psychiatry. Their primary methodology was to deal with repression. In retrospect I see their objective was to get me to deal with all those unacceptable desires and impulses I excluded from my consciousness. Those desires and impulses were natural, but I was taught otherwise. They were left to continue operating in the unconscious. The conflict had to be surfaced and cleared up.

I learned that the lesson about honesty Dad taught me regarding the Ray Parks beer bottle episode was needed, but the way he did it was harmful. It created a conflict! I wish he had said something about adolescence. If love is blind he could have allowed me to think I was okay, that what I did was normal childhood behavior. He could have told me about some of his childhood to illustrate. He also could have told me that we learn by making mistakes.

Sex was an example of a normal desire and impulse, but I was taught sex was bad. When normal thoughts of sex came up I tried to repress them. I became aware that almost every boy, when he reaches puberty, masturbates and it's normal. What a relief! I was doing it and I was normal! I also began to learn that sex is part of life, not all of life and that sex is not love. I learned that sex is an expression of an intimacy that already exists, rather than a way to become intimate. I also learned my obsession for sex was born out of my longing, my craving for someone to love me, someone to really care about me! Someone to hold me and let me know I was acceptable and loveable.

It was wonderful to learn these things! To learn that when I repressed a desire by trying to keep it out of my awareness, I did harm to myself. When emotions are redirected from the original object to something more acceptable or safer psychologists call it displacement and I had done a lot of that.

Visits with a psychiatrist amazed me. It was amazing how talking to a trained listener mirrored what I said in such a way that new realities developed.

Through displacement I focused on survival, which led to being self-centered. Self-centeredness led to delusion.

I set unrealistic goals. Not reaching the goals brought deep disappointment. These deep disappointments wiped out any value in any accomplishments I achieved. I simply didn't see any.

I learned repression had taken an incredible amount of my energy. I learned that through the years I kept my mind occupied so that a conscious realization could not occur. I had unwanted feelings and unconsciously worked to suppress them; feelings I was told were wrong and I should not have. Typically I substituted work to keep my mind occupied. I had a high tolerance for work and over time I found myself thinking about work 24 hours a day.

Neither Dr. Casey nor Dr. Bill allowed religion to come into our visits. Although it was never said they gave me the distinct feeling that more harm had been done in the name of religion than good. Hell, fire and brimstone, as well as blind ritualistic religion, creates a fear of open mindedness, it holds people back and keeps them from realizing their potential. I began to learn why people in our western culture take answers they are given as gospel and never question them. I did not know why I was different, I always had questions, questions, questions!

Once Dr. Bill and Dr. Casey satisfied themselves that I had dealt with matters of repression, they felt there was no need to come back. However, I knew something else was missing but could not figure out what. I had some answers but not the answer!

Dr. Barbara Andersen was more eclectic in her approach. She had been recommended to me by a business friend who had consulted with her.

I made rapid progress while going to Barbara Andersen. She promoted my quest for self knowledge. Over nine months she helped me educate myself in ways I never expected.

I learned that emotions are a gift of nature. They come and go at will. It's not that they come and go that is a problem. Problems develop only if we respond to our emotions incorrectly. Webster's Dictionary defines emotions as: an agitation; strong feeling; any disturbance. A departure from the normal calm state of an organism, of such nature to include strong feeling; any one of the states designated as fear, anger, disgust, grief, joy, surprise, yearning.

Dysfunctional family systems cause an incorrect way of dealing with emotions. Family systems perpetuate dysfunction when emotions and their components become contaminated. When natural emotions are over-ridden by negative emotions, healing becomes critical or negative emotions continue, and become automatic.

I learned I had always tried to control my emotions. I also learned I had been mislabeling my emotions as well. I sometimes got excited about a project and misread the excitement as anxiety. I filled my mind with work to avoid, or displace having to deal with my emotions.

I began to learn a new skill by first attempting to slow down my mind. This helped me start identifying my emotions. Emotions can bring pain and I always tried to avoid or escape it. I often wished I could have been taught that pain is a gift, if used as a signal to change. As Seigel said, "It can bring growth and development."

"Paul, you never talk about your Mother, tell me about her," Andersen started our session. I had to take a deep breath to think of a response. "My Mother really doesn't register in my memories. She was always there, just simply there. As I think about it, the only memories that come to mind involve my Father. Mother suffered his wrath just like the rest of us. Other than that she's a blank."

Barbara said, "Paul, I'd like to explore your relationship with your mother over the next few weeks."

Over the next three or four weeks we explored the relationship and as we did some anger I had at Mother surfaced. I found I had been, and was angry with her! Angry because she not only did not stand up to my father for us, the children, but used him as a threat to get us to do what she wanted.

During a recent visit with my Mother I discussed this issue with her. "Mom, why didn't you stand up to Dad for us, why didn't you, when you saw him at his worst, take up for us?"

She began to cry, "Son, I've wanted to talk to you about this for a long time and didn't know how." She wiped her eyes. "Your Dad was twenty-one years old when I married him. I had just turned sixteen. He treated me like a child then and that never changed. I was like one of you kids. I was as afraid of him as you were." I understood instantly! How could I be angry at her anymore?

What she didn't say, but I knew, was that women of her era in rural Oklahoma, the buckle of the Bible belt, were treated with no respect. Behaviors had been passed down generation after generation without change. Those folks followed the Old Testament and women in the Old Testament didn't fare well! Mother saw her father treat her mother the same way she was treated. It's all she knew.

My education from the psychiatrists convinced me my parents were the best they could be considering the circumstances and era in which they developed. The times and geographic part of the country in which they lived dictated what they would ultimately be. Their ability to help their children develop for adaptability to a transient society, was impaired. Today it is my belief they were the best parents they could be.

Mother and I had a great visit during the three days I spent with her. I found she and I were alike in many ways. It was interesting after all the years of thinking I was like Dad to find that she and I had more in common, and that our personalities and temperaments were much alike. These conversations were the first I ever remember that were substantive with mutual caring and sharing. She sacrificed for her family and cared about her family in ways I never knew.

Dr. Andersen helped me in many other ways, but she especially showed me how I had been living my life like a sprinter who can see the finish line; his race is over quickly. A long distance runner can't see the finish line and his race requires pacing.

The bottom line for me was that Andersen helped me see that I had always been hard on myself by trying to be perfect and control events. This practice had taken a heavy toll! I finally accepted that it was okay to stop. To finally stop!

MEDITATION

There is a story about a man riding a horse at full speed. Another man, standing by the road, yells, "where are you going?" The man on the horse yells back, "I don't know, ask the horse."

There are many out of control horses that we ride in our lives. I needed to come to a full stop to identify my horses, the ones I couldn't control, and meditation helped me do that.

Meditating is the practice of quieting the body and mind, focusing the attention inward. When I meditate I block out the world around me. Meditation allows me to coordinate at three levels and promotes awareness of what is going on with my mind, emotions and body. Physically I start to relax and continue mentally relaxing, as my busy thoughts grow quieter. This allows me to get in touch with the spiritual side of me.

Like some people I always thought meditation was silly and frankly a little weird. Its always been easy for me to condemn things I didn't understand. I thought I already knew the answers!

Today, I know the present moment is all that we have.

The past is gone. To fret over it is useless, since the future hasn't arrived yet, to fret over that is useless as well. If we deal with the present moment properly, the future will be pretty much as we would like it to be. Meditation allowed me to get to the present moment. To meditate can simply be reflecting or pondering over what you plan and project in the mind. As I take a simple walk in the woods viewing and experiencing the scenery, as I walk thoughts of the past or future that come to mind are allowed to come, but when they do I go right back to focusing on what I projected in my mind.

When I meditate I use the meditation I learned from a Buddhist monk named Tich Nhat Hanh.

(Take a deep breath in and say) Breathing in I calm
    my body
(Breath out and say) Breathing out I smile
(Take a deep breath in and say) Dwelling in the
    present moment
(Breath out and say) I know this is a wonderful
    moment

Projecting Tich Nhat Hanh's words on the mind, taking the breaths he recommends, repeating this several times takes you out of the past and away from the future. It brings you back to the present moment. As I get quiet I see what my state of mind is. I see what my emotions are doing and what is going on with my body. A calming effect comes and my anxieties begin to diminish. My mind slows and if I'm agitated, the agitation subsides.

At first it was very hard to meditate. The race my mind and emotions ran tended to agitate my body in such a way that merely to sit down was a chore. As I stuck with trying to meditate however, my reflection and contemplation slowly transformed my consciousness and forced me to new insights and new realities. Totally new insight came, bringing liberation and freedom!

The courage to try something new paid off!

DREAMS

Until I began dream research I did not know, and found most people did not know, why they dream. Our dreams cause us anxiety much of the time and nightmares especially raise our anxiety levels. I was bothered by my dreams; It was because I couldn't control them. Not understanding something also bothered me, and I sure didn't understand dreams!

Carl Jung, a pioneer in modern psychiatry did much work with dream analysis and interpretation. He believed the mind works on "laws of compensation". The conscious and unconscious play critical roles in the proper balance of the total self. The unconscious creative source of all evolves into the conscious mind and into the personality of the individual. When they are in the correct balance with each other neurosis and other disturbances don't exist. Jung felt the ability to analyze and interpret dreams could help keep the balance maintained. He felt that was critical.

Carl Jung developed a set of symbols and language now commonly used in psychotherapy circles. Symbols and dream language must be understood if one is to analyze and interpret dreams.

Robert A. Johnson, a Jungian analyst in his book *Inner Work* used dreams and active imagination for personal growth as a theme. He said, "Despite efforts at self knowledge only a small portion of the huge energy system of the unconscious can be incorporated into the conscious mind or function at the conscious level". Therefore we have to learn to go to the unconscious and become receptive to its messages. Later in the book he said, "The unconscious is a marvelous universe of unseen energies, forces, forms of intelligence, even distinct personalities that live within us. It influences us in ways that are all the more powerful, because they are unsuspected."

Raising the unconscious to the conscious can be done by interpreting dreams. I found when I was willing to learn the symbolic meanings of dream images, I could interpret many of my own. I also found a tremendous release, and many of my fears disappeared.

I repeatedly dreamed I was making love to my secretary. I knew some people have dreams that are pleasing and try to realize the dream in their waking moments. In fact I was tempted to try, but I could not because to do so would violate my conscience. Yet I obsessed about it.

To find in dream symbolism that my secretary was a symbol for my feminine soul image, my anima (see *Inner Work* by Johnson) and what I really was doing was trying to get close to that side of myself was illuminating! The recognition released me and it was really good to be released.

I learned that each male has 60% male chromosomes and 40% female chromosomes, and each female has 60% female chromosomes and 40% male chromosomes. This information wasn't readily talked about in Avant, Oklahoma. It's an over simplification to say men have a female side and women have a male side, but true never the less.

Another example: I had dreams while running for public office that I was in various states of nakedness. In one dream I was giving a speech to a political gathering and all of a sudden my shirt came off. My suit coat stayed on, but my shirt popped out from under my jacket. I left the convention room to get another shirt. As I left the big room, I encountered this giant, 14' tall, dressed in white, male figure, with an aura of light all around him. He said, "Hello Paul."

I knew him instantly, but did not call him by name. "Where have you been?" I asked.

He said, "I've been to a dance here in the hotel. There is going to be another one Saturday night, why don't you go with me?" The dream ended as I woke up.

I learned that when a person dreams he or she is naked or partially naked, in dream language this means your persona isn't adequate for the role you are attempting to play. My persona was not suited to run for public office.

The giant figure I encountered in the lobby was God! He was saying Paul, it's okay to play, you don't have to be a workaholic all the time, it's okay to dance. Prior to this dream, I had been working very long hours, as well as making a decision to run for public office.

Dream interpretation opened a new, wonderful, mystical world that gave me liberation and freedom. I learned about the anima, animus, persona, self, ego, and shadow. What I learned transformed my fear of dreams.

I consider myself lucky. Pain pushed me to grow and develop! It helped rid me of the pain dreams had brought in the past.

IMAGERY

Imagery, in my opinion is still in its infancy, though it is being used across the United States more frequently. However, it is still not broadly accepted by medical people.

I did not find imagery to be a readily available tool. A layman, unless supervised by a professional skilled in symbolic meanings, is not able to get much from imagery.

Siegel and Kubler-Ross use imagery in their workshops. They both use drawings in their imagery healing work. They helped me benefit from imagery.

I also attended imagery work shops at the 10th annual Common Boundaries Conference in Washington, D.C. Over 2,000 people attended, over one half being psychotherapists.

The Siegel and Kubler-Ross exercise in drawing imagery I benefited from was to take a sheet of white typing paper, lay it vertical in front of me, then with crayons, draw myself. Once my drawing was complete, symbolic meanings were used to interpret it. I found the drawing to be revealing in important ways! For example, I ran out of space on the sheet of paper and didn't have room to draw legs. This meant that I had been cutting my legs out from under me. That of course is what I had done most of my life and explained why I always went 360 degrees.

During my quest I found imagery cross checked conditions I found through psychotherapy and other means. For example, I could not see or believe I had been cutting my legs out from under me, why would I do that? The answer is I was doing it without realizing it and had to be shown several ways before I could see this paradigm in action!

STAGE II

With Bill and Casey I learned about repression, its effects and to some extent, the role it played in my life. From Andersen and her mentoring I went further down the road toward self-knowledge. After all was said and done I still knew there was a missing link. My quest continued, I continued to search.

Unknowingly I was about to learn that self-knowledge was not the missing link. The missing link would reveal itself through "The Twelve Step Programs", spawned by the Alcoholic Anonymous organization. Although I was not an alcoholic, I considered myself an addict.

My missing link had been grace! I needed it and it would only come from a loving Higher Power, through community.

Through the twelve steps as practiced by A.A. and its offspring, I found a spiritual program. A program which did not allow religion to be discussed just as Bill and Casey wouldn't. The old negative religious tapes from my early Avant education could not be played here. I began to find grace with and through others.

Two books helped me to understand addictions and how to deal with them. One was *Stage II Recovery, Life Beyond Addiction* by Earnie Larsen. The second was by Gerald G. May, M.D. called *Addiction and Grace*.

From them I learned about the nature of addiction and also that we're all addictive.

It was a revelation to learn that the treatment of addiction is gaining more acceptance and has now been included with repression for treatment by the psychiatric community.

Gerald May defines addiction as "any compulsive, habitual behavior that limits the freedom of human desire. It is caused by attachment, or nailing of desire to specific objects.

The word behavior is especially important in this definition, for it indicates that action is essential to addiction."

May also said behavior like "thinking, memories, fantasies, ideas, concepts, and certain feeling states can be attachments, and one can become fully addicted to them. We have all experienced obsessive thoughts. Some of us might even admit to having been addicted to certain moods—depression, shyness or cynicism."

He went on to say there are five essential characteristics which mark true addiction: 1) tolerance, 2) withdrawal symptoms, 3) self-deception, 4) loss of will power and 5) distortion of attention.

I found that when put to the test, I was addicted to obsessions about sex, worry, work and cigars. I had lost my freedom to these idols. Further, when I gave one up I found something to substitute in its place. I began to find when I gave up an object of addiction I also needed to deal with the loss of self-esteem that resulted. I also needed to deal with the root of the pain to avoid going to another object of addiction. An example of the root of my pain is my compulsion about trying to prove my Father wrong about me, and winning just a little of his acceptance!

Even now I hear the ominous words of condemnation my Father's stern voice imparted to me; his voice demanding, "Stop crying," "Be a man," the hurt, anger, rage and humiliation still burn in my heart. More than forty-seven years have passed since the clog dancer performed with the schools western band and in front of the student body, yet the look of my sister and brother's glare, the sound of my Father's voice and his attack, the throb of my black and blue feelings, remain sharp and clear today. They are the first things I can remember. They are the first bits of visual, verbal and emotional water, filling my empty vessel. A vessel I have come to know, as me, by my ability to remember.

My sisters and brothers were treated much the same way as I was, yet they revered Dad and held him up as a great man. Once, while at a co-dependents meeting I asked the group leader why, in an abusive family do some of the children revere and praise an abusive parent, while in the same family one child will tell it like it is.

He said, "Okay Group, what's the answer to Paul's question?"

The answer yelled out was, "Denial!"

The leader said, "Why denial?"

The answer came back, "Because the ones denying can't, and won't face pain. They repress the fact the abuse existed to avoid pain." To cope with repressing pain I had developed compulsive, habitual behavior.

To help stop compulsive, habitual behavior, I first had to identify it as being just that and I also had to accept the pain inducing feelings that came from denying the behavior. The feelings that said in painful ways, "Paul, you can't stop this behavior, its who you are and you have to have it." The important thing to know is you can't stop the feelings but you do not have to act on them.

I now began to learn new behavior and unlearn the old ones through grace. A spiritual program was necessary to give me support. The support I needed to make progress and recover. The twelve step program was able to do something for me that my religion couldn't.

I knew I was making progress when the delusion and denial caused by my addictions started to clear up. Some liberation came and I began to have clarity of vision.

I learned my new found clarity of vision had to do with my addiction to work. The realization came that my way of getting attention and praise was through work. My way of trying to anticipate and avoid physical and mental abuse was to impress others, especially my folks, with my ability at work. At a very early age I unknowingly had become an over achiever. Through the years I unknowingly filled my mind 24 hours a day to displace other painful thoughts or feelings. When I was younger the imbalanced life wasn't noticeable, but now it had reached the point that it had to be brought back into balance.

My new found liberation brought freedom and allowed me to redirect my God given gift of desire. The redirection to healthy desires began to bring renewal and regeneration.

Clarity of vision and freedom showed me that love—unconditional love and freedom—is why we were created. When we attach ourselves to an object, use it as an idol, our freedom is lost. Our ability or freedom to love is lost as well!

Dealing with addiction and grace played a part in bringing me to the place where the Bible and Church have new found meaning. Both became important sources for helping me deal with life.

CHAPTER NINE

THE TWELVE
STEPS

God grant me the serenity
To accept the things I cannot change
The courage to change the things I can
And the wisdom to know the difference

by Reinholt Niebor

The twelve step programs of recovery were first introduced in the 1930's by Alcoholics Anonymous. Since then their principles and the steps have been adopted by dozens of organizations whose members want to recover from smoking, over-eating, co-dependant relationships and the like.

Alcoholics Anonymous was adapted from a Christian revival organization referred to as the Oxford Group. (See *Serenity, A Companion for Twelve Step Recovery* by Hemfelt and Fowler.) The Oxford Group emphasized the following:

1) Complete deflation (of false pride)
2) Dependence and guidance from a higher power
3) Moral inventory
4) Confession
5) Restitution
6) Continual work with other suffering persons

Alcoholics Anonymous is a spiritual program, but not a religious program.

211

Mike Smith introduced me to the twelve steps. Mike, a member of a twelve step program, practiced the twelve steps. The reading materials he gave me and the reading materials I purchased outlined a program of recovery I could consider.

My Quest brought me to the Twelve Steps and I found reading about them beneficial. However, recovery required more than reading, it required participation—I found real healing comes by participation in community.

After researching different twelve step programs I determined that Emotions Anonymous represented the best program for me.

Courage to attend was a real problem! I wondered—what if I saw someone I knew there? What would people think? and all those other questions our culture conditions us to ask.

Humiliation or desire for liberation? Did I desire liberation enough? The answer was yes, if there was a chance this recovery program might help me I had to try!

STEP ONE

"WE ADMITTED WE WERE POWERLESS OVER OUR EMOTIONS—THAT OUR LIVES HAD BECOME UNMANAGEABLE."

I had been trying for a lifetime to control (people, places and situations) everything. It is now clear to me that coming out of an abusive family system I needed to be in control to limit the hurt which could be inflicted. It was my self-protection.

What I didn't know was that I had become totally self-centered and crossed the line of what I could or should control. An imbalance had developed without my realizing it. Obsessive and compulsive control had become my life. The struggle took me to an emotional bottom.

My actions, stemming from self-centeredness were dominated by my emotions. My emotions were controlled by my addictions. Sexual thoughts, work and tobacco were my idols, or my gods, and I spent all my time with them!

Mike Smith knew I had hit bottom, but wisely he didn't tell me. He merely shared information on the spiritual program.

Admitting I was powerless, that my life had become unmanageable was humiliating. Our Western Culture, my Avant culture, dictated, "Be strong—if you work hard enough or long enough you can do anything you want to in this world." The Avant culture or "I can whip you" mentality did not tolerate admission of weakness or defeat!

How could I humiliate myself by admitting I had warped my mind? That my obsessive and destructive thinking had gotten me to the place where only an Act of God could remove it, all of my will resisted. The bottom line was, if I wanted any chance of liberation and regeneration I had no choice, I had to take the chance. I was powerless, why not admit it. My life was unmanageable!

My addiction cycle was a 360 degree experience. It always started with pain. I reached out for sexual thoughts, tobacco, or work. I received temporary relief and negative things happened. A guilty conscience (shame), low self-esteem developed, and I was back to the beginning.

Step One called me to do less, to yield, to surrender, to let go. In the past fear of withdrawal and denial kept me in the addiction cycle. Both were so subtle I didn't realize what was happening. I soon learned that the painful feelings that always started the cycle didn't have to be acted upon. Once I quit denying the problem it was easier to face the withdrawal symptoms.

I began to realize I was powerless over other people. The only person I could change was me. I realized striking out against employees and my family wouldn't solve my problems and further that they weren't the root of my problems. I learned that trying to control situations was a waste of time. A traffic light isn't going to change, until it changes. My surrender began to change despair to hope. Reaching out for help brought some hope.

STEP TWO

"CAME TO BELIEVE THAT A POWER GREATER THAN OURSELVES COULD RESTORE US TO SANITY."

This step marked the end of my old life and the beginning of my emergence into a new one. It took a gradual transformation for the beginning to start, but it did start, and it came by being a participant. I went to meetings!

The Emotions Anonymous meetings spoke to the importance of believing in a power greater than ourselves. The higher power could be a traditional God, the Emotions Anonymous group, nature, or anything I could accept as being greater than me.

Now that I freely admitted I was powerless, and understood what that meant, I sought a new source of strength and power to take charge for me and make me whole and well.

My church experience from Avant along with the hypocrisy, bigotry and condemnation that I saw in our mainline churches did not allow me to have the church as my higher power. The traditional God, the one I was taught hurled hell, fire and brimstone was not an acceptable higher power. What was I to do? What would be my higher power?

The Emotions Anonymous people did not tell me I had to believe anything, just to participate with an open mind. The Emotions Anonymous book read, "With belief comes faith, a willingness to trust in the unknown, to trust a higher power to restore us to that sanity we so desperately want."

"Believing in a power greater than ourselves is different from having faith in a higher power. We cannot claim faith if we talk about fear and anxiety at the same time. Faith comes as we see God working in our lives or in the lives of others. Faith is commitment and belief in a power greater than ourselves. Our higher power finds us right where we are; we do not have to find him. If we have difficulty finding our higher power, we can begin by trusting another human being.

"Self-centered people have a hard time not playing God. To let go and let God is the test!" You have to give up control.

The addiction cycle for most people cannot be broken without yielding to a power outside themselves.

Some conversions are dramatic. Mine wasn't. It began gradually and continues. A spark came at my very first meeting. I felt God's presence—He was there. The caring, sharing and loving support I saw and felt showed me God surely was there, only a real God could cause what I saw and felt! I now had identified my higher power!

Experience has shown me that the God I came to believe could restore me to sanity is very different from the God of my heritage. Turning my will over to and trusting his will was another matter.

STEP THREE

"MADE A DECISION TO TURN OUR WILL AND OUR LIVES OVER TO THE CARE OF GOD AS WE UNDERSTAND HIM."

Until Step Two I never understood God! The twelve step program gave me the freedom to re-frame my concept of God. Having faith in a higher power or God, I found didn't mean I allowed him into my life. The missing key was willingness. Willingness could not come until I took myself out of the center of the universe and left that spot to its rightful owner—God! I discovered that the more I concentrated on myself and fought with my feelings, the more fears and anxieties developed.

Acceptance of myself and others, including my situation, was required and is the basis of the first three steps. This did not mean I had to be apathetic or give up. It meant accepting myself and saying this is the best I can do today. Acceptance freed me to begin to change.

I would not be able to live by self-will and self-centeredness anymore, they had driven me to self delusion and self pity. I had to trust! I had to start by trusting another human being, trust in God could not start until that happened. When I surrendered myself with my symptoms and feelings, only then could anyone help.

Step Three is often called the "turn it over step." The first two steps involve reflection and acceptance. The third step requires action, the action of giving up self-sufficiency and self-centeredness.

My willingness to turn it over began at my first Emotions Anonymous meeting. I was ready to get out of the drivers seat. Over the next several months a new understanding developed, I did turn it over. Each day the pressure comes to take control back, but I resist the feelings, I don't have to give into them. As I resist, the presence of God helps me lose my fear of yesterday and tomorrow. I find I'm living one day at a time. I now find I am freely given what I was unable to find on my own.

STEP FOUR

"MADE A SEARCHING AND FEARLESS MORAL INVENTORY OF OURSELVES."

Unknowingly I had been denying my emotional pain. I kept thinking something was wrong with me. I had to find it, fix it and go on. The denial of emotional pain drove it from my conscious mind. Denial protected me from being hurt consciously but also kept me from finding, facing and releasing my negative emotions. It kept me from self-awareness—the key to recovery.

The poet, Robert Bly says, "Denial stands for amnesia, forgetfulness, oblivion. A woman is sexually abused at four and forgets the event entirely until she is thirty-eight—and there is no blame for oblivion, denial means we have been entranced; we live for years in a trance."

I needed to better understand the word denial and its definition. By definition, denial is a refusal to admit the truth or reality or it can be an assertion that an allegation is false. You deny realizing the problem exists. I was accused of denial but had not understood how it was applicable to me.

I discovered that different people with different personalities approach new realities in different ways. Some people are flexible, so its easy for them to accept and assimilate new and different ideas. I have a more set personality, therefore it is harder and takes me longer to incorporate changes in my thinking. I had to accept this truth to break down my denial. My new found openness allowed self-awareness to begin. The deepest reasons for my past actions and attitudes began to reveal themselves.

I became aware that the most common symptoms of emotional insecurity are worry, anger, self-pity and depression. I had every symptom. Awareness would have shown me these symptoms stem from causes within me rather than without.

I had been stuck in part because I felt my emotional pain, and the need to manage it developed, causing me to deny it. I was subliminally afraid to look at it for fear it would become worse. I came to know recognition and acceptance were the key to stopping denial.

You must raise to the conscious mind issues that are festering in the sub-conscious and that's what the fourth step does. Identifying harmful conscious issues of an emotional and behavioral nature is also what the fourth step does.

You take a fourth step inventory the way a business takes inventory. "You take an honest and non-judgmental assessment of all stock on hand." You look for the good (character attributes) as well as the bad (character defects).

A moral inventory made me think of honesty, lying, cheating, and stealing. I always viewed myself as highly moral and was proud of that part of my heritage. I came from people I thought were moral! I learned, however, that morals involve much more. They include our prejudices, intolerance, criticisms, fears and guilts, as well as selfishness, egotism and resentment.

My morality came from my childhood beliefs and attitudes. My moral inventory had to include guilt, shame and embarrassment for deeds stemming from my thoughts, feelings and childhood experiences. I had to stop repressing my shame and guilt. I also had to stop judging and rejecting myself and others.

This inventory was just the beginning of what has to be a

lifetime practice for me. Anger, self pity and resentment have to be recognized and worked through, this keeps new attitudes and behavioral problems from developing. You must remember this process is the way your defects of character develop.

I identified my defects of character by listing my resentments and abnormal or irrational fears. I continued my inventory by using the seven deadly sins, pride, greed, lust, anger, gluttony, envy and sloth as a guide. We all tend to avoid the extreme of these but fail to look at the subtle ways they trap us even when done in moderation. These have to be listed and reviewed. Where we have been selfish, dishonest or inconsiderate and where we have hurt ourselves or others have to be listed.

My first attempt at taking an honest inventory showed me I really hadn't understood the word honesty. Sure I didn't lie, cheat or steal, but I wasn't completely honest, particularly with myself. One example of the type of dishonesty I am referring to was in my work habits. I told myself that working twelve to sixteen hour days was necessary and that one day it would stop. It never did. I also told myself I could stop smoking any time I wanted. I couldn't. My dishonesty with others surfaced in subtle ways like managing how I appeared to others. Pretending to know more than I did is an example.

My second attempt at taking an honest personal inventory helped me learn the real meaning of the word honesty. It also revealed and made me more aware of my humanness. It helped me learn that each of us is given desire, needs and freedom as part of our nature. Instincts for survival, food and shelter, are part of those desires and needs. We also have the natural desire for companionship. Sex, material and emotional security are part of these gifts as well. All are necessary and right.

Problems develop when our desires begin to drive, dominate and rule our lives. Emotional problems, in large measure are caused when behavior becomes compulsive and habitual, thus limiting freedom. Freedom is lost when desire becomes obsessively attached to an object, like tobacco, alcohol, worry, etc.

My task in the fourth step was to root out the idols which warped me. By discovering these liabilities I moved toward correction.

STEP FIVE

"ADMITTED TO GOD, TO OURSELVES, AND TO ANOTHER HUMAN BEING THE EXACT NATURE OF OUR WRONGS."

The twelve steps ask us to behave in opposition to our tendencies; all twelve deflate the ego. This is necessary to reduce self-centeredness. My own self-centeredness brought a paranoia which inflicted constant tension and fear. The resulting pain caused me to unknowingly try to escape reality through my addictions.

I was shown that sharing with another person gave me a truer picture of myself. I was also shown I could not make progress until I shared my honest inventory with someone else. I developed an ability to forgive others; an important part of the process of my being forgiven.

Some of my fifth step work was unknowingly done with the psychiatrists I saw and that had been painful and humiliating. Sharing with God and another human being was even tougher! The psychiatrist was paid and there was something about paying someone for help and keeping a confidence that helped me think I was still in control.

It seems since my birth my energy, curiosity and risk taking had gotten me into trouble. In retrospect it is clear it scared the hell out of my Father. His need to control me was magnified by my risk taking and experimentation personality traits. Clog dancing at the high school when I was six years old, picking up beer bottles at Ray Park's barn, masturbation and drinking near beer at Fair King's grocery store, had all been problems. They were all a normal part of childhood, but a problem for him.

Clog dancing in the high school with a corn cobb pipe in

my mouth and masturbation both involve toxic shame. I was made to feel I was no good and that I was the problem. I was made to feel the deed wasn't the problem, I was! Going in to Ray Parks barn and pouring out a full bottle of beer to get the bottle redemption money was wrong and involved shame. In other words it was a deed that was wrong, my brothers and I needed to learn that it was wrong. Drinking near beer involves shame and was a deed that was wrong, not because I drank the near beer but because I charged it to my father's account without permission. I was punished for drinking it, not for charging it to his account.

Like all children I needed to learn right from wrong, but also like all children I had the gift of natural shame. My conscious told me when I was doing something wrong.

John Bradshaw, in his book *"Homecoming" Reclaiming and Championing Your Inner Child* talks about shame and toxic shame. Shame and toxic shame are different. Shame is that painful emotion excited by a consciousness of guilt caused by a shortcoming or an impropriety. Shame, real shame, is a gift of nature. Toxic shame is that painful emotion excited by a consciousness of something being wrong with you. The deed or what you did is not the correctable problem, you are the problem which is not correctable. Toxic shame is induced, most of the time unknowingly, by ignorant relatives or parents.

Most of us learn as children, when we confess our shamefulness, we feel cleansed and relieved. When legitimate shame is confessed we feel good, but how do we confess toxic shame?

In Step One I admitted powerlessness and came to understand it. In Step Two I became willing to identify and acknowledge my self will was out of control. In Step Three I turned my will over to God's care. In Step Four my inventory on paper showed me my current situation.

Step Five gave me another opportunity to take a leap of faith. It was necessary that I expose my deepest secrets and thoughts to another human being and to God.

I spent a lifetime building protective shields. The problem was in doing so I hid from myself the real nature of my problems. This resulted in the sapping of my energy from constant tension that resulted.

Like many men in our culture I thought admitting weakness was going against the grain. Sharing my dirty laundry with someone else brought fear and trepidation. The guilt I felt wouldn't allow exposure. It was guilt that someone told me about, not natural guilt. A guilty conscience causes fears to multiply.

I identified the addiction and wrongs I had done to others, now I had to acknowledge them.

The objective in taking Step Five was to 1) reduce shame 2) express grief which expels fears and resentments. 3) practice honesty in all that I did. I always knew that, at a minimum, honesty implied a refusal to lie, cheat or steal and I had faithfully followed that practice, but I didn't know the expanded definition of honesty included the rigid practice of refusing to deceive in any way. Like most people I had not and did not practice the expanded definition of honesty faithfully.

I had in fact been dishonest when I tried to control and manage the impressions I made on others. It was as if I said if they knew the "real me" they wouldn't like me.

My neighbor once jokingly asked me if I mowed my lawn in a suit because I always seemed to be in a suit. His question subliminally meant, "Stearn's, don't you ever let your hair down?"

Behavior of this type was developed out of my dishonesty. It bred self pity and delusions of personal grandeur. The pain that resulted kept the addictions going. In turn the addictions isolated me and kept the guilt flowing.

False pride helped me to avoid acknowledging my whole self. The negatives, as well as the positives.

Shame supports denial and sharing with another human being breaks denial! Humility comes from acknowledging and sharing our deepest secrets and weaknesses. This in turn gives us an awareness of what and who we really are.

Discovering the exact nature of our wrongs and sharing them also brings us out of isolation and rids us of loneliness.

This act takes our spiritual beliefs and turns them into spiritual experiences.

I took Step Five with a friend of over twenty years.

Step Five opened my heart to another human being. I experienced the feelings I had suppressed long ago. Step Five brought to me self-awareness which came in the form of wonderful Epiphanies.

STEP SIX

"WERE ENTIRELY READY TO HAVE GOD REMOVE ALL THESE DEFECTS OF CHARACTER."

Was I ready to depend on God after all these years of trusting no one including him? Was I ready to give up trying to control? Was I ready to point myself toward perfection, walk in that direction, even haltingly?

Willingness to have God remove my glaring destructive defects came easily. I was willing to give up cigars for example. However, my willingness to clean house totally was somewhat questionable. Did I even know what all my defects were?

I had inventoried and identified all the character defects I could the first time I did Step Four. Now it was time to strive to remove my defects. Perfection is not possible but to strive for becoming centered or balanced is.

I initially found that subliminally I didn't want to be any more perfect than I needed to be to get by. I also found that as I practiced the program more defects came to my consciousness. In some cases I saw behaviors in a different light, which then showed them as defects. It was clear to me early on that spiritual and moral progress was not going to come quickly and easily.

My feelings of being superior to someone else had been okay but now would have to stop. I had to stop claiming ambition as being different than greed. The gossiping hooked to anger had to stop.

I listed and prioritized my defects, then began work on them one at a time. They had not been acquired all at once and my willingness to let them go wasn't going to happen all at once. I continued to work at being willing. I knew that until I became willing and made an attempt my defects weren't going away.

I found it was important for me to recognize balance. God gave us desires and instincts. The problem comes when they have grown so insatiable they drive us, and the imbalance takes away the gift of freedom.

Recovery for me is to take the effort to evaluate, balance and adjust to a healthy expression all my God given desires, needs and instincts! The only rule I now follow is not to identify a defect and state that I will not give it up.

STEP SEVEN

"HUMBLY ASKED HIM TO REMOVE OUR SHORTCOM-INGS."

The transformation I began would not be complete unless I could turn over to God all of my character defects. Only when that was done could I be an effective instrument of His will.

Submission is the price to be paid for humility and I didn't have experience submitting to any one or anything outside of myself. When I first began, submission was impossible! I might lose my precious control. At that point I didn't know my control was an illusion.

I had been humiliated through the years, now I was developing humility! My self respect returned as I identified defects and placed them in perspective. Faith began to develop each day as positive experiences came as a result of Steps One through Six. With self respect, faith and humility I asked God to remove all the shortcomings I was aware of and help me identify those I might still have.

Comparing myself to others was an everyday part of my life. That brought with it a feeling of inferiority or superiority. These feelings cloaked a character defect, and for me to understand this took some time and education.

Recognizing character defects was helped by getting outside myself to look in. The outside part was supposed to be the non-judgemental, non-critical observer. When a defect in feeling or a behavior was detected by the observing part of me I could send a call to my higher power to remove it.

STEP EIGHT

"MADE A LIST OF ALL PERSONS WE HAD HARMED, AND BECAME WILLING TO MAKE AMENDS TO THEM ALL."

I thought 'here comes some more pain!' Facing people you've hurt is very hard. The courage I needed didn't seem available.

My first list did not contain my name and my sponsor called to my attention that my defects probably had affected me most. I should be on the list. The list also contained more people than it needed to, I came to understand that my self centeredness had given me an exaggerated importance of every word I had uttered and deed I had done. My sponsor showed me how many on my list really hadn't been hurt by me.

What did amends mean? To make amends is like an amendment, which is to modify or change a relationship. It meant I had to acknowledge what I had done, accept full responsibility for it and make a commitment to change my behavior. I needed to promise to try never to repeat my harmful action.

My list disclosed to me harm I did deliberately and harms I didn't realize. Harms because my thoughts were on myself.

STEP NINE

"MADE DIRECT AMENDS TO SUCH PEOPLE WHERE POSSIBLE, EXCEPT WHEN TO DO SO WOULD INJURE THEM OR OTHERS."

Confession is good for the Soul! The anticipation of doing it however can be very stressful. I didn't look forward to the conversations and meetings I was to have.

I started making amends, but I knew that I ran the risk of some amends not being accepted and I also knew not to expect reciprocity. The wonderful thing I found as I did my direct amends was that with each one I lost some guilt and resentment and gained some self-respect, courage, confidence and self-esteem.

My Father was on my list. To make amends I went to his grave site, and had a long talk. I did not ignore, excuse or condone his abusive behavior to me, but I took back the negativity I contributed to the relationship. My Mother was on my list. We had discussions which led to a relationship that I feel good about now. I've also begun changing my relationship with my sister and brothers.

Making amends went better than I expected. The discussions were excellent and some new relationships developed. All of the "making of the amends" to all of the people on my list began to free me from the bitterness I had carried around for so many years. In freeing me a healing began that continues and I felt what spirituality was like. A perspective came I had not known before.

STEP TEN

"CONTINUED TO TAKE PERSONAL INVENTORY AND WHEN WE WERE WRONG PROMPTLY ADMITTED IT."

I now realize that coping with life is a lifetime process and the journey has no arrival point.

Step Ten helps me to maintain what gains I made in Steps One through Nine. It helps me maintain the ground I have gained. A spot check inventory of my needs, feelings, methods of meeting needs, and boundaries tells me if I'm staying in the proper balance. I also check my status with God.

My spot checks disclose relapses, which I accept as inevitable, but usually identify quickly. As relapses occur the spot check allows me to see it is not the end of the world, but rather that I am human. My humanness shows me if I'm setting realistic goals. It shows me if I'm expecting too much from others and myself. Finally, the spot check allows me to take prompt action to get back on the track.

STEP ELEVEN

"SOUGHT THROUGH PRAYER AND MEDITATION TO IMPROVE OUR CONSCIOUS CONTACT WITH THE GOD OF OUR UNDERSTANDING PRAYING ONLY FOR KNOWLEDGE OF GOD'S WILL FOR US AND THE POWER TO CARRY THAT OUT."

Most of my life prayer meant asking for relief. I bargained to relieve me of a situation—I did not pray for God's will.

I didn't know that prayer could be honesty about the way I felt and asking God to help me. He knew my needs already, I don't need to go to him for those.

Meditation didn't mean anything to me until Barbara Andersen introduced me to it. The most significant meditation I discovered was, "The Serenity Prayer."

"God grant me the serenity to accept the things I
cannot change, the courage to change the things
I can, and the wisdom to know the difference."

Praying and meditating brought my emotions into balance. I communicated with God in a way I never had before and as a result hopefully I am intuiting what God wants for my life.

Step Eleven took me out of the drivers seat and gave God the opportunity to provide the power for my life. Step Eleven also provided a daily spiritual maintenance.

Initially I was frightened God was going to lead me in a direction I didn't want to go. After awhile I realized that

God's will and direction does not necessarily dictate a radical change. He gives us free will to choose, but our choices don't always go beyond ordinary responsibilities.

STEP TWELVE

"HAVING HAD A SPIRITUAL AWAKENING AS THE RESULT OF THESE STEPS, WE TRIED TO CARRY THIS MESSAGE TO OTHERS, AND TO PRACTICE THESE PRINCIPLES IN ALL OUR AFFAIRS."

My spiritual awakening came! It did not come all at once, but its profoundness is no less important to me. It could more appropriately be described as a transformation.

My Quest brought me back to the beginning. Earlier in my life God and the church were central. They both were lost in a religiosity that was against my nature. A new basis for living developed, one in which I am not alone. I still have feelings and urges I don't like, however, I accept them and don't act on them as often. Having God's help has eased my burden. The pain that brought me to my spiritual awakening was truly a gift for with it came joy, serenity and peace.

The Twelve Step Program participants often use a slogan—'You can't keep it unless you give it away!' That's what this step is all about, giving it away.

My first attempts to carry the message to others were feeble. I found myself inadvertently trying to control again. Rather than merely telling others of my positive experiences, I tried to sell the program. My job is to carry the message by answering questions about the program or telling of my experiences, but not to go further. It was better to convey the message by the way I lived my life.

Volunteering at a local hospital gave me an outlet to do community service. Giving myself away brought personal satisfaction. My volunteer work helped break down my self-centeredness and find what is important in life. When you visit with someone your own age who has terminal cancer you begin to understand your problems aren't so bad. Isolation is something I was good at, but now I don't need to do that. This new found intimacy and connection brought me out of isolation.

New knowledge, growth, and development helped me with healing insights. Watching other people change broadened my understanding, and introduced life as a process. With God's direction I want to be useful to Him and others along my journey.

CHAPTER TEN

THE NEW PARADIGM

ON PROGRESS
Paul W. Stearns

Why does destruction seem so sudden
Was Mt. St. Helens destruction
Why does construction seem so slow
Was Mt. St. Helens construction
Why does destruction seem so slow
Was the Grand Canyon destruction
Why does construction seem such a wonder
Was the Grand Canyon construction
Did you ever dig a ditch
You can see where you're going and where you've been
Did you ever contemplate
You can't see where you're going or where you've been
Is a human being progress
Is a human doing progress
Are you a human being
Are you a human be-ing
I'm under construction

Wonderment was all about me and my quest led to new doors. Each one I opened brought new revelations! Each book I read, each new contact brought new illumination. I learned that it's not what happens to you but who you are, and it's not what happens to you that matters, but what you do with what happens to you!

It became apparent to me winning the battles I wanted to win required changing my behavior and re-evaluating what I valued. The old paradigms of looking to the outside had to die to make way for the birth of the new. The new was to look within. Clinging to the old was doing great damage to me. Nature shows us that death and rebirth happen naturally. Snakes shed their skins for renewal. Trees die in the winter to give new birth in the spring. Humans with free will, particularly in our culture, tend to resist natural changes that are needed. The need for these natural changes, for the most part, are unrecognized by most people.

Mythology, psychiatry, the twelve step programs of spirituality, all led me to revaluate religion. They also played a role in the development of my new paradigms.

The test for my new paradigm would be pragmatism. History is replete with renewal and regeneration. Regeneration is always cleansing, and usually dangerous. It is as risky as wing walking.

The old barnstormers said the first law of wing walking was never let go of what you've got until you've gotten hold of something else. The problem is sometimes in getting to the new there is a certain amount of time spent in mid-air.

Some people have demonstrated time and again a capacity for improvisation, self-renewal and self-transformation. You have to evaluate if you want to go through life changing little and being passionless.

MYTHOLOGY

Robert Bly says mythology confirms the power of ancient stories to guide, to heal, and to convey the deepest truths.

Through mythology I saw that we have our own spirit, and our spirit is linked to a strong need to express our interconnectedness to other living things. Jung talked about a collective unconscious we all share and in which we participate. It is illustrated by our universal language of music, art, religion, poetry and myths. They give us symbols through which we see our connection with each other, and all of nature.

It is clear to me we are all equal and dependent on each other for our individual contributions.

In his book called *Seeds For The Spirit*, Paul McElroy repeats a story Alfred Noyes told in *The Last Voyage*. He tells of a little girl who was taken ill on board ship in mid-Atlantic. After examining the child the ship's physician determined he couldn't save her but that Dr. Marlowe at Johns Hopkins might. Dr. Marlowe was also somewhere on the Atlantic, soon a tiny spark pierced the wide darkness of the howling sea and the two doctors, (the ship's physician and Dr. Marlowe) were in communication. Dr. Marlowe advised to operate.

One fellow passenger hearing the news remarked to another, "You think they'll save her?" "Yes," came the reply, "they may save her, but who are they?" Will it be the ship's surgeon, Dr. Marlowe, the radio operators, or the captain? Yes, in part, it will be all of them, but it will also be a host of known and unknown down through the ages who helped perfect medical science, nautical science, and the wireless. Thousands of people worked together to make possible that successful operation in the mid-Atlantic.

To be one of thousands who work together to help make possible some worthy event in our day—that is our opportunity! The part we play in the Great Design may be inconspicuous, but it may nevertheless be essential to the fulfillment of the kingdom.

Within our Western Culture there is a strain of humanism that does us a disservice by fostering the idea that we are creatures of our own creation. This results in an individualism that does not recognize our interconnectedness. Further it does not recognize our dependency on each other, as well as our Creator.

Since the founding of our republic—the republicans and the Puritans gave us the individualism we all take pride in.

This individualism, with the founding fathers concept of

community, held them in good stead. However as our country developed, moving from an agrarian society to a industrial society, to the information age, the founding fathers concept of community has broken down.

Individualism is getting us in trouble with ourselves. It causes isolation and tears at the fabric of our interconnectedness. To cope (the birth of) psychiatry came into being.

Joseph Campbell, the great mythologist taught that throughout all time man has been on a journey. Each person is called to a quest, an individual journey. In his book, *The Hero With A Thousand Faces*, Campbell called man's journey a "heroes journey". The key is to 'follow our bliss'. Following our bliss means that we are going where the deepest part of us wants to go. The soul is directing our minds and body. Campbell says, "Don't be afraid to follow your bliss and doors will open where you didn't know they were going to be."

I have come to the view that all of life is a Quest. A journey where the deepest part of us, our essence, wants us to go.

Looking back I can see I had been following my bliss in my chosen career. Unexpected doors had opened for me throughout my life. Although I was afraid most of the time I met life head on and took up the challenge. I made some mistakes. I now see that I went 360 degrees in some experiences instead of making linear progress. So okay, I can now change that and go on.

Campbell talked about three major parts of a "Heroes Journey":

1. Preparation for the journey, which had to do with development and learning to be secure and successful in the world.
2. The second stage is the journey itself, or becoming real, through encountering the deepest mysteries of life.
3. The third and final stage is the return to become ruler of ones kingdom by learning to express one's authenticity, power and freedom in the world.

The third stage is the one I'm telling you about. I am looking at the mysteries, learning who I am and expressing it, because I have a freedom I never knew before.

My preparation for my journey was done in Avant and although I was physically strong, my ego development was contaminated. I could not be secure. My over achievement helped me accomplish a lot but I didn't feel successful.

The second stage, the journey itself, was a time of confusion and sometimes stumbling, fearful all the while. It never occurred to me there were deep mysteries to contemplate. I was trying to survive!

Much of Campbell's work took him through the research of Sigmund Freud and Carl Jung. They looked to mythology in their psychiatric path finding. Both dealt extensively with the human life cycle.

Freud dealt primarily with infancy and the adolescent part of our lives; the half of our lives when we identify with our bodies. Jung dealt primarily with the second half of our lives, where we should be identifying with our consciousness.

Mythology, according to Campbell, shows that the powers which rise out of our deeply felt, creative experiences, the powers which give each of us meaningful purpose and direction represent significant matters. Matters of life and death. To ignore them is to do so at the risk of our greater health.

Campbell goes on to say that mythology shows us that in earlier cultures we can find role models to learn from and we can admire the traditions of manhood passed down generation to generation. Along the way our western culture stopped role modeling and mentoring. The word apprentice lost its meaning. When role modeling and mentoring aren't done we are cut off from a deeper sense of who we are.

Joseph Campbell defines 'myth' in the strictest sense as referring to interlocking stories, rituals, rites, customs and beliefs. They give a pivotal sense of meaning and direction to a person, a family, a community or a culture. He further said, "Myth is the cultural DNA, the software, the unconscious information, the program that governs the way we see 'reality' and behave." All myths deal with transformation of consciousness—transformed by trials—tests or certain illuminating revelations. Trials and revelations are what it's all about."

The myth offers security and identities, but it also creates selective blindness, narrowness, and rigidity because it is intrinsically conservative. It encourages us to follow the faith of our fathers, initiate the way of the culture's heroes to repeat formulas and rituals exactly as they were done in the old days. Such conservatism can work so long as no radical change is necessary for survival.

When I left Avant I had to make radical changes but didn't realize it.

Personal myths or stories can be examined in various ways. Psychotherapy and the twelve step programs are two of the ways I used. Using psychotherapy and twelve step meetings I could be in community and mirror with other people the forbidden or untold stories of my past. I found a safe environment, a loving, caring environment. One in which I told my darkest thoughts and fears. Suddenly when I told a story the spell of the past was broken and I felt and saw something new. Community with the kind of conversation I've just described allowed me to discover and cherish what I had in common with other human beings—my own uniqueness. The community I've described became a healing body. I found mythological stories, mine and others, to be powerful guides to the life of my spirit.

Campbell taught, "The ancient myths were designed to harmonize the mind and body. Myths and rites are means of putting the mind in accord with the body and the way of life nature dictates."

Ancient myths from both the hunter and planter cultures are replete with stories of death and rebirth. They teach us about dying to birth the new! The ancient hunter and planter cultures had relationships to their plants and animals controlled by spiritual beliefs. The taking of life from the creation was a form of tampering with the sacred circle, which is the relatedness of all things. For this reason animal and plant populations were continually evaluated and actions taken to insure the continued existence of these things.

I found studying mythology liberated me from my past erroneous teachings. The delusions created by those erroneous teachings began to fade away.

RELIGION

Defined as a system of beliefs, and the way it is practiced, religion all too often, in my view, cripples the spirit. All religions should be guides for the spirit. However, in my own experience, I seldom saw religion offered as a guide to the spirit. The spirit slept or was stunted in most of the situations to which I was exposed!

I feel there are two reasons why the religion I've been exposed to is deficient. The first is that in Avant, and Oklahoma in general, religion is a rigid system of beliefs passed on from generation to generation. Beliefs that are legislated, not heart felt. There are few places in Oklahoma that you can go and call the Bible a myth without getting into a fight. There a myth is understood to be an unfounded story. I know the Bible to be a myth, but also know that doesn't mean the Bible isn't true.

I believe true religion comes from the heart. A deep relationship with God brings peace, joy and love to people. Fear, guilt and meanness have no place!

The second reason is that in my view the rituals of religion should be enactments of a heartfelt response. All too often they are ritualistic without passion!

Jesus said the two most important commandments are first, "Love the Lord your God with all your heart and with all your soul and with all your mind and with all your strength." The second, "Love your neighbor as yourself."

Two key words are here—love is the first. Webster says, "Love is a feeling of strong personal attachment induced by sympathetic understanding, or by ties of kinship." The second is heart—the vital inner, or chief part of anything; the seat of emotions, affection.

Today's religious institutions seem to have a hard time touching the human heart thereby inducing love. Passionate, compassionate love!

Campbell in his *The Message Of The Myth* compares the creation story of Genesis with creation stories around the world. "Because the world changes, religion has to be transformed and new mythologies created. People today are stuck with old metaphors. Any myths that don't fit their needs, these needs, not met, can do harm."

The psychiatric community has long found some religion to be at the root of mental disorders. It finds people who need to grow spiritually are often held back by their religious backgrounds. Some religious systems don't allow the open mindfulness necessary for people to reach their potential.

SPIRITUALITY

My struggle laid me low, it humbled me! I was vulnerable, finally vulnerable to the possibilities that new insights and realities brought.

The spirit was within me all along, waiting for me to recognize it, from my own free will. All I had to do was be open to accept and show a glimmer of trust and the spirit would awaken. I began to feel a connection with my own individual essence and a new mindfulness developed. It was born out of the new awareness that my spirituality was rooted in my body and this mindfulness impacted my aliveness!

The Greek philosopher Epictetus said, "The fool looks to the outside for benefit or harm, he thinks what is out there makes him happy. The philosopher looks to himself. The wise man looks to his own heart! If there is joy to be found it is within."

A personal transformation became possible as a result of exhaustion. I surrendered and let go. I got out of the drivers seat! Only then did my higher power take over. The barriers I had all of my life were finally down and God willing, I will keep them down.

My pilgrimage became clear. I experienced the sublime and it was then I saw the immortal part of me.

The quest I had been on slowed me as a person, so that finally, I was on a pace physically and mentally to touch, feel, and become knowing.

You look but do you see? You listen but do you hear? A vacuum that allowed my spiritual side to awaken also allowed the conditions for the death of the old and the birth of the new. It was not without pain and I can't tell you the split second when I knew I belonged. I just knew in my bones that I was one with all and all was one with me. I finally found the answer, the reason I never felt at home. I had been looking out in the world instead of looking within myself. My yearning, searching, looking for the arrival point had been fruitless, until the spiritual world in me was discovered.

I enjoy my new feelings of awe and reverence. The change of state I am still experiencing gives me continued hope and faith that the delusions, hostilities and desires of the past can be completely eliminated over time.

My transformation continues. Dealing with the old is less than it was and the new grows daily. With God's grace my progress continues.

CHAPTER ELEVEN

THE WONDER CHILD

THE INNER CHILD

Paul W. Stearns

The spirit is like an inner Child
The inner Child wants to be heard
The inner Child can be repressed
The inner Child can be wounded
The inner Child doesn't like being hurt
The inner Child can recover
The inner Child wants a safe home
Home is a spiritual place—we find peace
when our spirit settles safely home
My Child hasn't had a home.

"Paul" is my wonder child, the six year old inner child I recovered. I re-connected with him for the first time since 1943 in the Yosemite National Park. I was watching a great waterfall and in deep contemplation!

While watching the waterfall, I suddenly understood the concept of "powerlessness." The powerlessness we try to fill with tobacco, alcohol, food obsessions, sex, work or excessive control. Watching the giant waterfall coming off the mountain and contemplating the beautiful, vast mountainous landscape brought a major sense of wonder. Thoughts came of the passage through the Custer National Park and about the American Indians. Thoughts of the image I saw of

239

a famous Indian chief, named Crazy Horse, being carved in a majestic mountain. The image being carved is grander in scale than Mount Rushmore. Caught in the mood which came from the sense of awe and wonder, I let go. Lansing and work did not exist for those moments. All the anxiety, pain and despair were washed away! I felt the reverence and spontaneity of a child! Letting go accelerated the recovery of "Paul."

The time Lib and I spent in one of our country's beautiful National Parks began the peeling of layer after layer of betrayal, broken trust and rejection.

My first contact with "Paul" was on that mountain, and it was as clear as a radio station signal when you're in the same city as the station transmitter. But the contact didn't last!

Although the first contact with "Paul" was fleeting, I felt the marvelous freedom that comes with letting go. Only when I let my guard down did the spirit begin to guide me. I was in touch with myself and the people around me. I knew instantly that the "over control" I exercised all those years had been spiritually deadening. It had brought a self-centeredness which I subliminally used for protection. Since 1943 that self-centeredness caused me to take everything personally. I became hypersensitive to my surroundings, other people and how they reacted.

On that day a mountain refreshed me spiritually. When I got home my personal growth continued as I attended Emotions Anonymous meetings and heard other people share their feelings.

At the meeting I heard an "Elderly Lady." She poured out the pain she suffered at an early age from a father and brothers, repeatedly raping her. I then shared my feelings and some of my pain with the group. I trusted them! It has been said we start to trust God by trusting another person. That day was my beginning! I had an emotional reaction and the clear sense that God was present in that room through those people. When I left the meeting I felt cleansed. A new framework for God started to be built, to replace what I had been taught.

The recognition that you have a problem is a giant step toward solving it. The recognition of what all the betrayal, broken trust and rejection had done to me became clear. The walls I built, the layers of protection I surrounded myself with had served to close my spirit, hide my inner child. Recognizing my problem helped a grieving process begin, this was necessary for my recovery. But what did I have to grieve?

Educators tell us that by the time we reach fourth grade, each has assimilated from our environment how we are expected to act and who we are expected to be. We then know what is expected of us from our families and communities.

In my own experience, my family culture advocated positions that went against the true nature of a human being. What was taught me and expected of me was out of sync with my true nature. The instincts and emotions my creator imbued me with were altered. I was not allowed to let them develop naturally. To some extent I became dysfunctional. The contamination had to be purged if I was to become a fully functioning person. We are not likely to be who we really are, or find our selves until we purge this contamination!

The concept of an inner child in us all surfaced initially during the reading I did. The authors advocated reclaiming that special part of us. That part of us that, if we listen to it, can lead and guide us safely through life.

That part of us that knows the crowd is wrong, that also knows that the barriers we've allowed to be raised are barriers society imposes on us. These barriers imposed through peer pressure, these barriers become so formidable that instead of fighting them, we embrace them.

I encountered "Paul" again and for a prolonged period at a Kubler-Ross workshop on grief. He was introduced to me in such a convincing way I fully accepted he was the wounded side of me submerged below all those layers of protection. My acceptance became childlike and an innocence returned. Barriers began coming down. The barriers that destroyed the part of me that:

1. Could act with spontaneity from the heart
2. Could be curious and observing, having an active imagination
3. Could experience deep involvement in activities losing track of time and external events
4. Could be non-judgemental and open minded about others and oneself
5. Valued playfulness for its own sake
6. Had a willingness to look foolish, make mistakes laugh at oneself

That part of me was weighed down by "shoudas," "oughtas" and "supposed tos."

Finding and reclaiming my inner child was a gradual process. It was also a lot of hard work!

Kubler-Ross says: "we must heal our unfinished business. We must work through and release pain, fear, guilt, and anger accumulated over a lifetime. Resolving these repressed emotions leaves us feeling free and able to live happy, loving lives, at peace with ourselves and others."

I have found that intellectual awareness is merely the first step in a process of change. We have to overcome subliminal resistance to acknowledge the issues we deny exist. Only when we acknowledge these issues and only when emotional distaste for these issues develops can we move on to lasting behavioral changes. My own intellect caused me to use therapeutic logic, but my emotions resisted. My progress started when, at the grief workshop, I raised hidden unconscious issues to the conscious level. My wonder child helped me in this process. As I allowed him to help, I found 'the road forward was the road back'!

To reclaim our inner child we need to understand some basic things. Kubler-Ross also says:

1. From birth to the age of six months we are concerned with our physical body and begin to get in touch with our five senses; sight, hearing, taste, touch and smell.
2. From six months to six years of age we discover

our feelings and what kind of feelings are in our families. We deal with "I want, I need" and sharing issues. It's at this time we begin to repress and stuff our feelings.

3. From six years to sixteen years of age we deal with adolescence. The years we find that we make decisions or they are made for us. During these years we can be made to feel stupid, dumb, and can be ridiculed.'

4. From sixteen years of age and beyond we ask 'why am I and what's my relationship to the world'? Spirituality becomes an issue.

From Jung I learned that human beings have four gifts which make up our temperament:

1. Thinking
2. Feeling
3. Sensing
4. Intuition—Spiritual

An educated person is strong in one of these areas and weak in one. I was weak in feeling. The object is to strive for balance for wholeness. You need to look at these areas and see where you might be incomplete. The weakest of the four, if strengthened, is where healing will come from.

Human perfection and family systems that are perfect don't exist. Parents can, and do, make mistakes and abuse does happen.

The Kubler-Ross workshop addressed the issue of children from dysfunctional or abusive families. They described children when little as being powerless and helpless, but they know at a deep level they have physical needs which should be met. Not getting their needs met, never being touched, being beaten, and being told 'I did it all for you' they become victims of self blame. They say to themselves 'I must be bad for mom and dad to do this to me'. John Bradshaw calls this toxic shame.

Children were described as having become victims and

enter a triangle. The bottom part of the triangle represents being a victim. We later become caretakers, which is one side of the triangle and often escalate to be perpetrators, which is the other side of the triangle.

Victims of self blame who feel unlovable and bad adopt new roles to survive. The 'A Plus Red Cross Caretaker' is what you become. You are efficient, put others first and work hard, because it's all your fault. "I'll fix it!" You as victims don't need anyone else or any help from anyone. You think others need you. If you work harder and harder you get rewards and get your needs met. The problem that develops, as in my case, was that after so long a time working twelve to sixteen hour days, I got tired and angry. Numbness set in. No matter how hard I worked it was never enough, I had to do more.

When you get tired, angry and numb you get set on automatic pilot. After awhile you can become a perpetrator, a little Hitler, a blamer. The perpetrator seeks out people to blame, becomes a critic.

The fuel for the triangle is shame, guilt, denial, fear and low self esteem. To exit the triangle you must acknowledge you are not responsible for when you first became a victim. You must, however be responsible for what you do with it. You can say no thanks, you can ask for what you need and express how you feel. This allows you to leave the triangle. You can learn who you really are and give yourself permission to be how you want to be. This requires testing new ideas and putting them through the tumbler, as Kubler-Ross calls it. Although the tumbler may be a little painful the end product will be polished.

It has become clear to me now, more than ever before, why so many in literature talk of their pilgrimages as being journeys across deserts or vast wastelands. Without a guide that's what it was for me until I recovered my wonder child.

The little child of my youth still existed. That divine part of me that spoke and acted spontaneously from the heart. That little boy at age six who became a clog dancer with a corn cob pipe, who drank near beer at Fair King's grocery, who got homesick trying to make the wheat harvest, who never saw his mother and father hug or kiss. The little boy who repressed all those incidents and those things which told him he wasn't worth anything, and from which he developed feelings of neediness, plus deep and abiding feelings of something being wrong and chronic feelings of not being safe in his world. The guilt and shame that followed led to a lifetime of over achievement and looking over his shoulder. His depression seductively whispered there could be no change, he was on his own.

In reclaiming my inner child I got in touch with my true self. I began to see that my head, that part of me that qualifies and rationalizes everything took over for the little boy in me way back. As I birthed the new, I let the old go, I developed a new, keener mastery of life, where I'm not being shaped, but with God's help, where I'm doing the shaping. Reclaiming my wonder child and finding my true self allowed me to identify my core issues. Those that in the future I won't allow to be compromised!

Someone once said, "The essential ingredient to greatness is passion." My wonder child is a great one because he brought back my passion!

Until now I had never understood when Paul said in Romans 12:2, "Do not be conformed to this world but be transformed by the renewing of your mind." It all begins with the mind.

You sow a thought, you reap an act
You sow an act, you reap a character
You sow a character, you reap a destiny
It all begins with a thought!

Author Unknown

I learned I wasn't responsible for what happened to Paul when he was six. I am however responsible to him during the recovery process. With his help I can watch my thoughts, my old ways!

Old ways, so ingrained, I thought I couldn't let them die.

Re-claiming our inner child and getting in touch with our true selves is not easy. However when we do, we can decide that some things, the core issues, can't and won't be compromised.

I'm now old enough, intelligent enough and big enough to give my wonder child the protection he needs, and by listening to him and following his guidance I know I will be safe. The Creator's gift of a natural emotion called shame will not allow him to lead me astray. One of the greatest Epiphanies from my quest is to finally understand completely what Jesus meant when he said, "Lest ye become as a child ye shall not enter the Kingdom of Heaven."

THE SPIRIT

Paul W. Stearns

Have you ever felt the spirit?
The missing factor in life sleeps in us all
The spirit awakens from time to time
It flows with aliveness for some
The breath of life, the actuating cause, the spirit is
The gift of deity, the spirit is
but you gotta take care of the spirit
Children feel the spirit
Dulled senses close the spirit,
Isolation and pain dull the senses
Sober mindedness is the incubator for the spirit
Consciousness reveals the spirit
Community consciousness is alchemy for the spirit
But you gotta take care of the spirit
Vulnerability is a pathway to the spirit
Humility is the door to the spirit
You have to die to the old to birth the new
Renewal—regeneration awaken the spirit.
You gotta take care of the spirit!

EPILOGUE

It has been three and a half years since my quest began. Jeff is now a senior at the University of Michigan with a grade average exceeding a three point. He settled in and is well on his way to Medical School to become a surgeon. Scott graduated with a Summa Cum Laude designation, sat for his Certified Public Accounting examination and passed all parts the first time through. He now works for Solomon Brothers, the New York based investment banking firm. His dreams since being a junior in high school have been realized and he now has bigger dreams.

Libby went on to become President of Child and Family Services of Lansing and President of The Southside Community Kitchen, also in Lansing.

Lib, Scott and Jeff walk their own individual paths and lead full lives.

When I began my quest I had no idea Webster defined "truth" as a transcendent fundamental or spiritual reality. My quest was to find the truth. I had hoped I could purge the pain I suffered from by releasing the truth. I also hoped to satisfy the longing and yearning that I had!

Through my own self-awareness I found that I'm not different. I'm unique, but not different. That is a transcendent fundamental. I no longer need to isolate myself. The walls I've torn down can stay down. This will continue to allow a natural connectedness to others, which truly opens my spirit.

Recovering "Paul" freed my spirit, that side of me that

needs acceptance and love! This acceptance and love, done in community, restored my natural joy, peace and harmony.

How do you tell or show someone who has never felt love that's what they are made for? How do you share with them that loving ourselves, our neighbors as ourselves and loving God is what they are made for? How do you convince them the transcendent fundamental or spiritual reality is love? Could the answer to all of these questions be "by example?"

During my quest I also discovered a "men's movement." Men across our nation who are on the same path. Their footprints lead to a common path.

I heard someone say, "Life is like walking in snow, every footprint shows!" We all are on our path and share it, bringing a certain uniqueness as our contribution. Allowing ourselves to be vulnerable to each other in love can heal us!

My reward has come in how I feel and, God willing, others, by what they see in me will attest my walls have come down.

COMMUNITY

Paul W. Stearns

God you have called me
You have called me in my pain
You have called me to humility
You have called me to be vulnerable
You have called me to compassion
You have called me so that I may see
You have called me to community

I alone must do it, but I don't have to do it alone!

APPENDIX

BOOKS

Alcoholics Anonymous
The Big Book. A. A. World Service

Alcoholics Anonymous
The Twelve Steps and the Twelve Traditions. A. A.
World Service

Anonymous
*"Conscious Contact" Partnership with a Higher
Power.* Hazelden

Anonymous
Stairway to Serenity. Hazelden

Anonymous
The Twelve Steps for Everyone. Hazelden

Anonymous
The Twelve Steps—A Healing Journey. Hazelden

Anonymous
Touch Stones. Hazelden

Bly, Robert
   Iron John. Addison Wesley

Bonhoeffer, Dietrich
   Life Together. Macmillan Publishing Co.
   The Cost of Discipleship. Macmillan Publishing Co.
   Meditating On The Word. Intervarsity Press

Bosnak, Robert
   A Little Course in Dreams. Shambhala, Boston &
   Shaftsbury

Bradshaw, John
   *"Homecoming" -Reclaiming and Championing Your
   Inner Child*. Bantam

Bridges, William
   Transitions. Addison Wesley

Campbell, Ernest T.
   Locked in a Room With Open Doors. World Books

Campbell, Joseph
   The Flight of the Wild Gander. Harper Perennial
   The Hero With a Thousand Faces. Princeton Univer-
   sity Press
   The Inner Reaches of Outer Space. Harper & Row
   The Power of the Myth. Doubleday
   Transformations of Myth Through Time. Harper &
   Row

Claypool, John R.
   Opening Blind Eyes. Abingdon

Cleveland, Martha
   *The Twelve Steps—Response to Chronic Illness & Dis-
   abilities*. Hazelden

Collins, Vincent P.
Acceptance—The Way to Serenity & Peace of Mind.
(Booklet) Abbey Press

Cordes, Liane
The Reflecting Pond. Harper/Hazelden

Dollard, Jerry
Toward Spirituality. Hazelden

Dunne, John S.
A Search For God In Time and Memory. Notre Dame

Felde, Leonard PHD
A Fresh Start. NAL Books

Fossum, Merle
Catching Fire—Men's Renewal & Recovery Through Crisis, Hazelden

Fox, Emmet
1. *The Emmet Fox Treasury—Five Spiritual Classics*
2. *The Sermon on the Mount*
3. *The Ten Commandments*
4. *Power Through Constructive Thinking*
5. *Find and Use Your Inner Power*
6. *Around the Year with Emmet Fox* Harper & Row
   Make Your Life Worthwhile. Harper & Row

Frankl, Victor E.
Man's Search for Meaning. Simon & Schuster

Friedman, Richard Elliott
Who Wrote the Bible? Harper & Row

Fulghum, Robert
All I Really Needed To Know I Learned In Kindergarten. Villard Books

Goldsmith, Joel S.
  Practicing the Presence. Harper & Row

Hanh, Tich Nhat
  Being Peace. Parallex Press, Berkley, California
  Present Moment, Wonderful Moment, Mindfulness Verses for Daily Living. Parallex Press, Berkley, California

Hay, Louise L.
  You Can Heal Your Life. Hay House

Hemfelt and Fowler
  "Serenity" A Companion for Twelve Step Recovery. Nelson

Hesse, Hermann
  Siddartha. Bantam Books

International, E.A.
  Emotions Anonymous.

James, Jennifer, PHD
  Success is the Quality of Your Journey. New Market Press

Johnson, Robert A.
  He (Understanding Masculine Psychology). Harper & Row
  Inner Work. Harper & Row

Jorklund, Paul B.
  What Is Spirituality? Hazelden

Jung, C.G.
  Modern Man in Search of a Soul. Harvest/ABJ Book
  The Undiscovered Self. Mentor

Krishnamunti, J.
Think on These Things. Walker Press
You Are the World. Walker Press

Kubler-Ross, Elizabeth
On Death and Dying. Collier Macmillan
Working It Through. Collier Macmillan

Kushner, Harold S.
When All You've Ever Wanted Isn't Enough. Summit
Books

Kytle, Calvin
Gandhi Soldier of Non Violence—An Introduction.
Seven Locks Press

Larsen, Earnie
Life Beyond Addiction. Harper & Row
Stage Two Recovery. Harper & Row

May, Gerald G., M.D.
Addiction and Grace. Harper & Row
Will and Spirit. Harper & Row

McElroy, Reverend Paul Simpson
Seeds for the Spirit "Devotions for Spiritual Growth"
Peter Pauper Press

Merton, Thomas
The Seven Story Mountain. Harcourt Brace

Menninger, Karl M.D.
Whatever Became of Sin? Hawthorn

Miller, Samuel H.
The Life of the Soul. Walker Press

Moody, Raymond A., Jr. M.D.
   The Light Beyond. Bantam Books

Nakken, Craig
   The Addictive Personality. Hazelden

Patterson, Ben
   Waiting/Finding Hope When God Seems Silent. Salt-shaker Books from IVP
   When God Seems Silent. Intervarsity Press

Peck, Scott M. M.D.
   People of the Lie. Simon & Schuster
   The Different Drum. Simon & Schuster
   The Road Less Traveled. Simon & Schuster

Pearson, Carol S.
   The Hero Within. Harper & Row

Potter-Efron, Ronald and Patricia
   Letting Go of Shame. Hazelden

Prevallet, Elaine M.
   Weavings A Journal of the Christian Spiritual Life
   1990. The Upper Room

Robertson, Edwin
   The Shame and the Sacrifice. Macmillan Publishing Co.

Schaef, Anne Wilson
   When Society Becomes An Addict. Harper & Row

Segal, Robert A..
   Joseph Campbell, An Introduction. Mentor Books

Simonton C.
   Getting Well Again. Bantam Books

Sheehy, Gail
    Passages. Dutton
    Pathfinders Bantam Books

Siegel, Bernie S. M.D.
    Love, Medicine & Miracles. Harper & Row
    Peace, Love & Healing. Harper & Row

Sinetar, Martha
    Do What You Love, The Money Will Follow. Paulist Press

Sussman, Corenlia and Irving
    Thomas Merton, A Biography. Macmillan Publishing Co.

Williams, Strephon-Kaplan
    The Jungian-Lenoi Dreamwork Manual. Journey Press

Zinsser, William
    On Writing Well. Harper/Collins

AUDIO and VIDEO TAPES

Bly, Robert
    The Naive Male Ally Press

Bly, Robert with Bill Moyers
    A Gathering of Men Mystic Fire Video

Borysenka, Joan PhD
    Minding the Body, Mending the Mind Simon & Schuster

Bradshaw, John
    Homecoming 1–10 Home Tapes

Campbell, Joseph
    The Hero With A Thousand Faces I & II
    Audio Renaissance Tapes, Inc.
    The Power of the Myth with Bill Moyers
    Mystic Fire Video
    The Message of the Myth
    The Hero's Adventure
    The First Storyteller
    Sacrifice & Bliss
    Love and the Goddess
    Masks of Eternity

Cayce, Edgar
    Understanding Your Dreams Audio Renaissance Tapes,
    Inc.

Hall, James A. M.D.
    Jung Interpreting Your Dreams Audio Renaissance
    Tapes, Inc.

Hanh, Tich Nhat
    Looking Deeply Parallex Press

Miller, Emmett M.D.
    Healing Journey Source Cassette Learning System
    The Source Meditation Source Cassette Learning Sys-
    tem

Miller, Emmett M.D. & Halpen, Steven
    Letting Go Of Stress Source Cassette Learning System

Thurston, Mark PhD
    Edgar Cayces Wisdom for the New Age (Soul—Purpose
    Tapes) Harper & Row Audio Cassette

STEPS TO
RECOVERY

THE TWELVE STEPS
OF ALCOHOLICS ANONYMOUS

1. We admitted we were powerless over alcohol—that our lives had become unmanageable.
2. Came to believe that a Power greater than ourselves could restore us to sanity.
3. Made a decision to turn our will and our lives over to the care of God as we understood Him.
4. Made a searching and fearless moral inventory of ourselves.
5. Admitted to God, to ourselves, and to another human being the exact nature of our wrongs.
6. Were entirely ready to have God remove all these defects of character.
7. Humbly asked Him to remove our shortcomings.
8. Made a list of all persons we had harmed, and became willing to make amends to them all.
9. Made direct amends to such people wherever possible, except when to do so would injure them or others.
10. Continued to take personal inventory and when we were wrong promptly admitted it.
11. Sought through prayer and meditation to improve our conscious contact with God as we understood Him, praying only for knowledge of His will for us and the power to carry that out.
12. Having had a spiritual awakening as the result of these steps, we tried to carry this message to alcoholics, and to practice these principles in all our affairs.

THE TWELVE TRADITIONS
OF ALCOHOLIC ANONYMOUS

1. Our common welfare should come first; personal recovery depends on A.A. unity.
2. For our group purpose there is but one ultimate authority—a loving God as He may express Himself in our group conscience. Our leaders are but trusted servants; they do not govern.
3. The only requirement of A.A. membership is a desire to stop drinking.
4. Each group should be autonomous except in matters affecting othergroups or A.A. as a whole.
5. Each group has but one primary purpose—to carry its message to the alcoholic who still suffers.
6. An A.A. group ought never endorse, finance or lend the A.A. name to any related facility or outside enterprise, lest problems of money, property prestige divert us from our primary purpose.
7. Every A.A. group ought to be fully self-supporting, declining outside contributions.
8. Alcoholics Anonymous should remain forever nonprofessional, but our service centers may employ special workers.
9. A.A., as such, ought never be organized; but we may create service boards or committees directly responsible to those they serve.
10. Alcoholics Anonymous has no opinion on outside issues; hence the A.A. name ought never be drawn into public controversy.
11. Our public relations policy is based on attraction rather than promotion; we need always maintain personal anonymity at the level of press, radio and films.
12. Anonymity is the spiritual foundation of all our Traditions, ever reminding us to place principles before personalities.

THE TWELVE SUGGESTED STEPS
OF EMOTIONS ANONYMOUS®

1. We admitted we were powerless over our emotions—that our lives had become unmanageable.
2. Came to believe that a Power greater than ourselves could restore us to sanity.
3. Made a decision to turn our will and our lives over to the care of God as we understood Him.
4. Made a searching and fearless moral inventory of ourselves.
5. Admitted to God, to ourselves and to another human being the exact nature of our wrongs.
6. Were entirely ready to have God remove all these defects of character.
7. Humbly asked Him to remove our shortcomings.
8. Made a list of all persons we had harmed, and became willing to make amends to them all.
9. Made direct amends to such people wherever possible, except when to do so would injure them or others.
10. Continued to take personal inventory and when we were wrong promptly admitted it.
11. Sought through prayer and meditation to improve our conscious contact with God as we understood Him, praying only for knowledge of His will for us and the power to carry that out.
12. Having had a spiritual awakening as the result of these steps, we tried to carry this message, and to practice these principles in all our affairs.

THE TWELVE TRADITIONS OF
EMOTIONS ANONYMOUS®

1. Our common welfare should come first; personal recovery depends on EA unity.
2. For our group purpose there is but one ultimate authority—a loving God as He may express Himself in our group conscience. Our leaders are but trusted servants; they do not govern.
3. The only requirement for EA membership is a desire to become well emotionally.
4. Each group should be autonomous except in matters affecting other groups or EA as a whole.
5. Each group has but one primary purpose—to carry its message to the person who still suffers from emotional problems.
6. An EA group ought never endorse, finance, or lend the EA name to any related facility or outside enterprise, lest problems of money, property, and prestige divert us from our primary purpose.
7. Every EA group ought to be fully self-supporting, declining outside contributions.
8. EMOTIONS ANONYMOUS® should remain forever nonprofessional, but our service centers may employ special workers.
9. EA, as such, ought never be organized; but we may create service boards or committees directly responsible to those they serve.
10. EMOTIONS ANONYMOUS® has no opinions on outside issues, hence the EA name ought never be drawn into public controversy.
11. Our public relations policy is based on attraction rather than promotion; we need always maintain personal anonymity at the level of press, radio, and films.
12. Anonymity is the spiritual foundation of our traditions, ever reminding us to place principles before personalities.

Reprinted and adapted with the permission of
A.A. World Services, Inc.